Caravan of Martyrs

Caravan of Martyrs

SACRIFICE AND SUICIDE BOMBING
IN AFGHANISTAN

David B. Edwards

UNIVERSITY OF CALIFORNIA PRESS

University of California Press, one of the most distinguished university presses in the United States, enriches lives around the world by advancing scholarship in the humanities, social sciences, and natural sciences. Its activities are supported by the UC Press Foundation and by philanthropic contributions from individuals and institutions. For more information, visit www.ucpress.edu.

University of California Press
Oakland, California

Library of Congress Cataloging-in-Publication Data

Names: Edwards, David B., author.
Title: Caravan of martyrs : sacrifice and suicide bombing in Afghanistan / David B. Edwards.
Description: Oakland, California : University of California Press, [2017] | Includes bibliographical references and index.
Identifiers: LCCN 2016045206 (print) | LCCN 2016046541 (ebook) | ISBN 9780520294790 (cloth : alk. paper) | ISBN 9780520967823 (ebook)
Subjects: LCSH: Martyrdom—Islam. | Sacrifice—Afghanistan. | Suicide bombings.
Classification: LCC BP190.5.M3 E39 2017 (print) | LCC BP190.5.M3 (ebook) | DDC 297.7/209581—dc23
LC record available at https://lccn.loc.gov/2016045206

Manufactured in the United States of America

26 25 24 23 22 21 20 19 18 17
10 9 8 7 6 5 4 3 2 1

To Hakim Taniwal and Naqib Ahmad Khpulwak

CONTENTS

ILLUSTRATIONS

PREFACE

The history of Afghanistan's bitter years of war can be told in many ways. It can be told as the story of poorly armed insurgents battling powerful armies. It can be told as a proxy war of superpowers and the meddling of regional rivals. It can be told as the story of fundamentalist ideologies struggling for the soul of a nation. *Caravan of Martyrs* chronicles the war in Afghanistan in relation to the sacrificial violence that has defined and dominated each stage of the conflict. The forms of sacrifice discussed in these pages are not just symbols or ancillary rites: they are the means by which the struggle has been articulated and carried out. As such, they have been generative of the conflict, and they have had their own transformative effect on how the conflict has evolved stage by stage over forty years.

Sacrifice has an important and long-established place in Afghan culture. As in other Muslim nations, Afghans remember the story of Ibrahim's sacrifice each year in their celebration of the Eid-i Qurban, the Feast of the Sacrifice, and, as long as anyone can remember, animals have been ritually slaughtered so that men can try to make peace among themselves and avoid losing their sons in feud (figure 1). These traditions live on, but they have been eclipsed by other forms of sacrifice that do not allow for surrogates or substitutions—sacrifices in which the victims are human beings. In some cases, they have been victims of war on whom the designation of martyr has been conferred after the fact. In other cases, they have been individuals judged guilty of moral crimes who have been executed in public spectacles of punishment and scapegoating, expiation and shaming. Most recently, the victims have assumed, or had thrust upon them, the role of burnt offering by means of a suicide vest or truck bomb.

FIGURE 1. Sheep sacrifice, Kunar, Afghanistan, ca. 2015. Photograph courtesy of Shahmahmood Miakhel.

This is a history not just of Afghans and Afghanistan. It is a history as well of outsiders, all of whom in their own ways have escalated the conflict and raised its stakes. The most important actors in this telling of Afghanistan's story are Arabs, far fewer in number than the Soviets and Americans who occupied the country but, in the end, perhaps more influential than either. Soviets and Americans affected the war from without and created the conditions within which the battle was joined. But Arabs—Afghan Arabs, as they came to be known—transformed the struggle from within, and they were instrumental in determining how and why the battle would be fought. Sacrifice was the catalytic agent they used to change the terms of battle and to turn the war in Afghanistan from a national struggle into the incubator for a global jihad.

The Afghanistan I write about in this book is not the same place that I first came to know forty years ago, nor is this the book I imagined myself writing, or would have wanted to write, when I set off on my journey. But it is the book that I have needed to write because it tells a story that has to be told. It is not a happy story, and it offers little in the way of hope or redemption in the end. But it is a true story, as true as I can make it out to be and as I perceive its truth, and it is a story that I have felt compelled to tell to do some kind of justice to what I have discovered in my travels in Afghanistan and Pakistan over many years.

My first awareness of Afghanistan came when, as a ten-year-old child, I received a postcard from my globe-trotting grandmother postmarked from Kabul. The city, she wrote, is "a *fascinating,* exciting, gay, colorful, *dirty, dusty* city—teeming with hundreds of different races, so one sees strange sights which are very exciting and all sorts of fun." The postcard showed a line of camels, and, when my grandmother got back to the United States and came for a visit, she told me of sitting up all night on the balcony of her hotel watching caravans unloading their wares in the bazaar below. That was in 1962. The next year, the Book of the Month Club delivered to our suburban home a copy of James Michener's *Caravans,* and I was hooked.

Most Americans now cannot imagine how a country like Afghanistan could inspire a lifelong fascination. Those who were fortunate enough to visit Afghanistan before it was ravaged by conflict are more likely to understand it. I had my chance in 1975, two weeks after graduating from college, when I flew to Luxembourg and then traveled overland to Kabul by train and bus, which in those days was a long but not overly dangerous journey. Indeed, one of the friends I met in Kabul had ridden on horseback most of the way from Herat. I taught in Kabul for two years, and, though the caravans no longer ambled into the center of the city during the night, as they did during my grandmother's visit a dozen years earlier, there were still plenty of camels and nomads to be seen in the countryside.

I have used the word *caravan* in the title of this book knowing that it might provoke some critical reactions. There is, after all, no more durable stereotype of Afghanistan and the Middle East. That is presumably why my grandmother could purchase such a postcard in the first place and why Michener chose the word as the title for his novel of a liberated American woman who takes up with a band of nomads in the Afghan hinterlands. Nowadays, Westerners have far more immediate and vivid images of Afghanistan, and, though some might believe that the society has regressed, no one thinks it is standing still. To the contrary, it is now imagined as a world apart for new and disturbing reasons. Today, the stereotypes attached to this beleaguered nation are of a very different sort, and, although many of those images still cast the place and the people as exotic, they no longer enchant.

I decided to use *caravan* in my title, regardless of its Orientalist associations, because it is a term used by the particular men I am writing about, who have used it in the same way I do: to signify the idea and image of people on a journey who are connected by a common purpose. I first encountered the expression *caravan of martyrs* (*shahidan-u karavan* in Pakhtu, *karavan-i shahidan* in Dari Persian) in a magazine published by one of the Islamic political parties in exile that arose in Peshawar, Pakistan, in the wake of the Soviet invasion of Afghanistan. The magazine was one of several devoted to commemorating the martyrdom of Afghans who had died fighting the Soviets. I came across the term a second time in researching the work of Abdullah 'Azzam, sometimes referred to as "the father of Global Jihad," who founded al-Qaeda in order to recruit and train Muslims from other countries to fight the Soviets in Afghanistan. One of the important works 'Azzam wrote to justify his mission was called *Join the Caravan.* In a similar vein, Osama Bin Laden used a 2007 video message to "the youth of Islam" to inform them that it was their duty "to join the caravan."[1] More recently, while researching the uses to which social media are put in forwarding the cause of jihad (see chapter 7), I found the term used in a variety of comments and memes uploaded to the Internet by jihad devotees (figure 2). I would argue that, for these ideologically motivated users of the term, it is precisely the stereotype of the caravan that appeals. Edward Said warned Westerners to be wary of how we perpetuated images of the East that refused to recognize the modernity and diversity of Muslim societies, but he did not anticipate how that very quality and sense of an unchanging common journey and purpose might serve the purposes of men determined to wage war against the West and to persuade their co-religionists that the only identity that mattered was that of believer.[2]

· · ·

In acknowledging the help I have received along the way, I should begin with the grandmother who sent me the postcard and the mother who subscribed to the Book of the Month Club. Would Afghanistan have loomed so large in my life if I had not first discovered the place at so young an age and from such consequential people in my life? Of my teachers, it is to Aram Yengoyan, Sherry Ortner, and Bill Schorger that I owe the deepest debts. Of my graduate student colleagues, the late Bill Kelleher is the one who helped me most to recognize the potential of anthropology as a way of seeing the world. In my two previous books, I have taken space to acknowledge many other debts of gratitude. Rather than repeat those names, I refer anyone interested to those books. The debts I owed then I still owe now, and the gratitude I felt then still holds strong today. But because this is a book on sacrifice and martyrdom, I need to repeat a couple of those names: those of Sayyid Bahuddin

FIGURE 2. "Caravan of Martyrs" Facebook meme.

Majruh and Hakim Taniwal, both of whom were good men who believed in Afghanistan and were willing to take risks in working to heal their country. Both died: Majruh at the hands of an assassin in 1988, and Taniwal in 2006, when he was serving as governor of Khost, by a suicide bomber of the sort I am trying hard to understand in this book. Both deserved the gratitude of their country, and both are missed by their friends and admirers. I have dedicated this book to Hakim and to Naqib Ahmad Khpulwak, who was teaching his class at the American University in Kabul the evening he was struck down by a suicide attacker in August 2016. Everyone who knew Naqib respected and admired him, and he too is deeply missed by his family and friends. Unfortunately, I never had the opportunity to meet Naqib. My dedication is a small gesture of respect to a man who—like Hakim—had other options but chose to help his countrymen.

I do not know how common it is for anthropologists to make one good friend in the field and to maintain that friendship for as long as Shahmahmood Miakhel and I have maintained ours, but that friendship has been not only the bedrock of my "fieldwork practice" but also an important and abiding part of my sense of who I am and what matters most to me. Shahmahmood has been with me in my explorations of Afghan culture almost from the start, not only on the interviews I conducted in and around Peshawar in the early 1980s but also in my study of the Kachagarhi refugee camp, where he lived at the time. Since then, he has accompanied me on many journeys in Afghanistan and elsewhere, and we remain colleagues, collaborators, and close friends. Whereas my life has proved relatively stable, with a long-term position at a liberal arts college in the United States, Shahmahmood's has taken him from the refugee camp to a taxicab in Washington, D.C., to a deputy ministerial appointment in Kabul, and most recently to the position of Afghanistan country director for the U.S. Institute of Peace. For all the help he has given me in understanding Afghan culture, as well as for the tolerance and forbearance he has shown in the face of my often-slow acquisition of insight and unintended slights, I owe Shahmahmood the deepest debt of gratitude, and I likewise acknowledge that my sense of just how important are the notions of debt and gratitude comes from him.

I want to give special thanks to Danish Karokhel, editor of the Pajhwok News Agency, who provided invaluable assistance in gaining access to materials related to contemporary suicide bombers and to Haji Sayed Daud, director of the Afghan Media Resource Center (AMRC), with whom I worked on digitizing the AMRC archive and who generously provided permission for use of photographs. I also thank those who have read and provided valuable comments on the manuscript at various stages of completion, including Michael Brown, Steve Caton, Noah Coburn, John Kleiner, Tom Kohut, Joel Lee, Shahmahmood Miakhel, Margaret Mills, and Greg Whitmore. I also want to acknowledge the assistance of Muhammad Amin, Mohibullah Amin, and Maryam Laly, who helped with translations; Lynne Withey and Reed Malcolm, my past and present editors at the University of California Press, for their support and encouragement; Erica Büky for her stern but thoughtful assistance in the final manuscript edit; and Julia Zafferano for her help getting the manuscript over the finish line. In my research for this book, which reaches back to the very beginning of my fieldwork, I have received support from a variety of institutions, including the Fulbright Commission, the National Science Foundation, the National Endowment for the Humanities, the Andrew Mellon Foundation, the Carnegie Corporation of New York, and Williams College, where I have been employed since 1989. I thank all of these institutions, and I am especially grateful that I had the good fortune to end up, through all the uncertainties of the academic job market, at Williams College, which has provided me with wonderful colleagues and students to assist my intellectual and material well-being. Finally, I offer thanks to my wife, Marketa, and our two children, Vilem and Tobias. My absences during the writing of this book have been more mental than physical, but they have still been real, and I appreciate their support and love more than they know or might have believed when I was nodding my head at their conversation while drifting among the still unwritten chapters of this book.

ONE

Sacrifice

THEN TO NOW

Nuristan, 1976

As I try to reconstruct the trajectory that has led to this book, my mind returns to the night I was stung by a scorpion by the side of the road on my way to Kamdesh. It was the summer of 1976. I was teaching English in Kabul and had taken a few weeks off to trek with two other young Americans with jobs in Kabul. I was living in a hotel down the street from the school, and Wakil, an Afghan who worked at the hotel accompanied us on the trip. He was taking us to his home in a mountain hamlet near the head of the Kamdesh Valley, in the region of Nuristan close to the border with Pakistan. We had hired a car and driver to get us to the town of Kamdesh, which was at the end of the motorable road. By evening, after an early-morning depar-ture from Kabul, we had made it most of the way to our destination, but when the driver noticed storm clouds ahead, we decided to stop for a few hours. I found a smooth spot on the ground, wadded my jacket under my head, and immediately fell into a sound sleep.

It was still dark when the driver woke us. He wanted to drop us off before sunrise so that he could make it back to Kabul by evening. When I sat up, I felt a sudden, stabbing pain in my knee. The lump inside my jeans felt hard at first, but as I pulled my pants down, it popped, leaving a cold smear along the inside of my calf. I felt a burst of sharp stings, like a million tiny splinters piercing every centimeter of skin from ankle to groin. By the driver's flash-light, I saw the pincers and crushed carapace of a large black scorpion, its innards dampening my leg.

My companions helped me into the Land Rover, cramming themselves into the rear compartment with our packs so that I could stretch out on the back seat. After what seemed like an hour but was probably less, the headlights revealed a sign with a large red crescent painted on it—a first-aid clinic. The driver ran to knock on the door. When he returned he was accompanied not by a doctor or medic but by a man in a large black turban. There was no doctor in residence, so the driver had been sent next door to the house of a mullah, who now looked at me blankly through the window of the car. He opened the door and positioned himself so that he could take hold of my injured leg without displacing the mass of black cloth that wound around his head. Then he started quietly chanting phrases that I later realized must have been verses from the Qur'an, blowing jets of cool air onto my leg and gently massaging my knee and thigh.

At first, even the sensation of his breath against my leg felt like more shards of glass being rubbed into the skin, but gradually the pain eased. After a while, he pulled himself out of the car and told the driver that the pain would soon go away. In fact, my upper thigh already felt better. My knee still throbbed, but the pain was now bearable. Maybe this was because of the mullah, but I also vaguely recall that one of my American friends offered me some antihistamine tablets, and I might have taken one of those while we were driving. At the time, it did not really matter why the pain had abated. I was able to walk without too much soreness by the middle of that morning and managed to continue the trip on foot, with only a short layover in a teashop in Kamdesh.

I did not yet know that I wanted to be an anthropologist, but this was my introduction to fieldwork and the start of a career-long effort to get behind the gaze of the man in the black turban. The next year, I was back home starting graduate school. I planned to return to Wakil's village in the high Hindu Kush to conduct my dissertation research. I knew that it would somehow involve Islam. In the event, my plans were never realized. It would be another nineteen years before I returned to that part of the country, and I would have to look elsewhere for the research project that would make me an anthropologist.

As I was finishing my first year in graduate school, on a beautiful spring day in Ann Arbor, Michigan, news came over the radio that military officers in Afghanistan had killed the sitting president and proclaimed a new state dedicated to freeing the peasants and workers from feudal bondage. Over time, the allegiance of the new rulers to the Soviet Union came into focus, but their message of ending oppression and sharing the wealth never took hold. By summer, the country was in open revolt against the new regime. The match that lit the blaze had been struck in the Kamdesh Valley I had visited two years earlier. The first newspaper reports attributed the violence to anti-communist "freedom fighters" intent on defending their country against communist aggression, but gradually it became clear that no matter who had ignited the rebellion, it was mullahs and other religious figures who had taken charge, and I wondered whether the mullah who had treated my leg was involved. The war forced me to reimagine what it meant to be an anthropologist. The prospect of study in a secluded mountain village was looking more and more distant, but, to a young researcher, studying a war of geopolitical consequence had its own appeal.

As you get older and try to make sense of your life, you inevitably read backward to your starting point. You look for telltale signs to confirm that who you have become was who you were meant to be, and what you have done was what you were meant to do. *Buud, na buud* (it was and it wasn't) is how Afghans say "Once upon a time." At the time, I imagined my trip to Kamdesh leading me toward a traditional anthropological career of fieldwork in a picturesque locale. Instead, it led me into a war zone and a conflict that continues forty years later, a conflict in which my own country became directly involved and sacrificed many of its own young people. One of them, Army Staff Sergeant Eric J. Lindstrom, was killed in combat near the village of Barg-i Matal, where we had spent a peaceful week hiking and swimming in the river thirty-three years earlier.[1]

Remembering the time before the violence and disruption, searching for pathways from then to now, I started to think back to the sacred words the mullah recited over my leg, words that had the power not only of representing a divine truth but also of conveying it materially, the mullah's breath a slipstream carrying sacred energy to heal an affliction. Until I started working on this book, that memory was not something I thought much about. Now I see that encounter as something irretrievably distant, a connection of a sort that is difficult to imagine in the present. Whether or not he was directly involved in what was to come, the mullah was at the epicenter of a conflict that has reshaped our world, a conflict justified, if not inspired by, the words he recited over my leg. At the time, they were words of healing; later they were turned to other purposes.

There were additional lessons to be learned from that night, lessons that it would take me some time to absorb. One had to do with the enormous gap that existed between the boulevards and pizza parlors of Kabul, the hippie hotels and tourist shops selling off the nation's heritage item by item, and the vast expanse of country beyond—a world of villages without electricity or running water, schools, or services. A representative from that world had gazed down at me on the backseat of that borrowed car, and it was that world that reacted with revulsion and outrage when the Marxist cadres announced that they were going to redistribute land and no longer allow the observance of traditional customs that had shaped rural Afghan society for generations. But, more immediately, what the mullah showed me when he sat beside me in that car was that modernity—in the form of medical care—coexisted in this world with the certainty of miracles, that God's presence in human affairs was not an abstract idea to be reflected on but a force to be reckoned with.

Peshawar, 1984

Anthropology found its footing as an academic discipline in the second decade of the twentieth century, when Bronisław Malinowski stepped ashore on the Trobriand Islands, set up his tent, and started taking notes. The discipline has changed since Malinowski's day. As the people traditionally studied by anthropologists have been displaced by economic, political, and ecological circumstances beyond their control, anthropologists have refined their methods in attempts to understand the diverse adaptations that humans have come up with to thrive when they can and survive when they must. One methodological response has been *multi-sited ethnography,* which attempts to capture the reality of people's lives in an era of migration and displacement.

The world is also a more violent place now than it was in Malinowski's time. Or maybe it is simply that, in the past, anthropologists were protected by their color and citizenship from the violence that afflicted the people they sought to study. Between roughly 1965 and 1978, a number of anthropologists managed to produce very good field studies in Afghanistan, with few mishaps beyond blisters and sunburns. I first lived in Afghanistan, working as an English teacher, when some of these anthropologists were still in the field. I entered graduate school with the idea of finding my own remote mountain village to study. With the outbreak of war, however, it became obvious that research of the sort I had envisioned was no longer feasible. Instead of working in a mountain village in the Hindu Kush, I found myself doing my dissertation research in the hot, dusty city of Peshawar, Pakistan, which had become the base of operations for many of the mujahidin parties organizing the resistance against the Marxist government and its Soviet sponsors.

Peshawar was utterly different from Kabul. There were restaurants in Kabul where you could order hot dogs and hamburgers. There were two discotheques, where Afghan couples danced next to expatriate couples, and out on the streets you could see Afghan women with hair uncovered, wearing blouses and skirts with sheer stockings. Women who dressed this way were a minority but not remarkable. The school where I taught was filled every day with young students, boys and girls, who were eager to learn English, and it was not a stretch to see Afghanistan as a nation on the move, a nation where the then rarely questioned promises of modernization were on the verge of being fulfilled.

By the time I arrived in Peshawar in 1982, the city was overrun with Afghan refugees. The population had doubled or tripled, and the vast majority of the refugees were from rural villages almost untouched by the modernizing efforts that had seemed so encouraging in Kabul. Most of the people on the streets wore country clothes. They were almost entirely men, and they had the manners of people unused to city life. When women appeared in public, they wore burqas and huddled together or walked a few steps behind their men. One of the most obvious differences between Peshawaris and Afghans was that the Afghans on the street rarely seemed to move very fast or to be traveling anywhere in particular. Most of them seemed unsure where they were going, how long they were likely to be there, or what to do in the meantime.

As it turned out, most of the Afghans were going to be there for a very long time. My own stay would be shorter, just over two years. I did not know at the time how long the Pakistan government would allow me to remain in country. I had been given a permit by one ministry to do research in a refugee camp, but when I arrived I was told that I would have to apply for a second permit from a different ministry. Not getting that second permit right away turned out to be a lucky break, because it allowed me to set my sights on a more interesting question, though vaguely defined and less clearly ethnographic in the Malinowskian sense: figuring out what the hell was going on in Peshawar. There were presumably any number of embassy analysts and undercover operatives trying to do the same thing, but to the best of my knowledge and for quite a long time, I was the only above-board, academically credentialed (or nearly), independent researcher in Peshawar who was interviewing mujahidin commanders and party leaders, visiting party headquarters and mujahidin training camps.

Perhaps because I was intimidated by the complexity of events in the present, I found myself oriented toward the past, specifically toward understanding the origins of the various Islamic political parties that had set up shop in Peshawar. Some were run by madrasa-educated mullahs, some by the heads of Sufi orders, some by former university students. None of these were people I had been aware of during my two years in Kabul. If I had been aware of them, I would not have considered them likely candidates to be running political parties, and I wanted to understand how it had come to pass that these people were now so much in the news and so clearly in charge; how it was that the war going on nearby was being called a jihad and that all the main actors in it were calling themselves mujahidin (though the American government insisted on calling them "freedom fighters"); and how it was that all these previously obscure leaders were claiming legitimacy for their efforts based on religious principles and aspirations that seemed to have little relationship to the democratic ideals espoused by my government, which was the one supplying them with most of their money and guns.

In a city swarming with refugees and in an effort to understand a phenomenon that we are all still trying to make sense of more than thirty years later, I developed my own fieldwork style, one that was part Malinowski, part Jimmy Olsen tracking down stories for the *Daily Planet*. It was immediately clear that this ethnographic research was not going to fit any model that I had read or heard about in graduate school. There was no "there" there, or, rather, there were so many "theres" that you could not keep all of them straight. There was no village surrounded by fields, no handful of characters who all knew and interacted with one another and whose interactions I could try to parse and explain. It was probably to my advantage that my graduate program did not require or even offer a course on research methodology. (The faculty apparently assumed that, after having read so many ethnographies, students would have absorbed by osmosis how to do field research—and if they did not have the wherewithal to figure it out, they were probably in the wrong line of work.) I can only imagine that if I had had a set idea in my mind about how to do fieldwork, based on the expectation of studying some well-organized community, I probably would have been overwhelmed by the incommensurability between what I had been taught and where I had landed.

One of the great virtues of anthropology is that it allows its practitioners to make it up as they go along. Other disciplines among those referred to as the social sciences try to conform to the model developed in the natural sciences. Anthropology, at least the variety I incline toward, recognizes that whatever theories you start out with will have to be reconceived as you get enmeshed in the research. The idea of testing a hypothesis is simply unrealistic and naive given the disparate and unpredictable nature of experiences you are likely to participate in, people you are likely to encounter, and events you are likely to witness.

In Peshawar, I set out to meet and interview Afghans whose ancestors had been involved in past jihads. My goal was to find out what Islamic politics had been like before in order to see if I could establish some connections to what it had become. History has always mattered to me—not so much the kind traditionally practiced by historians, which is to say accounts of notable people and events, but rather the *stories* embedded in history and the social realities those stories revealed. I hoped those stories could tell me about the way Afghans conceived of their own past and how it reflected the cultural values they espoused and the moral contradictions they grappled with.

Much of my first year was spent interviewing tribal elders and the sons and grandsons of Sufi mystics and Muslim clerics who had fought in earlier jihads. In the course of these interviews, the words *shahid* (martyr) and *shahadat* (martyrdom) kept popping up, but they were always on the fringes of what we were talking about, terms for the quotidian outcomes and local tragedies of historical battles now overshadowed by current struggles. My immediate concern was piecing together the names and affiliations, the events and chronologies, and trying to figure out how Afghans themselves made sense of the relationship of tribes and Islamic leaders and the state, how they knitted it all together into something like a history, and how that history helped them understand current events.[2]

Martyrdom was not the explicit focus of my field research. It was always in my field of vision, because it was a factor in how people dealt with grief and how they understood loss, but it was not what originally attracted my attention. One minor incident that brought martyrs and martyrdom forward in my thinking happened one day more than a year after my arrival in Pakistan, when I had finally received clearance to work in a refugee camp. I was sitting in the guestroom of an Afghan refugee living in the Kachagarhi camp, on the outskirts of Peshawar. While waiting for tea to be served, I noticed a magazine lying in the wall niche where the Qur'an was usually placed, and I started leafing through its tattered pages. The magazine commemorated members of Hizb-i Islami, the most radical of the Afghan resistance parties, who had died fighting the communist government. Some of those honored were rank-and-file mujahidin, others front commanders and subcommanders killed in battle. Others, dressed in sport coats, seemed to be students.

The articles that accompanied the photos told a story, or several stories. One was of the ordinary men who had been killed in the battle against the government, but the story that merited greater attention and importance was that of the university students who had joined the movement while still in school and had been arrested, imprisoned, and eventually executed. These students had larger photographs and more fulsome tributes than those awarded to front commanders, even though many of the front commanders had fought in combat against the Marxist regime while some of the students had done little more than hand out fliers on the street.

The fact that a whole magazine was devoted to martyrs, and the way their portraits were organized and arrayed, led me to pay more attention to martyrdom. It was still, at this stage, more a curiosity for me than a research focus, but I asked for and was given that magazine to keep. Then I started looking for others of the same sort, all of which I still have. (I analyze the content and imagery of such magazines in chapter 3.) Today, of course, such magazines are no longer novelties; they even seem somewhat quaint and outmoded among the proliferation of jihadist websites and social media apps that highlight tech-savvy videos of martyrdoms and beheadings of unbelievers. In 1982, however, the magazines signaled an important new stage in the cultural politics of Islamic resistance, one that would influence developments not only in Afghanistan but throughout the Muslim world.

Kunar, 1995

If my interest in martyrdom was awakened by a magazine, my broader interest in sacrifice—and how sacrifice and martyrdom are connected—stems from a trip to eastern Afghanistan in 1995. The Soviets withdrew from Afghanistan in 1989, and the various mujahidin parties had been fighting among themselves for power ever since. Eastern Afghanistan was experiencing an uneasy peace when I arrived. The parties were not openly fighting, mostly because they had divvied up power and spoils among themselves. One controlled the border crossing at the Khyber Pass. Another controlled the airport at Jalalabad. A third controlled the customs house in the city center. Five or six had set up tollbooths on the Kabul highway from which they taxed every car and truck passing between Jalalabad and the capital.

I was with my friend Shahmahmood Miakhel, who had arranged for us to travel with a former jihad commander named Abdul Wahhab to the Pech Valley, near the headwaters of the Kunar River. Abdul Wahhab provided a Toyota Hilux pickup truck and four well-armed men for our protection. Toward the end of our journey, we stopped for the night in Shahmahmood's village of Mangwal, on the eastern side of the river. After food and conversation, we bedded down on wood-and-rope *charpai* beds in the garden outside Shahmahmood's father's compound. Two men stood guard while the rest of us slept. It was a moonless night, and when one of the sentries returned to our encampment and tried to wake one of the other guards so that he could be relieved, the man rose from his bed with a start, grabbed the Kalashnikov under his pillow, and started screaming that we were under attack. All four of the guards seized their guns and started shouting. No one could see anyone else in the dark, and I rolled off of my bed onto the ground, making myself as small as I could manage while tensing in anticipation of the first shot. After an interval that was probably only seconds but felt much longer, the commander's voice rose above the others', restoring order. The shouting stopped, but talk took its place, punctuated by bursts of laughter before we all drifted back to sleep.

It was a minor incident, but it showed the fragility of peace in a land where so many men were armed and there were few to trust and many to fear. People were under tremendous strain to survive and keep their families safe. Although the communist enemy was gone, old animosities were still alive. Enmities in Afghanistan can be patched up, but they never completely heal, and it was one of those enmities from the war years that kept the commander and his men on edge on that moonless night.

The next morning, as we all sat drinking milk tea and gradually rousing ourselves for our onward journey to Jalalabad, Shahmahmood's father suddenly appeared from inside the compound pulling a sheep with a rope around its neck. The beds were pushed back into a circle. Shahmahmood's father matter-of-factly recited some prayers while stroking his beard, then calmly cut open the sheep's carotid artery, spilling its blood on the packed earth. Shahmahmood and I shared a look, nothing more, but I knew we were thinking the same thing: it was sheep's blood on the ground, but it could have been ours. That day the sheep was our *qurbani*—our sacrifice—for having stayed alive another day. That moment remains my own most significant experience of the power of sacrifice to ritualize and thereby exert some control over the wellsprings of fear at our own pending deaths that, from time to time, bubble up into consciousness.

The focus of most anthropological studies is meaning: what people say and what they mean when they say it, what they express in nonverbal ways, and the media through which they express it. Often neglected (because difficult to verbalize or measure) is the power of emotions: how emotions connect to meaning and how they bind people to the central symbols of their society. The divide between meaning and emotion is, of course, an artificial one. As Eva Illouz notes, "Emotions are cultural meanings and social relationships that are inseparably compressed together, and it is this compression which confers on them their capacity to energize action."[3] Such compression occurs most regularly and reliably in the context of ritual, where cognition, affect, evaluation, motivation, and the body are all simultaneously fused, resulting in the release of energy. No ritual has the capacity to release more of this energy than the ritual of sacrifice, in particular the sacrifice of living things. Sex is a mystery that can simultaneously delight and terrify us, but death on its own offers little in the way of beguilement. It mostly just terrifies us. Sacrifice seeks to achieve some leverage over that terror by putting death in our hands, allowing us to set aside and tidy the place where it happens, determine its timing, and assert its meaning. In so doing, we also harness, to some degree at least, the emotions it elicits.

I do not know whether Shahmahmood's father knew what had happened the night before he slit the throat of that sheep. It was an act he had performed many times before and would perform many times thereafter. I do not know whether he knew that he could have lost his eldest son hours before. Nor do I know whether the men we were with that day, men who had witnessed so much killing, had thoughts anything like mine. I had spent a long time among Afghans by that time, but I was a neophyte in their world of guns. I can only assume that they had had many closer calls. A better-prepared anthropologist would have thought to ask what they thought and felt about the whole affair, but I did not. Maybe I was still in shock myself, but the moment also seemed strangely private to me, a moment when I was lost in my own reflections, my own intimations of mortality. I did not speak of it even with Shahmahmood until much later.

I have said that death does not beguile, but maybe that is not entirely true. Maybe part of the attraction of sacrifice is that it brings us close to death—a place where some part of us desires to be or at least to know—letting us see into the abyss while keeping us far enough back to avoid falling in. Then again, maybe I am overthinking or attributing the wrong features to sacrifice. My own response to the act was personal and existential in character (how was it that I survived?) rather than religious (thanks be to God), and this seems an important fact to note. Just because it is a ritual and because it is framed by the recitation of religious verses does not imply that its power derives from or is exclusive to religious belief. To the contrary, it might be said that religion takes its power from the ritual act of sacrifice, not the other way around. It is through the appropriation of this act that particular religions gain much of their emotive power and their meaning, but sacrifice itself stands apart as an act that can be replicated, borrowed, and embroidered for different purposes by different bodies.

Kabul, 2003

I returned to Kabul on the second anniversary of the beginning of Operation Enduring Freedom, the U.S. attack on Afghanistan in response to the September 11, 2001, attacks. October 7 is not as memorable a day as September 11, and there were no ceremonies in Kabul to mark the date. For Kabulis, it was just another morning, and the streets were crowded. That is the first thing that struck me on my return—the traffic. It had been twenty-six years since I had last seen Kabul. Back then, I thought that I would be returning soon, but it did not work out that way, and the city I finally returned to was very different from the one I had left.

In the mid-1970s, the streets were crowded only on holidays, when people came in from the provinces to witness the government-sponsored festivities. On any ordinary day, there was never much traffic to speak of. In the two years following the Taliban's collapse and the arrival of the Americans, things had changed dramatically, and not all for the better. Take taxis, for example. According to one estimate, there were forty thousand taxis crowding the streets of Kabul in 2003. Many were right-hand-drive cabs brought in illegally from Pakistan. Even if you removed all the other vehicles—the trucks and the motor rickshaws, the prewar Mercedes minibuses, the Toyota Land Cruisers favored by expatriates, the Datsun pickup trucks formerly used by the Taliban police for their patrols, and the armored personnel carriers bearing the International Security Assistance Force (ISAF) peacekeepers who had replaced them—the taxis by themselves would have created tie-ups, because there were no functioning traffic lights and only ineffectual traffic police at most of the intersections in the city. In 1977, there had been more horse-drawn tongas than motorized vehicles. It is not just nostalgia that makes me think so: home movies shot by foreigners living in Kabul before the war show that the streets were empty, and the waters of the Kabul River, which by 2003 had been reduced to stagnant pools, still flowed fast and clear from the snowmelt in the mountains. The city had only half a million people then. By 2003, the number was closer to four million.

Kabul has always been dusty, and even the smallest wind whips up the silt of its worn-down hills. The dust hangs in the air all day, mixing with the diesel smoke; it settles at night, until the morning traffic sets it back in motion. When an inversion layer thickens the air, you do not want to go outside. Most of the foreigners who lived in Kabul in the years after the U.S.-led invasion, including the foreign businessmen who were making Kabul briefly into a boomtown, did not have to go outside—or not for long. They lived and worked in high-walled compounds with air conditioners, which were powered by generators when the electricity was down. When they had to travel, they moved in tightly sealed SUVs with drivers. The government elite lived and moved around in the same fashion.

When I came back to Kabul in 2003 to shoot a documentary film, I was staying not far from where I had lived when I was teaching English. But with the exception of a few places like Chicken Street, where all the tourist antique shops are located, and my old school itself, long since boarded up, not much of the neighborhood looked familiar. The compound we stayed in belonged to a wealthy Muhammadzai family, distant cousins of the former king. When the communists took power, the Afghan secret police (KHAD) confiscated the property. When the mujahidin came to power in 1992, their security service occupied it, and when the Taliban took charge, they gave the property to their Directorate for the Propagation of Virtue and Prevention of Vice. One of the buildings in the compound became a prison where they detained low-level "criminals" who had been picked up for minor offenses, such as trimming a beard or buying a video.

The walls of the building were covered with the scratched initials and messages of prisoners, and, out back, a foul smell still wafted from the pit latrine, though it had not been used for years. Snooping around the building, we found pots and pans left behind by the Taliban and even a fragment of a poem in Persian folded and pushed into a hole in the compound wall:

In my pen, no healing ink, only blood
On the walls of the oppressor . . . [4]

That was one reminder of the Taliban. Another was the strands of magnetic tape fluttering from electric lines in the streets, flung there by the morality police when they found a taxi driver listening to a forbidden Bollywood cassette tape.

But these seemed like distant reminders. The three of us making the film hired a driver to transport us around the city. In 2003, the security situation was very different from what it was to become in the following years, and somehow it seemed that the presence of the camera gave us permission to enter just about any place. Perhaps because they had been deprived of movies for so long, people appeared happy to see our camera. Perhaps they had just become used to cameras from all the news crews that had come and gone following the departure of the Taliban. Or perhaps they just did not know what to make of us—a middle-aged American man, an Afghan woman, and a young American cameraman. Whatever the reason, we never worried about our safety, whether we were filming in the currency exchange market in downtown Kabul, a shrine on the outskirts of the city, or a tiny factory making candied almonds deep in the center of Shar-i Kohna, the Old City.

When I returned a year later to teach a class on oral-history research at Kabul University, the situation was already more tense. While shooting the film, we had heard complaints from women students at the university who told us that the American soldiers treated Afghans like "wild animals," and they joked that, for all the talk of empowering Afghan women, all they had seen so far were useless projects to teach them how to do things like bottle pickles.[5] I didnot know if the complaints were fair, but the frustration was obvious. Foreigners seemed more oblivious. With the exception of the drivers and cooks and office staff they saw each day, foreigners were largely unaware of what was going on outside their tightly sealed cocoons.

That sense of separation began to evaporate, however, when the Taliban attacks became more frequent and immediate. In late August, shortly after I had arrived back in Kabul, a truck bomb went off a few blocks from where I was staying (figure 3). The target was the headquarters of DynCorp, Inc., which provided security for many of the top foreign and Afghan officials, including President Hamid Karzai. The blast had apparently been timed for the end of the workday, when DynCorp employees walked across the street from their office compound to their housing compound. When I reached the site of the blast a few minutes later, the tangled skeleton of the vehicle was still on fire, and a crowd had gathered to stare at the wreckage. I heard that a

FIGURE 3. Car bomb, Kabul, Aug. 2004. Author's photograph.

second bomb had been planted in a parked car nearby that was intended to go off a few minutes after the first, but for some reason it never detonated.

There was some dispute as to whether the driver of the truck had survived. A spokesman for the Afghan interior ministry said that the remains of the truck's engine had been found three hundred meters from the site of detonation and consequently that it was likely the driver had been killed in the blast. The Taliban spokesman, however, refuted this assertion, telling the press that the driver had used a remote-control device and had survived. The point is worth noting because, a year or so later, the Taliban spokesman would have taken the opposite tack, emphasizing the willingness of the bomber to blow himself up. Suicide bombing was the basis of an explicit strategy first championed by Osama Bin Laden in a February 2003 video that encouraged "martyrdom operations against the enemy." That same message was picked up by the Taliban, which began to initiate its own attacks, partly in emulation of similar attacks by insurgents in Iraq.[6]

Only two such attacks occurred in the first year after Bin Laden's video and three the next, but in 2005 there were twenty. The number shot up to 105 in 2006 and to 140 in 2007. Since that time, there have been, on average, around 100 attacks each year. The first wave of suicide bombings appears to have been carried out principally by Arabs; Afghans and foreign commentators familiar with Afghanistan initially observed that it was highly unlikely that Afghans would ever participate in such attacks, which were contrary to their cultural sensibilities. However, as the numbers climbed, it became clear that it was not just foreign fighters who were strapping on suicide vests and chauffeuring bomb-laden cars and trucks to their appointed destinations: Afghans and Pakhtuns from across the Pakistan border were in fact were responsible for the majority of these incidents.[7]

I have been around Afghans long enough to appreciate both their common sense and the pride they take in not being told by others what to do. Self-determination is a cornerstone of their cultural ethos, and the fact that Bin Laden and the Taliban were both championing suicide bombing seemed to me an insufficient reason to explain the fact that people were deciding to follow that course of action. Though there were undoubtedly some suicide bombers who were coerced or brainwashed, I could not believe that this was true of all of them. The decision to become a suicide bomber was still an individual one for most, and it was one that would have been unthinkable in the past. So why now?

MAKING SENSE OF SACRIFICE

The central question that has arisen out of my preoccupation with the war in Afghanistan—the question that is central to this study—is how it happened that men (and sometimes even women and children) would come to consider it a good thing to strap bombs onto their bodies, walk into crowded places, and trigger the bombs, knowing not only that they will lose their own lives but also that they will take with them a large number of strangers. That such things happen now gives those of us who have long worked in Afghanistan a feeling of horror and sadness. These events, which utterly contradict anything I would have imagined when I first set out on my journey of discovery, have made me question how much I actually knew about Afghanistan in the first place.

If the framework I have constructed over the course of two books and twenty years to explain what I call the moral fault lines of Afghan culture has any validity and utility, it must be able to help explain the unsettling reality of suicide bombing, and it must do so, first of all, in terms that make sense to Afghans themselves. This book differs from my earlier ones in its approach, but it shares with them the sense that understanding the present requires understanding the past. In keeping with that dictum, I begin by trying to get a fix on what sacrifice has meant and what it means today, and how it has been expressed from before the war until the present day.

Suicide bombing did not begin in Afghanistan. Incidents of intentional self-destruction took place in Sri Lanka and Palestine years before the first bomb went off in Afghanistan. But the fact that a phenomenon appeared in one country before it appeared somewhere else is not necessarily relevant to understanding the development in any given locale. Suicide bombing was not something that existed when I conducted my first research in the 1980s. It was not even imaginable, and it is insufficient to say that it was imported from someplace else. Techniques for constructing a detonator or sewing explosives into a vest might have been brought in from Palestine or Iraq, but, first, the idea of blowing oneself up had to find local adherents: it had to seem like a reasonable idea to some group of people. To assume that it was imposed on Afghans by others would be to deny them agency, whereas much of Afghan history pivots around the struggle for agency. Nevertheless, the role of outside actors cannot be ignored. In viewing Afghan culture as dynamic, it is necessary to understand that it has not changed on its own; isolated though it might have once seemed to Americans, it has been part of a global economy and subject to regional and international social and geopolitical forces for millennia.[8]

In coming to terms with the act of killing at the center of this study, it is important first of all to know what to call it. It is usually referred to as terrorism, but this term defines the act solely by its effect on others. *Suicide bombing* and *suicide bomber,* though imperfect, have the advantage of equivalence to the terms that Afghans themselves use, the most common of which—*intehar* (for suicide bombing) and *intehari* (for suicide bomber)—is a linguistic borrowing from Arabic that perhaps reflects the association of the act with its having been brought to Afghanistan by Arabs.[9] Terms I try to avoid here are "terrorism" and "terrorist." I do so not to deny that acts of suicide bombing create terror but because these terms prioritize the strategic objective and experiential consequences for others over the act itself and subsume the person responsible for the act within the outcome of his action. For the purposes of this study, I want to maintain the focus on the act itself and what leads up to it, rather than on the consequences of the act. This is not to deny that suicide bombing causes death and destruction and that it has the effect of terrorizing those who survive the act. It is simply to maintain an analytic division between the causes of the act, the act itself, and the consequences, a division the terminology of "terrorism" and "terrorist" erases.

My approach to the study of suicide bombing has been strongly influenced, first, by the work of Natalie Davis on the rites of violence in sixteenth-century France (1973). It was in reading Davis's seminal article that I first became attuned to the symbolic dimensions of violence (the "violation" that is inherent in acts of violence) and to the importance of not reducing violence to its instrumental effects. A second work to which I am indebted is Alan Feldman's *Formations of Violence* (1991) on sectarian violence in Northern Ireland. Feldman's work brilliantly demonstrates the importance of understanding the forms and relations of violence in and of themselves and of tracing how those forms change over time and how they change society and social persons in turn. In focusing on forms of violence rather than ends, I am concerned with the cultural logic that informs the act. Here, I have also been influenced by the work of Marshall Sahlins (1979) and the importance he ascribed to understanding what he has termed "the structure of the conjuncture" within which actions take place, particularly actions that mediate relations across cultures.

Sahlins introduced that expression to locate the analytical task of making sense of moments in which disparate aspects of history, myth, and ritual come together and collide, with sometimes catastrophic results. His example was the meeting between Captain James Cook and the Hawaiian islanders, a meeting that began with the Hawaiians' viewing Cook as their returned god, Lono, and ended with his death at their hands when he failed to follow their script. Although such episodes of cultural clash bring together elements that had not previously been in contact, creating unpredictability, they do not consist entirely of randomness and contingency. The "structure" of the conjuncture is provided by the codes, customs, and cultural understandings that people carry with them and apply to the problem the conjuncture has presented to them. These are not just clashes: they are also ritual moments, or moments of conjoined ritual. Cook, after all, was as determined to make the Hawaiians behave in what was for him and his officers the appropriately subordinate manner as the Hawaiians were to make Cook behave like a god.

A SIMPLE MACHINE

My approach to understanding the evolution of suicide bombing in Afghanistan follows Sahlins' model in its focus on ritual as the form through which the structure of the conjuncture is mediated. The ritual that I set out to understand, which I see as central to understanding the evolution of suicide bombing, is sacrifice. I am, of course, not the first anthropologist to find broad significance in this ritual. Sacrifice has a long history in anthropology; in fact, it could be argued that it was the enigma of sacrifice that brought anthropology into existence. That is to say, it was the inadequacies of earlier explanations of sacrifice (and of other mysterious, seemingly universal cultural forms like the incest taboo) that led scholars in the later part of the nineteenth century to come up with more sophisticated and empirically grounded modes of investigation and generalization in order to make sense of this ubiquitous but not easily definable or explicable cultural form: what it was, where it came from, and what diverse forms it took in the various cultures of the world.[10]

For all the effort so far expended, however, the meaning, nature, and function of sacrifice remain elusive. Part of that elusiveness might derive from linguistic indeterminacy. *Sacrifice,* after all, is one of those umbrella terms that can be used to describe everything from the story in Leviticus of the casting out of the scapegoat to purify the village of disease to the human-devouring ritual complex of the ancient Aztec to the act of a batter in baseball hitting a fly ball to deep right field in order to advance a base runner. Sacrifice explains the action of a mother who quits her job to raise her children, and it is invoked at every nation's parade to honor those lost in war. A firefighter who dies of smoke inhalation while putting out a blaze in an empty warehouse is praised for his sacrifice, and giving up a chess pawn to corner a bishop goes by the same name. The word is also used in reference both to the 2,996 people who died on the morning of September 11, 2001, and to the men responsible for their deaths.

The vagueness of the term does not account for the continuing interest in sacrifice. Rather, that vagueness is a surface effect that demonstrates the magnetic attraction of the concept and the abiding sense that there is something important lying buried beneath the layers of language and the multiplicity of usages. Like many of my peers in academia, I believe something is worth discovering there, though I am also cognizant of the danger that I may only add more confusion to what is already a tangled web of partial solutions. Scholars have tended to add more stories to the stack rather than clear out the clutter that makes it difficult to get to the bottom of the pile. Our stories, more often than not, have been of the "just so" variety or—again, as Afghans say—*buud, na buud:* it was and it wasn't. These stories come in the form of explanations of how our ancestors moved beyond the state of nature through various acts of collective violence.

One work that went against this theoretical obsession with uncovering the historical roots of religion and culture in an original act of sacrifice was published in 1898 by Henri Hubert and Marcel Mauss and translated into English as *Sacrifice: Its Nature and Function.*[11] Mauss is most renowned for another work—*The Gift* (1924)—written in the last years of his career. *The Gift,* one of the most influential works in anthropology, is credited with providing the discipline with much of its intellectual foundation. *Sacrifice* has not enjoyed as much fame or had the same sort of influence. However, it might be argued that, rather than *The Gift,* with its focus on precapitalist modes of exchange, *Sacrifice* has the most to teach us about the trials and tribulations of the contemporary world.[12]

Hubert and Mauss take as their starting point sacrificial rituals described in ancient Vedic and biblical sources, but they do not assume any evolutionary connection between these early examples and what comes later. As students and disciples of the sociologist Émile Durkheim, they are more interested in discerning the commonalities of ritual practice across time and space and developing propositions that could explain those unities in terms of both form and function. Given the authors' preoccupation with ancient texts and ritual forms, much of the book is of limited relevance to my project; however, its theoretical approach embodies features of signal importance. For Hubert and Mauss, the primary role of sacrifice is to establish a pathway between the sacred and the profane worlds through the mediation of a victim whose destruction gives this relationship material form. Creation of a communicative link between the profane and sacred realms demonstrates the reality of the sacred. A second feature is the tripartite structure of both the rite (entry, act, and exit) and the division of responsibility (among the *sacrifier,* the sponsor of the sacrifice, to whom the moral benefit of the act accrues; the *sacrificer,* the person who carries out the sacrifice; and the *victim,* the individual or object offered up and destroyed in the sacrificial act). Despite the set nature of the ritual's structure and personnel, the act could nevertheless be employed for diverse purposes, among them the fulfillment of an oath, expiation of a sin, and initiation of an individual to a new status, depending on how the parts of the ritual were arranged:

> According to the end sought, according to the function it is to fulfill, the parts of which it is composed can be arranged in different proportions and in a different order. Some can assume more importance to the detriment of others; some may even be completely lacking. Hence arises the multiplicity of sacrifices, but without there being specific differences between the various combinations. It is always the same elements that are differently grouped or developed unequally.[13]

Because the elements of the rite can be arranged in different proportions and orders, it can be employed toward, at the one extreme, "inducing a state of sanctity" or, at the other, "dispelling a state of sin."[14] The ritual can bring about such different effects because the pure and impure are not conceived as dichotomous but rather as aspects of religious reality that can be exerted for good as well as for evil, depending on circumstances:

> Thus is explained the way in which the same mechanisms of sacrifice can satisfy religious needs the difference between which is extreme. It bears the same ambiguity as the religious forces themselves. It can tend to both good and evil; the victim represents death as well as life, illness as well as health, sin as well as virtue, falsity as well as truth. It is the means of concentration of religious feeling; it expresses it, it incarnates it, it carries it along. By acting upon the victim one acts upon religious feeling, directs it either by attracting and absorbing it, or by expelling and eliminating it. Thus in the same way is explained the fact that by suitable procedures these two forms of religious feeling can be transformed into each other, and that rites which in certain cases appear contradictory are sometimes almost indistinguishable.[15]

There are obvious difficulties in applying this analysis to understanding the role of sacrifice and the rise of suicide bombing in the Afghan conflict. It is, first of all, not always possible to delineate a ritual structure in the acts of sacrifice I examine; indeed, the act is often perceived as sacrifice only after the fact. In such cases, sacrifice is less a ritual than a retrospective process of recognition and bestowal of status. Likewise, the demarcation of roles—of sacrifier, sacrificer, and victim—appears to break down or be nonexistent in many of the situations I examine, such as in cases that involve explicit self-sacrifice. Nevertheless, Hubert and Mauss's work provides an invaluable starting point for my analysis, most importantly in the way they identify in the consecration of the victim the reality of violence (an object once alive is now dead) and understand that it is this act of killing that establishes the reality of the sacred and its tangible and immediate relation to the world of profane affairs.

In adapting and applying the concept of sacrifice to the Afghan conflict, I build upon but also simplify the lessons of Hubert and Mauss. As theorists have always done, I borrow an idea or an image from one domain of experience to make sense of what eludes ready explanation in a second domain. Even in this digital age, theory building is an analog process, and we make strides by extending what we already know and understand into areas that we do not yet know very well and do not at all understand. This is a metaphorical process, and "paradigm shifts" arise from a combination of new facts, new ways of perceiving those facts, and new insights that bring into focus the underlying patterns that are there for the seeing in the right light.

The analogue on which I base my theory of sacrifice is the simple machine. Like other simple machines, such as levers, screws, and pulleys, sacrifice converts, directs, and amplifies energy. Parts can be added to the basic structure, the energy produced can be directed along different channels to different ends, and that energy can be enhanced by the manner in which it is contained and released. In viewing sacrifice as a machine, I do not imply an instrumental or functionalist view of ritual process. Machines do not always fulfill the purpose for which they were originally intended, and that original purpose does not always prove the best use of a machine or foresee what unintended uses it might be put to or what the consequences of its use might be. If all of this is true for the machines that we consciously and incrementally invent, how much more true must it be for machines that no one invents, but which are happened upon or borrowed from someplace else? In this sense, I see the uses to which sacrifice might be put—whether it be the promotion of what Durkheim called "mechanical solidarity," what Marxists might call the "mystification" of power relations, or any other possible purpose—as an appropriation, and one that is likely eventually to fail, given that any particular ritual can tap but will never exhaust the energy on which sacrificial rites feed.

The energy that fuels this simple machine is the act of giving something up, most significantly manifested in the act of killing something or someone. There are sacrifices that do not involve—or only minimally involve—the act of killing, but all involve an act of giving something up, and it seems reasonable to suppose that the energy released by the act of sacrifice is proportional to the closeness of the relationship between the thing given up (or the individual killed) and the ones who remain behind. The energy released by human sacrifice can be so great, in fact, that it can explode through the container meant to hold and channel it, and that possibility must be accounted for. All machines do break down over time. But the life of a machine can be extended through proper maintenance and care. It will break down faster if it is poorly maintained and overused. Likewise, if the ritual vessel that contains the energy released is not strong enough to hold it—if, for example, the violence inflicted appears unjust or arbitrarily applied—the energy can escape from the container, damaging the machine and indiscriminately spilling the residual contents of unsuccessful sacrifice (doubt, recrimination, and anger) out into society, with sometimes devastating results.

The machine I am imagining has just a few parts. These parts can be found anywhere, and when the machine breaks down, it can be readily rebuilt. Because of its simplicity, the machine can also be retooled to other purposes, particularly by a ritual engineer with a good understanding of the basic functioning of the machine. Then it can become a very different machine from the one it used to be, and it can be used to achieve very different ends. If, in the beginning, sacrifice was used to assuage grief, it can be transformed into a mechanism for bringing grief to others. As we will see, its force can be amplified to such a degree that it can also bring about levels of destruction that would have been unimaginable when the simple machine of sacrifice first entered human culture.

Just as physical machines require a means for harnessing and directing the energy released, so too with sacrifice. One might say that the energy is released by the machinery of sacrifice in two stages. The first stage, which involves the act of killing, happens within the container of ritual; the second, which involves the act of witnessing and absorbing the ritual, completes the transformation of a biological process into a social process. The act of killing thus creates the combustion, but the pistons that convert that energy into dynamic form are, first, the actions and words that accompany the act and, second, the perception by those witness to the act of what has taken place and the stories they tell about it. This second stage is the less predictable and more dangerous. The operators of the ritual attempt to follow the instructions and carry out the ritual as exactly as possible. They seek to demonstrate that they are the only ones entitled to conduct the ceremony and that they are doing it as prescribed by law and tradition. But the spectators of the ritual act might judge otherwise. They might notice mistakes or question the validity of the rite. A lot depends on circumstance. Do those conducting the ritual seem to know what they are doing? Are they using the right instruments and using them in the right way? Does the victim evoke loathing or sympathy? Do the members of the audience feel as though they are watching something they are part of, or something that is being imposed upon them? In most cases, the machine functions as it is supposed to, but the possibility of failure must be accounted for and remembered.

In my metaphoric model, the "sacred" can be thought of as the "surplus energy" that comes from engaging in a collective action, the experience of which seems to the participants to be greater than the sum of its parts and to come from somewhere else. Because we do not know what to call that surplus, we give it a name that associates it with something that we do not control, that comes from without, and that is inexplicable and therefore wondrous. That surplus can be greater than the force of arms, as people will fight to control its source in order to possess its power. To a great extent, that is the story told in this book. It is also the story of how something that begins simply and constructively becomes, through the efforts of those who would have that power for themselves, something both incomprehensibly complex in its workings and tragic in its consequences.

The language of sacrifice I am using here might seem quite different from that of Hubert and Mauss, but the similarities are more important than the differences. Following their lead, I see the role of sacrifice as communicative and affirmative of the role of the sacred in the everyday world, in this case the everyday world of violence and loss. That violence can be transmuted into sacrifice is what makes the sacred real and loss thereby manageable. Like Hubert and Mauss, I also believe that, though sacrifice has certain recognizable and standard components, it is mutable and can be deployed toward different desired ends. Where my conception of sacrifice would seem most to differ from theirs is in their specific concern with formal rituals. My notion of sacrifice is more sweeping and often makes no reference to a particular ritual act or to individuals who fulfill in any obvious way the ritual roles of sacrifier, sacrificer, and victim. However, I see these differences not as deviations but as adaptations of the original theory that help us to understand contemporary adaptations of sacrificial ritual.

Martyrdom is the most important of these mutations for understanding the conflict in Afghanistan. Although it might appear that the idea and ideal of martyrdom have a certain permanent and ineluctable quality—a person gives "the last full measure," and those he leaves behind honor his passing in a culturally appropriate fashion—the certainty and finality we assume to be inherent in death and its remembrance are, in fact, illusory.

Defining a death as an act of martyrdom has at least as much potential for introducing doubt and finitude as for creating certitude, both for those who are part of the society that has come up with that designation and for those of us on the outside who are trying to make sense of the act. What is martyrdom, after all? How is it constituted as a true act of sacrifice, and who has the authority to make that determination? Do you have to die fighting, or can you die on the way to the fight? Is it necessary to have made a prior commitment to fight in order to be judged a martyr? Are you a martyr if your intention is simply to gain fame for yourself as a brave warrior, or if your motivation is specifically to die?

These are matters for which there are no definitive answers, even from experts of various sorts. Questions of meaning provide extensive room for uncertainty, debate, and political maneuvering. Many of the most common answers to the simplest of these questions go back to scripture, which means that only Islamic authorities can provide accurate answers. However, the scriptures themselves are subject to multiple interpretations, and there is no certainty as to who has the authority to deliver these interpretations. Besides, people do not always want experts to tell them the answers when they have answers of their own. The net result is that martyrdom is both an ideal and a problem, and it is in the widening crevasse between experience and ideal that many of Afghanistan's most intractable problems have their origin.

Martyrdom is only one form of sacrifice. Another is the act of collective killing in which a "public" led by an "authority" (whether formally recognized as such or not) strikes down one or more of its members who have been judged guilty of a crime. Although the adjudication of the crime might be a legal matter, the public act of punishment can rightfully be considered a form of sacrifice, or, more specifically, of scapegoating. I will argue in chapter 4 that the Taliban adopted this form of sacrifice at a juncture when the machinery of sacrifice associated with martyrdom (a machinery that had helped to maintain the authority of the mujahidin parties during the Soviet occupation) had broken down due to infighting among the parties that had claimed the right to determine who was a martyr and which martyrs were more worthy of honor than others.

The Taliban period represents a time when martyrdom was eclipsed in importance by scapegoating rituals, but this was not the end of martyrdom.

Even while the Taliban regime was relying on acts of collective violence to solidify its legitimacy and power, so-called Afghan Arabs led by Abdullah 'Azzam and Osama Bin Laden were actively changing the way that martyrdom would henceforth be understood and deployed. No longer satisfied with the retrospective conferral of status on the dead, they affected changes in the sacrificial machine that made the martyr the willful agent of his own demise. Or, to use the terms of Hubert and Mauss, the martyr would henceforth take onto himself the roles of sacrificer, sacrifier, and victim, accruing to himself, as well as to the leader and group he represented, the moral benefit of his act of self-sacrifice. This was the pivotal moment in the history of sacrifice in Afghanistan, and it laid the groundwork not only for September 11 but also for the subsequent alterations and manipulations to the machinery of sacrifice that have been undertaken since that cataclysmic event, including most especially the advent of suicide bombing, the subject of the final chapters of this book.

TWO

Honor

THE DOG FEUD

It happened that Said Jan lived in one house, and next door was Zafar. There was a path between their houses. Said Jan wanted to put a wall there to have some privacy, and Zafar told him not to put the wall there. Said Jan said, "I am building it." Then Zafar said, "Don't build it." So Zafar's son, Askar, fired at Said Jan. With one shot, he was killed.

When they did this, [the religious figure] Sahibzada Sahib Ibrahim Jan came [to mediate], and the tribal council decided to send Benaris [Askar's brother] away. This man was exiled. Both Zafar and Haji Sahib [the father of Said Jan] promised to pay 20,000 rupees as a guarantee [of abiding by the truce]. At that time, 20,000 rupees was like 200,000 today. . . .

Time passed. Maybe it was two years. Maybe it was ten years. I forget the year. It was raining and there was snow. [Said Jan's brother] Mand Ayub Khan had a dog, and it was running around outside their compound. There was still a gun with that Askar who was the son of Zafar and the brother of Benaris. He aimed at the dog and fired. He shot it in the back. The dog was running around and howling. People up to Bar Saparai and Shinili could hear the howling of that dog.

So the dog was killed, and Askar went to his house. After some days, Askar's father became very sad because of what had happened, so he went to Khogakhel of Barai Mena and asked some of their "white beards," and also Sahibzada Sahib Ibrahim Jan, to accompany him. So he brought these people and he brought the women of his family with Qur'ans on their heads and one sheep as guarantee, and he came to [Haji Sahib] and told him that, "My son killed your dog, so I brought these people as guarantors and the sheep as 'uzr [sacrifice]."

Askar's father realized that "they will take revenge on us." So he brought a sheep as 'uzr. Our grandfather told Askar's father, "I accept your apology," but . . . [his son] Mand Ayub Khan told to his brother, "I swear by the

Qur'an that I won't tie my turban until I send that Askar with this dog into the ground."

Thus begins the story of a feud that would consume the Butikhel branch of the Mohmand tribe for over forty years. The story was told to me by an old man named Shahmund, one of Haji Sahib's grandsons, who was involved in both the fighting and the process of reconciliation. The story is too complicated to go into in detail, as it involves multiple lineages and crosscutting ties of kinship, with unfamiliar names popping up and then disappearing and tangential events unexpectedly wrapping themselves into the main history. I have read and reread the transcript of the interviews I conducted with Shahmund and his nephew, Muhammad Ali, many times. It is over sixty pages long, and every time I get confused by the names, which change in the course of the telling. Sometimes Said Jan's father is called Haji Sahib, sometimes Haji Reza Khan, sometimes just Reza Khan. The names used to identify all the actors in this drama can change with the circumstances being described.

As confusing as the story becomes when new characters and incidents are added to the string, one can discern an underlying structure. A dispute breaks out. A delegation goes out to ask elders and religious figures from surrounding villages to come and fix the problem. A truce is arranged, with steep monetary penalties imposed on any party to the dispute who breaks it. A larger tribal assembly (*jirga*) convenes to arrive at a solution that both compensates the victimized family for its loss and ensures equivalence. The focus of these negotiations is less on the punishment of individuals than on reasserting parity. An individual who causes a dispute might be viewed as a *badmash* (a bad person, a troublemaker) if he repeatedly causes trouble in a way that seems disconnected from any honorable intent. He might also be viewed as mad (*lewanai*) and therefore not responsible for his actions. But the goal is not really punishment of the individual and certainly not rehabilitation. There is no implication of sin, moral turpitude, or any other failing. Even when a person is sent into exile, it is not because of his character or the harm he personally has done to the community but rather because of the need to redress one family's loss by an equivalent loss to the family deemed responsible for the dispute.

In imagining the role of feud in Pakhtun tribal society from something like a native's point of view, it is important first of all to note that how it is viewed depends in part on generation. Young men are primarily concerned with their own reputation and are willing to take great risks in order to gain a name for themselves. Family disputes provide an ideal setting for pursuing their interests. They undertake actions that boost their personal reputation ostensibly to uphold the family name, but they sometimes do so in such reckless ways that the security of the family is jeopardized, whether they succeed or fail. Older men try to maintain the family name by managing the family affairs so as to strengthen the family's position and minimize its vulnerability to threats from others. This includes securing sufficient wealth to ensure the family's independence from others, negotiating advantageous marriage alliances, maintaining a guesthouse to offer hospitality to friends and allies who can be called on when needed, and participating in tribal assemblies in which they use their wisdom and verbal skill to persuade others of their point of view. Older men need young men to protect the family, but they also recognize that the same spirit that keeps enemies at bay can bring those enemies to their door.

Studies of Pakhtuns often begin with *Pakhtunwali,* the so-called tribal code of honor. However, this focus distorts the nature of honor in the tribal context, suggesting that honor is governed by a set of rules, observance of which ensures one's status. The conceptual basis of Afghan tribal society is better described by the term *doing Pakhtu* (*pakhtu kawal*), which conveys the idea that honor is founded in actions, not in rules, and in the evaluation of those actions according to principles that have been formulated through prior actions and the stories that are told and retold about those actions.[1] Many of the provisions of Pakhtunwali, in fact, relate not to the attainment of honor per se but to problems of maintaining relations in a society where personal reputation is paramount and there is no central authority to impose its will on recalcitrant individuals.

Rather than thinking of Pakhtun honor as governed by a code, it is better to think of it as a cultural conceptual space within which identity is negotiated. Referring to it as a code implies that it is straightforward in every instance to know what the proper action would be and to act accordingly. In fact, doing Pakhtu is highly complex and subject to contestation. It centers on a series of conceptual contradictions that have to be worked out in practice, not through any rule book. The most important of these contradictions centers on the contrary impulses toward self-determination and negotiated compromise. Thus, though much is made of the Pakhtun ethos of bravery and self-determination, there is a countervailing social pressure toward conformity and acceptance of social norms, as expressed especially in the jirga, the institution that punishes those who violate those norms. Too much self-determination, and the person is seen as arrogant (or a badmash) and is shunned; too much willingness to compromise, and a man is considered weak and effeminate. Too much social control, and individuals are discouraged from acting independently, with the result that the tribe itself becomes vulnerable; too little social control, and all brakes against violence fail. Managing these negotiations is a delicate business that is constantly subject to disruption and abuse. An important component of the process that keeps it on track is sacrifice.

Most rituals practiced by Pakhtuns that involve sacrifice are associated with Islam, and most are rituals that are also practiced by Muslims elsewhere. The general and most common term used to refer to sacrifice is *qurban* or *qurbani*, though other terms are also used that usually refer to particular variants of sacrifice.[2] Animal sacrifices are especially important and common: they typically involve slaughtering a sheep or goat, though cows, camels, and water buffaloes can also be ritually sacrificed. Like Muslims around the world, Afghans slaughter sheep in commemoration of Ibrahim's near sacrifice of his son, Ismail, at the time of the Eid al-Azha—or, as it is more commonly referred to in Afghanistan, Eid-i Qurban (Dari, "feast of the sacrifice") or Loya Akhtar (Pakhtu, "great feast"). Animal sacrifices also accompany important rites of passage, such as a male circumcision (*sunat*), the first head shaving of a male child (*sar kalai*), the anniversary of a relative's death, and the presentation of charitable donations, known as *kherat* and *sadaqa*.[3] Similar sacrificial acts can occur when a person returns home from a long trip or on the occasion of a tribal assembly's agreeing to the terms of a truce or of a punishment to be meted out against a person convicted of some sort of crime or trespass.

As in the case of the Dog Feud, a person, family, or group can indicate their intent to end a feud or otherwise sue for peace by offering a sacrifice to the other side, often by sending a delegation of women, accompanied by elders, to the compound of their enemies. The women carry copies of the Qur'an on their heads, an action that symbolizes the group's acceptance of the role of "petitioner" (if not of loser). The delegation also brings a sheep, referred to as 'uzr, as a form of apology. Sending a female delegation is, in effect, a sign of the petitioning group's offering up to the other side what is most valuable to them, namely the honor (*namus*) of their women.[4] The copies of the Qur'an that the women bring signal the sanctity and seriousness of their intent. Sending the women to the other side demonstrates the group's faith that the women's honor will remain inviolate. And just as female relatives exchange visits en masse on holidays, this movement of women is understood as the first in a series of friendly visits. Finally, the offering of a sheep as a material expression of the family's desire for negotiation is intended to seal the deal: by slaughtering the animal, the recipients indicate their willingness to accept at least a temporary truce, and this acceptance sets in motion the assemblage of a tribal jirga.[5]

In all these cases, sacrifice is used as a way of symbolically invoking Islam in the context of life events. Symbolically here could be taken to mean superficially, given our tendency to use the term symbolic almost as a synonym for meaningless. But symbolism here has a deep significance (as it does in Western societies as well, even if our sense of ourselves as "rational" beings sometimes occludes our ability to see that significance). Sacrificial rituals are offerings that refer an event to another domain of meaning. When a sacrifice is made at an *eid* feast, as part of a rite of passage, or to conclude a collective agreement, it works to sanctify and sanction the ritual being performed. However, to say that sacrifice only sanctifies and sanctions is to reduce to insignificance what sacrifice is and does. My interpretation of sacrifice as a machine for releasing and directing energy gives greater weight to the act, even in these relatively routine contexts. In relation to feud, nothing about what sacrifice does is routine: in essence, sacrifice provides the mechanism that mediates the essential contradiction between self-determination and social control. In this sense, sacrifice is a mechanism for changing the terms of social engagement from violence to negotiation. Sacrifice can thus be thought of as a form of metacommunication through which people involved in a dispute can switch frames—from one in which the appropriate action involves young men shooting at each other to an alternative frame in which older men decide how to reapportion resources in such a way that parity between parties can be reasserted.

The uses to which sacrifice is put in the tribal universe are associated with and gain their sacred character from Islam. The presence of one or more men whose status derives from Islam and who supervise the sacrifice (reciting the appropriate Qur'anic verses and sometimes cutting the animal's throat) provides the assurance that tribal practice is fully commensurate with Islamic belief.[6] However, this practical correspondence between tribal and religious practice obscures an inherent tension between honor and Islam.

Though rarely manifested as such, this tension becomes especially important in certain political contexts. The Pakistani anthropologist Akbar S. Ahmed argued that "Pukhtunness and Muslimness do not have to coalesce, they are within each other, the interiority of the former is assumed in the latter."[7] In one respect, this statement is adequate and accurate. Pakhtuns assume without question that belief in Islam is part of who they are. However, there are occasions when adherence to cultural ideals associated with Pakhtun identity can set in motion contradictions with ideals associated with Islam. None of the actions associated with feud are condoned by or in any way related to Islamic discourse and belief. Sacrifice is invoked and is thought of as providing religious sanction to the processes, but the symbolic expressions of sacrifice and uses to which it is put are idiosyncratic to tribal customs and institutions. In arriving at solutions to a conflict, the jirga adheres primarily to local precedents, collectively referred to as *nerkh,* and only secondarily to Islamic *shari'a* (or religious) law. The presence of religious figures in the jirga process provides religious sanction, their participation demonstrating that nerkh does not disagree with shari'a and therefore is acceptable. Throughout, Islam and specifically shari'a law remain in the background.

What is most striking, given that feuds involve matters of life and death, and specifically of killings in the name of a cause greater than the individuals themselves, is that those deaths never inspire the use of terminology related to martyrdom. I cannot recall a single account in which someone killed in a feud is referred to as a martyr. Nor, in these accounts, does one find concern expressed for the souls of the dead. Casualties in feud are buried with normal religious formalities, but there seems to be no greater need to explain or justify that death than there would be to justify a death from disease or a car accident. It might even be said that, in the tribal context, death by feud constitutes a death by natural causes. The most succinct expression of the disconnect between feud and martyrdom I have come across occurs when Sultan Muhammad Khan, a leader of the Safi tribe (whose career is examined in my book *Heroes of the Age*), finds his elderly father mortally wounded by cousins jealous of his power and wealth. With his last breaths, the father tells his son not to seek vengeance for him: "My son, God has given me paradise because I am a pure martyr. I have never deprived anyone of their rights, so be careful that you don't ruin the Day of Judgment for me." The son immediately rebuffs his father's dying request, making it clear that what he asks is inappropriate and irresponsible, given where and among whom they live: "The dead have no rights over the work of the living. I am alive. If I do not have the force and power in me to take revenge on one person for every bullet that has struck your body, then I would not be your son."[8]

The Safi War took place in the mid-1940s, roughly when the Dog Feud was heating up not far away in Mohmand. It is significant that this conflict is always referred to as a *jang* (war) and never as a jihad, because the protagonists—the Safi tribesmen who rebelled against the government—never succeeded in convincing others, or even themselves, that their actions were justified. In the controversy over these events, we can also see a shift in the calculus and meaning of sacrifice. As in the Dog Feud, the central actors in the Safi War came from one of the most isolated parts of the country—the steep, inaccessible tributaries on the west side of the Kunar River Valley—but the context was different. Tribesmen were defending their interests not against their kinsmen but against the state. The issue at the center of the conflict was conscription, specifically whether the Safis would continue to supply their quota of troops to the Afghan army on the basis of *qawmi,* by which the tribal elders selected the conscripts, or according to *nufus,* which gave the government the right to select men based on its calculation of the population in the area, thereby eliminating the role of the tribe as intermediary between its members and the state. I interviewed one of the four leaders of the Safi War in 1983, while conducting doctoral research in Peshawar. Aman ul-Mulk, like Shahmund and Muhammad Ali, my Mohmand informants, had taken refuge in Peshawar after the Soviet invasion. Like Shahmund, he was an old man by the time I met him, but his memories were clear:

> The Safi War started because of conscription. Before we had given qawmi, but the government wanted nufus. We sent elders and mullahs with the holy Qur'an to the government. "We cannot give you nufus. We can only give you qawmi." The government accepted this the first year, and we gave qawmi, and the Jalalabad Brigade was formed from this qawmi. The next year the government again wanted nufus, and again we sent *torsaree* [black-headed women] with Qur'ans on their heads to the government. . . . For thirty years, we gave qawmi to the government. From this qawmi, the Kala-i Jangi in Kabul was built. Then Sardar Lewanai [the so-called Mad Prince, Daud Khan], came to Jalalabad: "You must take nufus." We again begged Daud Khan, and we again gave qawmi, and from this qawmi, the gendarmerie in Jalalabad was built.[9]

As the government in Kabul gained strength, its demands escalated: it insisted not only that conscription be organized according to official calculations of population but also on taking twice the previous number of men.

This was too much, and the four Safi tributaries in the northern districts of the Kunar River Valley rose up against the government in 1945:

> When the fighting started, one mullah came and told us that Sardar Lewanai said that the Safi women would be sold for two paisa each and we will make a market to sell them. At that time, we had already started fighting in Salampur. When we heard what Daud Khan had said, we told ourselves that death would be better than having our women sold in front of us. The fighting became more intense from that point.

The conflict continued for eleven months, during which the tribe found itself with a problem beyond that of fighting a larger and better-armed fighting force: deciding whether they had the right to engage in this fight and, if so, how it should be fought.

> Mullah Sayyid Jamal was the big mullah. We asked him what we should do when *roza* [the month of fasting] came. If our dead would be spoiled [*kharob*], we wouldn't fight with the government. He gave a *fatwa* after three days: "You should keep the fast until the mid-afternoon prayer. After that, if you don't face difficulties, you should maintain the fast and make *niyat* [determine your intention]." [10] [He also decreed that] if twelve thousand people select a king [*padshah*], and the people accept the order of the king, the deaths of these people is not kharob. He was a big mullah, and . . . the other mullahs stood behind him, and he was in the front when he ordered all the others to accept it.

Based on Mullah Sayyid Jamal's fatwa, the tribe decided that it was not enough to fight the government as a tribe. Instead, they had to constitute themselves as a state, with the four leaders taking titles imitating those of the government they were fighting against:

> We called Amanat Lewana ["mad," parroting the popular epithet for the unpopular Daud Khan]. He was our prime minister. Shasawar was minister. Salimai was king, and I was minister of defense. We used these titles because we were fighting against an Islamic king. . . . The mullahs told us to select one elder and call him king, and if the government attacks beyond the road, then you should also attack them. In that case, your death does not become kharob. This king should order the people to accept his order, and your death would not become wrong. This order to fight was given to us by mullahs. The elders told us to accept these orders.

Ultimately, the rebellion failed. The government used artillery and superior weaponry to subdue the Safis, and, in a demonstration of the difficulties that would afflict the tribes in the region when the communists took power in 1978, a number of other groups in the Kunar Valley joined the army to fight the Safis on the promise that they would have booty to plunder. For my present purposes, what is most interesting about these events is the importance given in Aman ul-Mulk's testimony to the status of those who died fighting the government. Repeatedly during the interview, he brought up the subject and reiterated what Mullah Sayyid Jamal had told them: that if they had twelve thousand men behind them, and if they constituted themselves as a state, and if they were attacked, then their protest would become a jihad and their dead would not be "spoiled" or desecrated. The ultimate disposition of the dead in feud seems unrelated to the manner in which the death occurs, and the matter did not come up in the course of my many hours of interviews about the Mohmand feud. But when the Safis rose up against the state, it suddenly took on monumental importance. Thus, the Safi decision to commit to an uprising seems to have engendered a profound sense of uncertainty. They were in new terrain, and voices that had previously been carefully muted, the voices of religious leaders, rose up with new force and relevance.

Perhaps part of the explanation for this difference in attitude lies in cultural differences between the Safis and the Mohmands and in the roles of their religious leaders. But both tribes are famous for their adherence to tribal values of honor, and it is perhaps indicative of their shared concern for honor that both follow the custom of sending women with Qur'ans on their heads to end a conflict: in the first instance to negotiate a cessation of hostilities in a feud, and in the second to resolve a conflict with the state. The story of the Safi tribesman Sultan Muhammad Khan, who rejected his father's dying plea that he not take revenge for the father's murder, is also exemplary of the importance that Safis, like Mohmands, attach to the ethos of honor and their willingness to subordinate religious concerns to its dictates. Thus, there is at least circumstantial evidence that the difference lay not in the constitutions or attitudes of the two tribes but rather in the nature of the conflicts and specifically the uncertainty brought about by a tribe's taking up arms against the state. In this context, the tribes seemed to lose their natural confidence in the rightness of their way of doing things and turned to the outside expertise of religious leaders for counsel.

It is also perhaps significant that Aman ul-Mulk never used the term *shahid* (martyr) nor claimed that status for any of those who died fighting the government. The only concern he expressed was that their deaths would not be "spoiled," and he even seemed to concede in his comments that their decision to rise up against the government was unwise, if only because their efforts ultimately failed and all the leaders were exiled to the distant Shulgara district of northern Balkh Province. Still, the concern for the status of the dead, as dictated by religious considerations, seems a significant shift from the apparent indifference expressed by Shahmund and Muhammad Ali in their descriptions of feud. Although these examples cannot be held up as definitive, they illustrate the tension between honor and Islam. Before the onset of fighting in 1978, this tension was generally suppressed, but it became unavoidable when the tribes found themselves entangled with outsiders who made different claims to legitimacy, claims that created dissonance and uncertainty for those previously confident in the primacy and superiority of their own way of life.

TRIBAL POETICS

In *The Great War and Modern Memory*, Paul Fussell demonstrates that the transformation in British consciousness that occurred with the onset of World War I resulted in the disintegration of heroic sentiment and a necessary embrace of irony as the only way to express the unbridgeable disjunction between the reality of the soldiers' experience and the official reports and the enduring attitudes of those far from the front, who still believed that the war had transcendent meaning. Those who survived the conflict could never again completely believe what they were told by those in authority, nor could they entirely believe in the myths and axioms their society posited as the basis of truth and beauty.

In Afghanistan, too, a transformation came about based on the disjunction between experience and prior belief, but that transformation did not lead to irony. As in Britain, the principal casualty was honor, but in Afghanistan, the refuge was Islam rather than satire. Islam provided a template for understanding the conflict, at first in general terms but over time in the more concentrated figure of the martyr. This transformation is apparent in the same source that Fussell so adeptly taps: the poems written during the war and the changes revealed as the war progresses.

As elsewhere in the Middle East, poetry in Afghanistan is an important vehicle for the expression of cultural values and norms and political beliefs.[11] Its role in Afghan culture has been noted by a long line of scholars, beginning with Mountstuart Elphinstone in the early nineteenth century and continuing through a number of late-nineteenth-century writers, such as H. G. Raverty and C. E. Biddulph, whose preface to his 1890 anthology of Afghan verse contains the following observation:

> Afghanistan has always been a country abounding in rustic poets, and amongst a people absolutely devoid of any other form of literature the poetic has, as amongst most free and mountainous races, been ever the favorite mode of recording any forcible impression whether of a sentimental, historical or moralistic description which may have occurred to the composer.[12]

The poems I consider in this chapter have been transcribed and translated from Pakhtu-language cassette tapes recorded between 1978 and 1980 and offered for sale in the music bazaars in Peshawar and other market towns along the border. According to my informants, these tapes were produced by poets, musicians, and shop owners on portable recorders, without the assistance or control of any political party or government agency. Most of these cassettes were produced and purchased in what was then called the North-West Frontier Province of Pakistan and is now called Khyber Pakhtunkhwa, but the creators and most of the buyers came from the border provinces of eastern Afghanistan. Many of the cassettes were carried back to Afghanistan, where they were played with great frequency during the first months after the Marxist coup d'état, when people in the border region were deciding whether to openly oppose the government. One individual who was then living in the Mohmand territory along the Afghan-Pakistan border when the decision was made to attack the government told me that the poetic exhortations on the tapes played a significant role in galvanizing people to take up arms (figure 4).

For border Afghans, the most famous writer of political verse is undoubtedly the great eighteenth-century warrior-poet Khushal Khan Khattak, who is often held up as the exemplar of Pakhtun cultural values. On first sight, Rafiq Jan, the poet whose work I consider in this chapter, does not bring to mind a paragon like Khushal Khan, nor does he appear to be a man capable of influencing events or helping to spark a popular rebellion. Unimpressive in stature and humble in demeanor, Rafiq Jan, when I met him in 1984, was indistinguishable from tens of thousands of other Afghan refugees living in dingy apartments in the Peshawar bazaar. However, between 1978 and 1981, Rafiq Jan recorded over sixty poetry cassettes that were purchased, listened to, discussed, and memorized in villages close to the Afghan frontier, at a point in time when the residents of those villages were wondering just how they ought to respond to the new regime in Kabul. Rafiq Jan's poems helped

FIGURE 4. Afghan mujahid with tape player, Paktia Province, 1984. Author's photograph.

to provide answers, and they did so in a medium that Afghans were familiar with and that they knew and trusted. Rafiq Jan was not responsible for igniting the insurrection against the Khalqis. It certainly would have gotten started without him, but he did articulate a local vision that helped clarify the issues in the conflict for people at the time, and in retrospect his work helps us to see some of the ways in which the Khalqi revolution misjudged its audience and squandered its opportunity.

In the years before the April 1978 coup, Rafiq Jan wrote poetry in his spare time while making his living as a day laborer and small-time smuggler of goods between Afghanistan and Pakistan. He earned enough from his various jobs to purchase a tea shop in the Peshawar market, which he kept for some years before buying a shop near the Firdous Cinema that sold cassette tapes, mostly bootlegged soundtracks from Indian and Pakistani films. This relatively comfortable life was jolted by news of the Marxist coup. Though he had settled in Peshawar, Rafiq Jan still saw himself as an Afghan, and, the day after the coup, he took a bus to Kabul to witness events for himself, returning to Peshawar after seeing the smoldering tanks in the streets near the presidential palace. That summer, about the time of the first antigovernment violence among the Safis in the Pech Valley of Kunar, he returned to Afghanistan to attend his brother's wedding and again saw the transformations initiated by the Marxist regime. Shortly after this trip, he began to write what he referred to as "revolutionary poems," which he recorded in collaboration with professional musicians, who put the poems to music. These recordings were sold to Afghans who carried them back over the border. Soon they became so well known that he could return to his country only in secret:

> Taraki's government tried to capture me or my cassettes in Kabul, Barikau, the Khyber border post, up to Kunar and Asmar. They had tape recorders with them and they would listen to the cassettes to find out what was on them. They tried very hard to outlaw my cassettes from Afghanistan, and they arrested so many people for playing these cassettes. One time, Commander Abdur Rauf [the head of the Asmar garrison, who defected to the mujahidin shortly after the Soviet invasion] told me that the governor of Kunar told him just to capture my cassettes, not men.... The cassettes of my revolutionary poems had a very positive effect in provoking people. That's why the Khalqis were very angry at me.[13]

Rafiq Jan's sense of the importance of his poetry is not exaggerated, even if his fame proved short-lived. In the Mohmand area and elsewhere, cassettes of his poems began to appear in the winter of 1979, when tribesmen were meeting in jirga to decide whether to attack local government posts. The poems had the intended effect of casting the government in a negative light, reminding people of the obligations of honor, and inciting them to battle. The response justified Rafiq Jan's pride in having helped set the antigovernment insurrection in motion, at least in the border areas.

"WHO DOESN'T CARRY ARMS SHOULD NOT BE CALLED A MAN"

The first stage of the Afghan conflict was the briefest, lasting just over a year and a half. The Marxist regime that took power on April 27, 1978, immediately tried to mobilize popular support by initiating reforms designed to appeal to economically and socially marginalized portions of the population. That plan failed, and, within three months of the coup, locally organized groups in a number of areas had risen up against the regime.[14] In some areas, resistance was fomented and organized by Sufi brotherhoods, in others by local leaders or village councils. In the Pakhtun tribal areas along the Afghan-Pakistan border, the resistance was initially organized around the institution of the tribal *lashkar*—an army formed from young men representing the various patrilineal subdivisions of the tribe.[15]

Like Khushal's verse, Rafiq Jan's poems orbit around notions of individual bravery and generate their fervor from a combination of exhortation, denigration, and satire, the latter intended to illustrate the opprobrium that will be heaped on those who fail to show bravery in battle. An example of this style can be seen in the opening lines from a poem by Rafiq Jan in which the poet addresses members of the Safi tribe who were among the first to rise up against the government but who then fell quiet:

> Safis! Before you were heavy, why do you weigh so little now?
>   Don't be cautious, shoot all of the [Marxists] with your five-bullet guns.
> Safis! Before you were heavy, but now you are as light as straw.
>   Find for yourselves good guns and ammunition.[16]

In these lines, the poet introduces the contrasts that are elaborated throughout the poem between (brave) actions undertaken in the past by heroic ancestors and the inaction of those alive today. He goes on to implicate neighboring tribes and regions in a widening sphere of moral responsibility for the defeat of the government:

> Make unity, O Safi brothers, with the tribe of Jadid [Nuristan].
>   When you have become women, what can you expect from the Kunaris?
> In all of Kunar, there are no men, all are women.
>   Around the candle of religion, the Shunkraiwal burn themselves like
>   moths.
> . . .
> Why are you afraid, Shinwaris? Get up from your sleep, wake up!
>   You must go on the path of your ancestors.

The rhetorical structure of praise and rebuke employed here is reminiscent not only of earlier poets like Khushal Khan but also of the two-line verse form known as *landai*. Primarily associated with women and the difficulties, ambiguities, and unrealized desires they experience, landais also provide a warning to men that their actions will be judged. Landai are not attributed to individual authors; their anonymity only reinforces the warning, making it appear to be the consensus of society as a whole, an expression of what will be said behind a man's back, if not to his face, if he fails to act according to cultural expectations:

My lover fled from the battle.
　　Now I regret the kiss I gave him yesterday.[17]

Oh, my love! Sacrifice your head for the homeland.
　　Don't leave me to the taunts [*paighur*] of my girlfriends.

Who doesn't carry arms should not be called a man.
　　It is better for him to put henna on his hands and make-up on his eyes for
　　　the young men.[18]

The political salience of the landai form is best seen in its association with the perhaps apocryphal Afghan heroine Malalai, who is said to have averted a rout of Afghan forces in a battle with the British in 1880 by attaching her veil to a spear and shaming the nearly defeated Afghans into counterattacking. The story has endured, and its implicit message that it is better to die in battle than endure the unending stain of cowardice is expressed in an oft-quoted landai:

My beloved, if you do not fall a martyr in battle at Maiwand,
　　By God, someone must be saving you for a life of shame.

Malalai is more than simply an Afghan version of Marianne, the French icon of liberty. She has a particular symbolic resonance because of the dynamics of honor and shame that underlie her gesture. Attaching her veil to a spear shows a willingness to sacrifice everything, including her own feminine honor, to defend her homeland. The immodesty of the act demonstrates to the men that it was a desperate measure undertaken only as a result of their own inaction, and the shame that she risks by removing her veil is their shame. Once the dishonor has occurred, honor can be restored only by a compensating action that is likely to lead to death. Every retelling of the story reinforces the message that even victory will not entirely wipe away the taint of cowardice.

Although the story of Malalai has been frequently deployed as a patriotic legend, its significance is deeper: it speaks directly to the relationship between death and dishonor. As such, it can be seen as a template for Rafiq Jan's poetry. As with the landai, Rafiq Jan's poems tell of the rebuke that will fall on those who fail to fight bravely to defeat the Marxists. Unlike the anonymous poets of the landai, however, Rafiq Jan identifies himself and assumes the position of moral arbiter. This pose is acceptable because it is assumed not by an individual who is situated in a particular nexus of tribal relations but by the figure of the poet, whose position transcends particular rivalries. As the poet, Rafiq Jan is careful not to identify with or condemn any one group. They are all equally subject to honor and praise as well as rebuke and warning.

Of particular importance to this study is how Rafiq Jan positions himself in relation to Islam and specifically how he invokes the terminology of martyrdom, which in the following stanza is insinuated into the spaces between ancestral veneration and a satiric gibe:

> As good swordsmen were their fathers, so are their sons.
> The martyr is that one who is sprayed by the enemy's bullets.
> Martyrdom is chosen by those youths who don't care about food.
> When the people of Kandahar eat food, they lick the dishes.

These lines evoke the centrality of tribal—as opposed to Muslim—identity in the ethos of the resistance in this first stage of fighting. Among tribal Pakhtun men, their status as Muslims is taken for granted. Their identity as *men,* on the other hand, is much more tenuous and subject to forfeiture should they fail to act as expected. Since a man's status as a Muslim is ultimately a matter between him and God, the poet need not address the issue. However, a man's honor is a matter between him and his peers, and therefore one about which poets have a great deal to say, regarding both the ideals of honor and whether they have been upheld by the men whom the poet addresses.[19]

The almost cavalier mention of martyrdom in this verse—encased as it is between a reference to swords as weapons of war and a joking reference to the uncouth behavior of Kandaharis—tells us, first, that honor is the poet's primary concern, but it also demonstrates that widespread violence had not yet been unleashed on the country when the poem was written. Rafiq Jan was not yet aware of how warfare had changed since his grandfather's generation. His images of battle come from hearing old stories and poems rather than from actual experience. At this point in history, honor still took precedence over Islam, heroism over martyrdom. For the individual warrior, the aim of combat was not to achieve a specific military objective or even to kill as many enemies as possible; rather, it was to gain renown and avoid shame. Like a matador in a bullfight or a Plains Indian warrior "counting coup," the tribal warrior was expected to come within a footfall of death before artfully pulling back. The final stanza of the poem demonstrates the poet's willingness to risk all:

I am Rafiq Jan, and I weigh my poems on a true scale.

I will keep reciting these [lines] even if my flesh is roasting on the fire.

Rafiq Jan and other poets use Islamic terms to describe those willing to sacrifice themselves in the first stage of the anti-Marxist uprisings. They are characterized as *shahidan,* "martyrs," those willing to bear witness through their actions—but *what* they are bearing witness to is not self-evident.[20] If anything, it would appear that they are bearing witness to their own claim to honor and respect and to their fear of the shame incurred by cowardice. In this sense, the logic of this exhortatory poem is the logic of feud. It attempts to channel the energy of the traditional rivalries between individual warriors and tribes into a common struggle against the forces of the state. References to martyrdom in this poem are not only disconnected from any actual experience of death but also subordinate to and supportive of the ethos of honor, just as rituals of sacrifice are subordinate to and supportive of the ethos of honor when tribes engage in feud. Thus, Rafiq Jan's poems make no suggestion that men go into battle in order to please God or to earn their place in Paradise. Rather, they emphasize that if a man does not go into battle, or if—God forbid—he shows cowardice in the face of live fire, he will be subjected to the taunts of his peers, which, for a man of honor, would be a fate worse than death.

JANG TO JIHAD

One of the striking features of feud is the importance of proportionality. One death requires another to maintain the balance on which social life depends. But different lives have different value: men's and women's, elders' and children's, those of occupational specialists who live and work among a tribe and those of members of the tribe. It is the job of the tribal assembly to make determinations about value, and they do so as soon as possible after an act of violence so that the reckoning is precise, timely, and credible, and to prevent or at least scale violent retaliation. Feud is not so much about violence as it is a way of ensuring balance and the possibility of community while still allowing the autonomy of individual action that honor requires.

The war that began in 1978 forever changed that reckoning, and it did so on a variety of levels, including that of weaponry. Before the war, the bolt-action Lee-Enfield rifle was the weapon of choice for tribesmen, and it was a weapon well suited to the culture, in that each shot fired required the deliber-

FIGURE 5. Afghan mujahidin with weapons, Paktia Province, 1984. Author's photograph.

ate pulling of the trigger. Shots could be fired in fast succession, but each shot involved the action of aiming and shooting. Although cross fire could result in unintended casualties, complicating the allocation of responsibility, it was nevertheless possible for jirgas to keep score and ensure that violence was kept under control. As the war escalated, however, considerations of parity and balance were abandoned. One reason for this was the changing weaponry with which the war was fought.

Of particular importance was the proliferation of Kalashnikov AK-47 machine guns that—owing largely to U.S. government support—began to show up about the time I began my fieldwork. Unlike the Lee-Enfield, the AK-47 can shoot long bursts with a single pull of the trigger. It is also less accurate. In feud, these characteristics would be destabilizing, making it likely that larger numbers of people would be killed or wounded. For the purposes of the war, however, they were an improvement, allowing a small number of men to lay down a field of fire to protect their position. Other weapons also began to appear on the battlefield, such as rocket-propelled grenades (RPGs) and a variety of heavy machine guns that were effective in ambushing armored vehicles and—to some extent—protecting mujahidin bases from air attack (figure 5).

FIGURE 6. Victims of Soviet bombing, ca. 1986. Photograph courtesy of Afghan Media Resource Center, Kabul, Afghanistan.

These weapons gave the mujahidin a chance against their far better-armed enemy, but they also fundamentally changed the management and consequences of violence. With the increase in scale and speed of firing, it became more difficult to know who had done the killing and therefore more difficult to narrate the deaths or explain the fates of those who were killed. Feuds evolve gradually over long periods, and the stories told about them emphasize the preparations for violence more than the violence itself. Firefights happen quickly and in such a way that no one really knows what transpired. Heroic acts could still take place, but it is often difficult to sort out the heroic from the accidental, and heroes are less likely to emerge than victims. A burst of bullets fired from a distance leads to someone getting killed. Who did the killing is not clear. What is clear is that someone has died. Even more destructive of the heroic ethos was the kind of war that the government unleashed, which included the use of helicopter gunships, high-altitude bombers, heavy artillery, antipersonnel mines, and even chemical weapons. The Afghan army had included mechanized elements and combat aircraft for some time, including during the Safi War discussed earlier in this chapter, but the

Afghan military was neither so advanced nor so murderous as the Soviet version, which could rain destruction from great distances and reduce villages to rubble in a matter of minutes, killing men, women, and children indiscriminately (figure 6).

Facing this new kind of warfare, so savagely removed from anything they had ever experienced or heard of, poets backed away from the kind of playful satire and goading that seemed appropriate to the first period of the uprising. Poets, it appears, came to realize that they were now engaged in a different kind of conflict from any in their personal or collective memory. It was an existential crisis, a contest for the soul of the nation. The dynamics of the first stage of the war were those of feud and honor, and the underlying logic of feud and honor is conservative: it is the logic of equilibrium. This conflict would be longer and bloodier than any before it, and its outcome was far from certain. Even if he did not recognize the full extent of the change or the duration of the conflict his country was facing, Rafiq Jan did understand that something fundamental had changed and that this change had to be accounted for. As he told me when I interviewed him, Afghanistan had entered a "time of Islam":

> [The people] have acted bravely and have stood firmly against the enemy, so now they are beautiful. . . . They have sacrificed their blood. They have become martyred. They have lost their hands, feet, land, and houses, but they are still fighting. So now it is not the time to taunt or jeer. Now it is proper to praise them because they are facing their enemies without fear.

Rafiq Jan's concession to the exigencies of the conflict is also a concession to Islam. After the Soviets invaded, the names of specific tribes largely disappeared from verse. It no longer mattered what the Mohmand or Shinwari or Khogiani were doing. Whatever identity they might have possessed in the early days of the war was fractured through the efforts of the Islamic political parties to insinuate themselves into the fabric of the tribe and manipulate local rivalries to their own advantage. The locus of honor itself shifted from the tribe to political party, from tribal warrior to mujahid, from the act of killing to that of being killed.

Before the war, martyrdom was not emphasized. To say that a man who has died in a tribal dispute is a martyr is to imply that those who killed him are infidels—and also not Pakhtun, because Pakhtun identity presupposes Muslim faith. This association broke down as the war progressed, and, as that fissure widened, the role of sacrifice also changed. Before the war, sacrifice had been invoked, in Hubert and Mauss's words, to renew "that character, good, strong, grave, and terrible, which is one of the essential traits of any social entity."[21]

Sacrifice bound individuals through a shared respect for the social whole, without compromising their autonomy of action or their honor. Hubert and Mauss discern the balancing function that sacrificial rituals played in ancient texts, but the same wisdom could be applied to tribal society as it existed through the early stages of the conflict:

> [Individuals] find in sacrifice the means of redressing equilibriums that have been upset: by expiation they redeem themselves from social obloquy, the consequence of error, and re-enter the community; by the apportionments they make of those things whose use society has reserved for itself, they acquire the right to enjoy them. The social norm is thus maintained without danger to themselves, without diminution for the group. Thus the social function of sacrifice is fulfilled, both for individuals and for the community.[22]

Sacrificial rites of the old sort continue to mark important life events, and they are still offered as a way of expressing personal, familial, and societal gratitude to God for bounties received, however modest those bounties might be. Likewise, sacrifices are performed as part of truce negotiations, as they have been in the past. But, with the escalation of violence, the sacrifice machine that had long served to maintain social harmony and balance was turned to other purposes. There had always been emergencies in the past when the language of Islamic jihad was invoked, but those disruptions tended to be short-lived, and they never threatened the moral détente that existed between Islam, tribe, and state. The war that began in 1978 destroyed that balance. We do not know whether the change is permanent or whether the ballast of tradition is weighty enough to swing the capsized boat upright. We do know that the changes that have taken place since the war began have been epochal and unprecedented, and at the center of those changes is the figure of the martyr.

THREE

Martyrdom

WAR TRANSFORMED THE ETHICAL CONTOURS of Afghan society. The central values of honor and kin loyalty that held sway early in the conflict were soon competing with a different ethos. Making sense of that transformation requires recognition of the diminished role of tribes in the wake of the Soviet invasion in 1979 and the expanding power of the Islamic political parties that took root in Peshawar and spread their influence across the frontier into the Afghan heartland. The inability of the tribes to either combat the government or resist the inroads of the Peshawar parties led to the diminution of their role in the conflict. As tribes ceased to be the operational center of the antigovernment resistance, men who wanted to participate in the fight had to join one of the parties, abide by their rules, and obey their leaders. Tribal solidarity was loosened, as was the importance of tribal leaders. New loyalties emerged, not only to political parties but also to those with whom the fighters were sharing the challenges and deprivations of combat. The physical landscape itself changed as well. If the village had been the hub of communal life before, for those engaged in fighting, the center of activity and symbolic locus became the *sangar* (a "trench" or "bunker"), the space where the front both prepared for and fought its battles (figure 7). In this chapter, I consider the growing importance of martyrdom in defining this transformation, and I examine some of the ways in which the Islamic political parties took advantage of martyrs and martyrdom to augment their own power.

FRIENDS AND MARTYRS

The poetry composed in the second stage of the war—after the initial, naive optimism of the first uprisings but before the resistance parties in Peshawar

FIGURE 7. A sangar (a trench or bunker as a place of battle). Photograph courtesy of Afghan Media Resource Center, Kabul, Afghanistan.

began to exert control over the meanings of the war—shows a marked contrast in how death is understood and how it is commemorated. In contrast to the earlier verse, with its emphasis on honor, the poetry composed during this stage of the conflict is characterized by a focus on martyrdom. Most of these poems—at least among the examples I was able to collect—have a generic quality. They tell the story not of particular individuals but of martyrs in general, and they replace the rhetoric of heroism with a more plaintive form of expression, as in the following poem written by a poet who identifies himself as Gul Sha'er:

> Today, there is a battle against the infidels which is jihad.
>> Oh, I am going to the field, my father!
> I am going on the path of God and His Prophets,
>> There is a battle against the infidels which is jihad.
> . . .
> Today, our sisters and brothers have been martyred in the wild mountains,
>> There are flags waving in all the cemeteries.
> Martyrs don't need to be washed and shrouded,
>> They are the garden flowers.
> Today, I will martyr myself, and I will definitely go to Paradise.
>> Today, if you are martyred, there is no answer, no question.

FIGURE 8. Flags over a martyrs' cemetery. Photograph courtesy of Afghan Media Resource Center, Kabul, Afghanistan.

For anyone who doubts this, there is God's Book,
    There is Doomsday, the punishment of sinners, Oh God, the torment!
Gul the Poet announces the truth and gives you good advice,
    The person who is wise will accept this advice.[1]

If the tone of the earlier poems of tribal rebellion was uniformly strident, the tone here is far more subdued, the intent seemingly almost pedagogical in the sense of informing the listener of the significance of something they had previously been unaware of or to which they had not given much thought. In Rafiq Jan's exhortatory poems, battle was heralded as an opportunity for young men to fulfill the expectations of their forefathers by performing glorious deeds and splitting open the skulls of their enemies. Here, the prospect of going into battle is more frightening because the material consequences of warfare have already been experienced: the martyrdom of sisters and brothers, and flags waving over graves (figure 8). War is no longer history to be recalled, nor is it a sought-after moment in the future when young men will have the opportunity to prove themselves in battle. Under the bombardments unleashed by the regime, women were being killed as well as men, children as well as adults, the elderly and infirm as well as the fit and able.

In Rafiq Jan's verse, Islam is a subordinate symbolic element within a structure that achieves its most potent effect not through declarations of piety but through the dynamic opposition of warring tribes, of past and present, and of individuals besting their rivals in the struggle for honor. Islam, of course, is also an important component of Rafiq Jan's early vision, because adherence to Islam is a source of unity between tribes and regions; moreover, it provides the ultimate justification for going into battle and the reward for those who die in combat. But in the early poems, unity derives from the assumption that all those listening to the poem share a concern for honor and reputation. Islam serves more as a symbolic backdrop and legitimizing stamp for what people are being called on to do rather than the immediate motivation for doing it.

Over time, however, the situation began to change. War became an immediate reality rather than a historical abstraction, and it bore no resemblance to what people might have pictured from listening to stories of their grandfathers' brave deeds or the poems of Khushal. This was a kind of industrial combat in which machines did most of the killing, and there was nothing heroic in the manner of dying. This was not death by intent and action but, as often as not, by chance. In this context, Muslim identity and Islam's promises to its followers began to matter more and more, and a radical transformation began to occur in the significance of the conflict people were involved in and their own role in that conflict.

Although the form of combat was impersonal, the losses that people suffered were not, and poetry became a medium for expressing the intimate nature of grief. This transformation is apparent in the following verse by a poet named Gauhar. Although it still enshrines an ideal of heroic action, it is of a sort utterly different from that of earlier poems:

O, famous Martyr—your name is spread throughout the world.
    O lucky Martyr—you brought faith into the world.

You watered the garden of Islam with your blood.
    O battered Martyr—I keep your memory alive.
I sacrifice myself for every drop of your blood.
    O Martyr—I sacrifice for your blood-red trench.
. . .
You martyred yourself, but your widow and children stay in sorrow.
    O Martyr—you sacrificed yourself to learn the grief of the oppressed.
Your body became a sieve from the bullets.
    O Martyr—your blood says "Allah Akbar" every moment.
. . .
I send greetings to your soul every morning and evening,
    I kiss your sword in the trench, O Martyr!

I, Gauhar, pray for you every moment.
O Martyr—your rank will be high on Judgment Day!

Gauhar's verse is striking not only for its emphasis on self-sacrifice but also for how it deviates in its rhetoric from earlier poems like Rafiq Jan's. Thus, the martyr commemorated in the poem has acted with bravery, but he has performed in this way not to gain honor for himself or even to defend his homeland but, more abstractly, to "water the garden of Islam" (*ta de islam baghchah sairaba krah*) and "learn the grief of the oppressed" (*ta de mazlum la ghama ta kralo khabar shahida*). The poet also does not laud the active deeds of the martyr but instead emphasizes what has been done to him: "your body became a sieve from the bullets" (*ghalbail ghalbail dai tul surat shu pa gulaiu bandai*). Finally, the poet has left the venerable central character of the poem unnamed. In all of these ways, the poem evinces a departure from the poetic rhetoric and cultural ethos that informed Rafiq Jan's work.

In the tribal universe, one fights and risks death so that one's deeds will be recalled and enshrined in verse and story, thereby ensuring that the hero's memory will endure beyond his death. In this poem, however, the dead man is placed in a category—that of martyr—that obviates even the mention of his name or recitation of his acts of bravery. Immortality in the tribal universe is very much identity and deed dependent. The immortality of the martyr does not depend on his name or fame, those of his forebears, or his place in a tribal lineage. Rather, the martyr and his acts are known to God, and that knowledge, in the final analysis, is sufficient. As before, poetry serves to incorporate events in a language reflective of and committed to a vision of moral order and political action, but there is a difference here that has to do with the experience of war, the grief evoked by that experience, and the need to seek out a larger symbolic framework that will make that grief both endurable and significant.

Whereas Islam provides the framework for understanding the sacrifice of the unnamed martyr, the poem's central preoccupation is death itself. The dominant images are of blood and flesh mangled by the machinery of modern warfare: machine-gun fire and bombs. The poem thus combines a sense both of indeterminacy (in that the martyr is unknown) and of the vivid immediacy of a death that has been witnessed—or, perhaps more accurately, the experience of gathering the body parts of many martyrs for burial after an attack. The gruesomeness of the imagery is shrouded, however, in the speaker's idealization of the martyr, an idealization that calls to mind the image of "the Beloved" in Sufi poetry.

In these poems, the audience is intended to understand that the beloved one is God, but the language and imagery are so intimate and suggestive that carnal and divine love overlap and fuse, the spiritual dimension gaining emotional power from the personal. The same can be said of many of the martyr poems composed during the early stages of the war in which the imagery of blood and mutilation fuses religious symbols with a homoerotic tenderness that reflects the close male camaraderie that bound many of the mujahidin groups. In this sense, these poems can be connected to an important theme of Pakhtu culture: the veneration of the friend (*dost* or *rafiq*), memorably expressed in the poetry of Rahman Baba, the second great Pakhtu poet after Khushal Khan:

> True friendship's first condition it must be
> > That come what may, they will burn together.
> Separation from the friend
> > For one moment is like Judgment Day.
> Should their love take them to Hell,
> > For the friends, Hell is paradise.[2]

In the view of Charles Lindholm, who conducted ethnographic research in the Swat Valley in the 1970s, the Pakhtun ideal of friendship is much more intense than the casual concept of friendship that generally prevails in Western cultures, at least in part because friends stand outside the rivalries, obligations, expectations, and jealousies that otherwise pervade tribal life:

> Friends should be together constantly; they should completely trust one another and reveal all their secrets to one another.... The friend should be willing to sacrifice himself in total devotion to the will of the other. His affection must be spontaneous, without reservation, and all-consuming. The true friend is called "naked chest" because the hearts of both parties are bared to one another, thus sweeping away the pervasive secrecy and mistrust of ... society.[3]

Jihad replaced the social basis of tribal society, centered on a set of kin relations that were determined at birth, with a society of male brothers-in-arms whose responsibility to each other was based only on their commitment to a common cause. There was a kind of romance attached to these relationships—in a society in which heterosexual romance was largely precluded, even if poeti-

FIGURE 9. Burial preparations. Photograph courtesy of Afghan Media Resource Center, Kabul, Afghanistan.

cally and narratively imagined.[4] Male friends trust one another and owe no obligations to one another except those of loyalty. Such friendships had always been valued, as Lindholm demonstrates, but war increased their frequency and importance. The catch, of course, was that many of these brothers-in-arms died. The poetry of martyrdom reflects the grief associated with the loss of friends in battle (figures 9 and 10). But the transformation of the idealized friend into the idealized martyr transmutes that grief into hope, not only of a peaceful reward for the dead but also for future reunion.

The closeness of the male bonds expressed in these early martyr poems is also associated with the liminal space in which these relationships were forged, a space set apart from the world of the family and kinship responsibilities. With so many women and children in refugee camps in Pakistan, many villages were sparsely occupied, and the mujahidin groups themselves, which usually stayed on their own bases in the mountains, were made up almost entirely of men. Thus, the mujahidin for the most part lived in a hermetically sealed world of male relationships. These groups were structurally different from the earlier lashkars, which likewise had been composed of males, but nearly all of the members of the lashkars would have been kinsmen, connected by tribal genealogy and the hierarchies, obligations, and expectations that accompanied kin ties. Mujahidin groups, however, were

FIGURE 10. Afghan mujahidin praying at a martyr's grave. Photograph courtesy of Afghan Media Resource Center, Kabul, Afghanistan.

generally not organized along tribal lines. A large percentage of mujahidin in a particular group might be from the same area and even the same tribe, but tribal relationships were not specifically marked or relevant. Indeed, the Islamic parties downplayed the significance of kin ties, seeing them as contrary to and in some cases even subversive of the party and its leadership. The world of the mujahidin group, then, was one of male comrades, not of tribal cousins, who had left their families behind.

Most mujahidin groups moved back and forth each year between Pakistan, where they spent the winter, and Afghanistan, where they returned each year in the spring for the "fighting season." This movement was often ritually marked by the mujahed passing under a Qur'an held by his father or mother, the idea being that he was passing from the realm of peace (*dar al-Islam*) to the realm of war (*dar al-harb*). Often the lone object carried by the mujahid would be a woolen shawl (*patu*) in which he carried his food when he traveled, from which he gained some warmth when it was cold, and in which he was likely to be shrouded if he was killed. The central symbol of the liminal space of the dar al-harb was the sangar, which was usually thought of as a trench, often dug out of the side of a hill and fortified with stones, in which mujahidin waited to attack or withstand an attack from enemy forces. On a symbolic level, the sangar also connotes a place betwixt and between—a place outside the village or the city, a place from which attacks were mounted and repelled.

The sangar was outside the bounds of the domestic world overseen by women. Women might bring food to the fighters in the trench, but they did not stay there long because the sangar was the domain of men. As Gauhar's poem demonstrates, it was also a domain saturated in the imagery of blood and, in that sense, a liminal zone between life and death, between the sufferings of this life and the futural promise of eternal life in paradise. Consequently, those who inhabited this world did so in a state of preparedness and expectancy for the moments of violence that would signal their transit to another world.

The centrality of the sangar as a symbol in the emergent poetry of martyrdom can be contrasted with the central spatial symbol in tribal poetry and tribal culture generally, namely that of *watan,* or homeland. The term "watan" is used in a variety of contexts, including as a synonym for Afghanistan generally, but its emotional resonance is in relation to the land that the tribe itself owns, occupies, works, and defends. The English translation is, for once, on the mark, because the centerpiece of the homeland is "the home" itself. Unlike the image of the sangar, which emphasizes death, watan is more than anything an image of life. It is the place where children are born and within which the time one spends on Earth is passed. Both symbols carry with them the possibility of violation and death. The watan, after all, is where the ancestors are buried, and it is the space that others might at any time seek to take away and that the men who were born and raised there must be willing to give their lives to protect. But, unlike the sangar, which exists in the no-man's-land of war, watan symbolizes the land of living that must be defended from the threats of death.

The watan is also a fixed space. It can be expanded to include larger territories up to the limits of the nation itself, but it does not go beyond those borders. Sangar, however, is not fixed, and as the conflict continued and particularly as it spread to battlefields other than the mountains of Afghanistan, sangar was to prove a highly adaptable and useful metaphor that could be applied to a wide variety of spaces and places and to different sorts of combat. The sangar could be any place—as we will see—from a marketplace to a jet aircraft to the pages of Facebook. Always, though, an essential feature of what sangar has signified has been the quality of liminality—of being betwixt and between, of being materially in one place but spiritually in another, of living but being always prepared to die—and in that sense it has been critical to the evolution of martyrdom.

INSTRUMENTALIZING MARTYRDOM

The early poetry of martyrdom reflects the personal experience of loss and the attempt to transmute grief into meaning. The personal dimension of loss and its expression in poetry would persist as the war continued, but death quickly became politicized as some among the political parties vying for advantage in Peshawar came to recognize in the dead bodies that were piling up across the border an instrument that could be used for political purposes—as the raw material for creating a cult of martyrs that they could control. By dictating the meaning ascribed to those deaths, the parties could harness its energy to bolster a larger narrative developed by and for the interests of the parties themselves. To explain this process, it is necessary to consider the context in which this new sacrificial machine was constructed.

Following the Soviet invasion, the exiled Islamic political parties based in Pakistan (and, to a lesser extent, in Iran) assumed an increasingly important role in organizing, financing, and leading the anti-Marxist resistance. In addition to receiving assistance from Pakistan and other foreign powers, the exiled parties were able to capitalize on their religious authority to claim leadership over the scattered purposes and forms of local insurrection. With people throughout Afghanistan seeing the enemy as an infidel regime and looking to religion to validate their losses, the parties gained an edge in defining the conflict for their own ends. Although the various parties all claimed Islam as their calling, they had different credentials on which they based their claims to leadership. Thus, the two parties led by hereditary Sufi leaders (*pirs*) premised their right to command on the charisma inherited from their saintly forebears. The parties led by well-known clerics based their authority on their role as interpreters of scripture. This much was straightforward. The parties with a problem were the Islamist parties, which had no obvious basis for claiming authority or for expecting ordinary Afghans to follow them.

This problem had first revealed itself in 1975, when the leaders of the Muslim Youth Organization (*sazman-i jawanan-i musulman*) based at Kabul University audaciously and naively set off for their home districts to raise local insurrections, thinking that, because of the widespread dissatisfaction with the government, the people would take up arms and follow them into battle. They further thought that they could coordinate a number of popular insurrections simultaneously in different provinces and in conjunction with a military coup d'état in Kabul. Events did not go the way they anticipated. The local people for the most part ignored the students, in some cases even turning them in to the government. These experiences taught them a lesson not only about preparation, logistics, and organization but also about the importance of propaganda.

Martyr Magazines

Whether with strategic ends in mind or not, Hizb-i Islami and Jamiat-i Islami, the two offshoots of the Muslim Youth Organization and the most radical of the parties that set up shop in Peshawar, came up with at least a partial solution to their legitimacy problem when they began producing illustrated magazines.[5] The numerous copies of these magazines that I collected in the spring of 1984 all came from Afghan refugees in Pakistan, where they were published in large numbers and widely distributed at no charge. I have been unable to determine how extensively they were disseminated in Afghanistan, but I know from interviews and videos made at the time that mujahidin groups carried copies of these magazines with them when they crossed from Pakistan to their home country at the start of each fighting season.[6]

Most of the magazines were published in Dari and Pakhtu, though some also appeared in Arabic, Urdu, and English. These foreign editions contain articles about the party sponsoring the magazine and highlight recent battlefield successes. The magazines in Dari and Pakhtu have a different focus and seemingly a different purpose, most importantly the commemoration of martyrs killed in the struggle against communism. One such magazine is *Sima-yi Shahid* (The Visage of the Martyr), published by Hizb-i Islami. In keeping with its general theme, each issue of *Sima-yi Shahid* consists largely of obituaries and other pieces related to martyrs and martyrdom, including panegyric poems on particular individuals and battles, and theological commentaries and pronouncements on achieving martyrdom in Islam and the rewards awaiting martyrs in the next world. Although Hizb-i Islami condemned the sort of tribal poetry that Rafiq Jan produced, and Rafiq Jan himself told me that he stopped composing poetry because of threats he had received from the party, the magazines published by Hizb-i Islami also contained poems celebrating specific martyrs and martyrdom. One is a panegyric with the title "In

Praise of the Heroic Martyrs of the Thirtieth of May," honoring members of the Islamist movement who were arrested by the government, tortured in the infamous Pul-i Charkhi prison in Kabul, and later executed:

> What doves, so full of hope, that flew from the nest.
>> What brave men, all of whom went with legends in their hearts.
> Don't ask me about these guerrilla fighters.
>> By God, my words cannot tell the story.
> All are Afghan lions, all are saviors of the age.
>> All are possessors of faith, all are the lights of this house.
> . . .
> What brothers were these, so full of dignity and virtue.
>> For their decency, they have a home in the hearts of people.
> For Commander Abdul Hadi, for Pilot Ziauddin,
>> My heart is aflame, the grief is caught in my throat.
> For Sial Khan Mangal, who was the flower of courage,
>> Blood and tears are flowing from the corners of my eyes.
> In memory of Nadir, for the pain of separation from Qadir,
>> Night and day, commemorate them with poetic songs.
> In memory of Amin, so full of life; for Munib, whose character was like a precious gem,
>> Listen to my solitary song, it is a poem [ghazal] of love.
> For Shakur to Agha, all of them strivers for the movement,
>> If I judge, it must be with complete purity and sincerity.
> . . .
> Pul-i Charkhi prison was a place of knowledge and mastery
>> In a time of terror and cruel torture.
> All of them had these qualities, all of them had their strengths.
>> All of them became martyrs and warrior symbols.

One striking aspect of the poem is how much it resembles earlier poems celebrating martyrs. The adjectives and tropes used to describe the dead, the forms in which the poet addresses his listeners, and the ways in which he characterizes the poem itself have all been borrowed from panegyrics that go back to the early history of Islam and are especially associated with celebration of the Prophet Muhammad (*moulud*). The principal elements that set the Hizb-i Islami poem apart are the inclusion of the date of the executions in the title, the fact that one of the chief virtues of those who died was their participation in the Islamist movement, and the significance attributed to the prison as a site of struggle.

The Pul-i Charkhi prison, in particular, was a vital symbol of Hizb-i Islami's history and sacrifices and fundamental to its claims to leadership.

Many of its founding members had been arrested after Daud Khan seized power in 1973, and most of these were killed after the Marxists took power in 1978. The prison is described in a rich, metaphoric language as a place of despotism and suffering but also as a place of instruction. Prisoners learned from each other, with the more experienced and knowledgeable prisoners teaching the others. Moreover, the deprivations of the prison provided the means for deepening the prisoners' spiritual awareness and bringing an ever more profound realization of the limits of temporal power for the devout Muslim.

In the poem, the prison functions for the prisoner much as the isolated chamber (*chilla khana*) functioned for the Sufi, or the mythical cave of divine revelation functioned for the Prophet Muhammad: as a place of ascetic retreat where the devotee confronted both fear and temptation. Suffering confers spiritual authority. Sufi miracle stories reveal the power gained through total submission to God and the pir who heads the Sufi order. For the leaders of the Islamist parties, the lessons of the prison are transmitted through narratives of state-inflicted hardships and suffering published in the party magazines. The difference is that, whereas the Sufi metaphorically slays his material self in order to enliven his spiritual self, the prisoners were literally executed, and the lessons to be learned must therefore be communicated by and to surviving party members.[7]

This brings us to what is arguably the most important feature of the magazines: their use of numerous illustrations, the most dramatic of which are always the front and back cover illustrations. Some are hand-colored images of combat, with skies tinged an apocalyptic orange. The cover of one issue of *Mithaq-i Khun* (Oath of Blood) shows a crudely drawn image of a young man in prayer, a bloody stump where his head should be, his hands holding the head aloft in an offertory gesture (figure 11). More typical are studio portraits of young men in coats and ties, the photographs blown up, airbrushed, and color-tinted to highlight the subjects' blushing pink cheeks and piercing eyes against lurid backdrops (figure 12).

Inside the magazines, the lead articles are always eulogies for the individuals depicted on the front and back covers. They show how the events of the individual's life are given meaning by the final sacrifice. Subsequent obituaries are progressively less detailed, with the ordinary martyrs being grouped toward the back of the magazine under headings such as "Meet the Martyrs of the Path of Truth," "Sacrifices on the Path of God," and "Rose-Colored Shrouds from the Trench of Truth." These sections feature photographs accompanied by short obituaries that include the individual's name, father's

FIGURE 11. *Mithaq-i Khun* (Oath of Blood) cover illustration, vol. 1, no. 11, Mizan 1360 (Sept.–Oct. 1981), publication of Jamiat-i Islami Afghanistan.

name, place of residence, some brief details of his life and death, and finally a more or less formulaic denunciation of the enemy and a slogan in praise of Islam. A final section of obituaries is dedicated to those for whom no photograph could be found. These are relatively few, however, since most Afghans at least had photos of themselves for use on their Afghan or refugee identity cards, and these are the photographs most often used in the magazine.

In these memorials, status is determined by seniority in the movement. Consequently, those honored with a cover photograph are invariably young student leaders who were imprisoned by the government in the early 1970s

FIGURE 12. *Sima-yi Shahid* (The Visage of the Martyr) cover illustration, vol. 2, no. 9, Sinbula, Mizan, Aqrab, 1360 (Aug. 23–Nov. 21, 1981), publication of Hizb-i Islami Afghanistan.

and died in prison before the onset of the fighting. Typical in this regard is the tribute paid to one Miran Gul, reproduced in full here from an issue of *Sima-yi Shahid*:

Miran Gul, son of Baz Gul Khan, was born into a poor and religious family in 1330 [1951] in Ganggul village, Pech Valley. He received his primary education at elementary school in Barkendai. In 1346, he went to Kabul to attend Rahman Baba School.

Corruption and communist activities motivated him to join the mujahidin. The mujahid brotherhood assigned him to discipline and recruit mujahidin. He was very good at his job. During that time, the government authorities witnessed growth in the numbers of the Mujahidin and their influence. The government decided to stop them, and Miran Gul and a few of his friends were accused of a murder and were sent to prison. He was found not guilty and later released from the prison. After his release, he continued his political struggle. After graduating from Rahman Baba High School, he went to Gardez Province for a teacher-training program. However, he was sent to prison once again. After his release, he continued his political struggle aggressively until his completion of the training program. After he finished that program, he became a teacher in Kunar Province. And even in Kunar, he continued his struggle. He worked with the local people and the mullahs in the mosques and worked toward unity. During that time, President Daud came into power. Miran Gul was once again, for the third time, arrested by the government. He was kept in Kunar Jail for some time. Then Nangarhar's Governor Wasifi requested the government to send him to Dehmazang prison.

In 1357 [1978], when the communists reached their power through coup, they started to execute people. And Miran Gul was martyred by these communists. In 1358 [1979], he was martyred. When he was being executed, he said his final goodbyes to his friends and said to them, "Those who say, when disaster strikes them, 'Indeed we belong to Allah, and indeed to him we will return,' are the ones upon whom are blessings from their Lord and mercy. And it is those who are the rightly guided."

Miran Gul's long service to the party, the manner of his sacrifice, and his suffering as a repeat prisoner in the jails of the oppressive regime put him in the first rank of martyrs. It is also a mark of his importance and devotion that Miran Gul joined the party at an early stage, before the jihad proper had commenced. Precedence was of prime importance to Hizb-i Islami. Lacking the traditional claims to authority—Sufi lineage, clerical training, or tribal standing—they had to make the most of what they had, and chief among the virtues they could point to was the fact that their organization had been the first to raise the banner of jihad against the government.

Next in order of precedence after party loyalists like Miran Gul, front commanders who died in battle could count on obituary notices of modest length. Following them were ordinary mujahidin who died in the fighting (figure 13). Of greatest significance in determining this ranking were not the martyrs' feats of arms but rather their service to the party. An individual who had fought for five years at the front ranked behind a student who had been arrested for handing out leaflets back in 1973. Thus, boys with peach-fuzz

FIGURE 13. *Sima-yi Shahid* (The Visage of the Martyr) obituaries, vol. 2, no. 9, Sinbula, Mizan, Aqrab, 1360 (Aug. 23–Nov. 21, 1981), pp. 88–89, publication of Hizb-i Islami Afghanistan.

mustaches and cast-off Western sports coats are celebrated above turbaned warriors. In the party cosmology, the pen was mightier than the sword; the obedient party functionary was greater in stature than the tribesman willing to defy his elders to make his name in battle.

Viewed in this light, the organization of obituaries was not an abstract semantic matter: it was of immediate political significance. Through its practices of commemorating and arraying the dead in hierarchical order, the party gave to a conflict with a thousand scattered purposes and contentions a single voice, narrative, and moral message. Although some might have viewed this act of intervention as an arrogation of social prerogative—in Afghanistan, as elsewhere, it is the family's right and honor to commemorate the dead—they had to accept the party's usurpation of this role for the simple reason that to challenge it would have been implicitly to denigrate the status of the martyrs. In accepting the party's role in this matter, however, the survivors were also playing into the party's larger purpose, which was to legitimate its own authority while insulating itself from political attack.

Photographs played an important role in this process. The vast majority of Afghans were illiterate and therefore largely impervious to the propagandistic effects of print, which was the preferred medium of communication for the university students turned politicians in Hizb-i Islami and Jamiat-i Islami. Writing, printing, and distributing pamphlets was where they got their start, but that mode of insinuating themselves into the political process, which had been so effective for them as an underground movement in Kabul, was less effective in terms of developing a mass movement in exile. In this context, photographs became an especially important tool for the party in its efforts to expand party membership beyond the limited base of educated young people (which had been its original source of support as a student party in the late 1960s) to the far larger body of uneducated rural villagers who were suspicious of political parties in general.[8] Photographs of the war dead appealed to this audience because they were not "about" ideology or theology but about relatives and friends who had died in the fighting. They confirmed to bereaved viewers that their dead were in fact Islamic martyrs.

Equally effective and commonly featured were images of the wounded— old people and children who had lost limbs, for example—photographs of bombed houses and destroyed villages, and photographs of burned copies of the Qur'an, which were also considered (when destroyed in battle) to have been "martyred" and were duly shrouded and given burial rites in the same fashion as human martyrs. Such religiously tinged commemorative practices affirmed the authority of the party as the temporal arbiter of God's judgment. In essence, the martyrs became the emblems of the party's legitimacy: arrayed in formation on the pages of the magazines (as they might be arrayed before God on Judgment Day), they became unwitting agents of the party's quest for political primacy.

The popular veneration of martyrs had existed independent of the parties. Wherever mujahidin and civilians died as a result of enemy action, the terms and symbols of martyrdom were invoked. The sacralization of martyrs began as a personal project to dead family and friends and as a response to the catastrophe that had befallen society as a whole. Poetry offered succor to the bereaved by giving them assurance that dying could be a good thing. It taught people what that good thing was and glorified the dead by associating them with it. The genius of Hizb-i Islami and Jamiat-i Islami, the two parties that most actively and effectively deployed martyrs in their publications, was to recognize the political potential of those commemorative acts and displays (figure 14).

FIGURE 14. Hizb-i Islami meeting, 1986 (poster of "Shahid" Abdur Rahim Niazi, founder of the Muslim Youth Organization, in background). Photograph courtesy of Afghan Media Resource Center, Kabul, Afghanistan.

Saints might have largely disappeared from the scene, but martyrs replaced them as foci of popular veneration and as nodes of divine power. In the past, people might have flocked to the shrines of dead saints. Many continued to do so, but the Sufi orders that kept that tradition alive were less present and important in this context. Martyrs filled at least part of the gap, as reminders of divine presence, and, whereas shrines provided a more concentrated and distilled indication of God's power, the abundant, scattered, and multiplying graves of the martyrs spread that power more evenly through space. Even when travelers did not know the identity of those buried in a particular graveyard, the flags fluttering above the many new graves that kept appearing made apparent and provided a continual reminder of loss and of redemption.

Under the party's direction, the diffused locus of the cult of martyrs was redirected and harnessed. Just as the parties, with the connivance of the Pakistan government, had secured for themselves the right to determine who was and who was not a refugee, offering those so identified an identity card and, with that card, the privilege of living in a refugee camp and receiving regular rations, so in determining who was and who was not a martyr, and identifying those selected in their magazines, the parties afforded themselves the right to accord to those so identified the greatest treasure of all: the right to enter Paradise and to receive the endless bounty that Paradise offered. This might seem an abstract concern and a highly problematic assumption—if not a usurpation—of authority. However, under the circumstances and with so little to hold onto or look forward to in the world as it existed, this promise— as contingent as it was—at least offered something tangible, visible, and hopeful amid all the destruction and bleakness.

In the words of Henri Hubert and Marcel Mauss, those whom the party celebrated as martyrs passed back to the party the "sacred character of the religious world," providing it an aura of sacrality that it would otherwise have lacked and would have had no credible right to claim for itself.[9] Recognition of this possibility for authenticating an otherwise uncertifiable claim to precedence through the invocation of sacrificial rite would have profound implications going forward. In a sense, it could be argued that turning the battlefield dead into martyrs allowed Hizb-i Islami and Jamiat-i Islami to transform sacrificial rite into sacrificial writ insofar as they leveraged the moral capital they claimed for themselves as "sacrifiers" into the right to command others to do the parties' bidding and to determine the course, conduct, and ultimate consequence of the conflict.

A Rulebook for Jihad

The martyrdom magazines were one important element in a larger publishing project undertaken by the Islamic political parties in Peshawar. The majority of Afghans in the 1980s were illiterate, as they are now. The parties undertook not only to enhance literacy but also to make the illiterate increasingly dependent on and subservient to those who could claim mastery of the written word. One prong of this project involved establishing the legal basis for how to conduct jihad, an example of which can be seen in a pamphlet titled *Mufti sangar* (Legal Expert of the Trench).[10] The pamphlet, in compact and portable form and written in simple prose, was intended to address the practical problems mujahidin might encounter in combat situations. Much of the text is in a question-and-answer format and addresses a variety of mundane problems: What do you do when there is no water available for the required ablutions before prayer? Other questions relate to the complex interactions and moral conflicts that arise in warfare: If a civilian is wounded or killed, or civilian property is accidentally damaged or destroyed during an attack against the communists, are the mujahidin responsible? What do you do to a woman or child who is discovered spying?

In addition to addressing the practical problems of living in a combat zone and managing conflicts in a religiously sanctioned manner, the pamphlet provides a conceptual framework for society in the midst of jihad. This begins by defining jihad itself and the conditions under which participation in the jihad is required for some (*farz kifaya*) and for everyone (*farz 'ain*). Thus, for example, when some Muslims are unable to defend themselves against infidels, those who are able must assist in their defense. The obligation is greater for those who are close by; for those at a greater distance from the threat, assistance is not compulsory. But the pamphlet states that the participation in jihad becomes obligatory for Muslims everywhere if Afghanistan on its own proves unable to resist the atheist government alone.[11]

Mufti sangar also provides guidance for mujahidin on how to carry themselves, when and how to pray, and—perhaps most important—whom and how to obey. Much of the text is devoted to the subject of authority: who holds it, how it is obtained and forfeited, who is required to obey, and the nature and limits of obedience. All of these matters were significant in establishing a legal basis for diminishing the authority of tribal leaders. By carefully defining the territory of the jihad, the nature and duties of individuals in times of war, the correct observance of those duties, and the structure of authority under these conditions, the parties created an infrastructure to challenge not only the Marxist state but also the local tribes in whose territories the mujahidin traveled and operated and on whose support and benevolence they relied.

Mufti sangar also addresses the status of martyrs. The first chapter of the pamphlet deals with the categorization of martyrs according to the Hanafi school of jurisprudence that holds sway in most of Afghanistan. Fifty such categories are spelled out, including those who die to protect *mal* (property), *izzat* (honor), and *namus* (women, land, guns); those who die trying to kill an oppressor; those who die at the hands of a robber; and those who are injured in battle but later die of their wounds. Most virtuous of all are those who are killed while affirming their belief by reciting the *kalimah allah* ("There is no god but Allah, and Muhammad is His Prophet"). The pamphlet also discusses the preparation of martyrs' bodies (which are not to be washed); the proper burial garb of the dead (they should remain in the clothing in which they died, but they may also be wrapped in a shroud [*kafan*]); and the prayers to be recited when they are interred. For communists killed in battle, the pamphlet stipulates that, though the bodies should not be mutilated, they should not be afforded the dignity of a religious burial. They should be neither shrouded nor laid to rest within a Muslim cemetery. Instead, they should have dirt thrown over them in an unceremonious fashion, just as you would do with "the body of a dog."

These precepts and proscriptions related to martyrdom reinforce the commemorative power of the martyr magazines. If those magazines provided a platform for glorifying those whom the parties judged to have died in defense of Islam and the party, then *Mufti sangar* can be seen as providing the legal infrastructure by which the party arrogated to itself the authority, once held by the tribe, to make and fine-tune those judgments.

The fact that the instructions were in writing, even though most of the people who became subject to them were illiterate, was not necessarily a deficiency. To the contrary, it may have increased their power, particularly since they were heavily annotated and supplemented in Arabic script. Even to those with only the rudimentary mosque education that most Afghans receive, this script would have been recognizable and associated with religious authority. Many Afghans wear protective amulets, consisting of sacred words written on paper that is folded and tucked inside cloth and leather packets and worn around the neck. Those who can claim to read those words, recite them, and interpret their meaning have additional authority. Before the war, the authority conferred by literacy and religious knowledge was offset by other considerations, such as ancestry, land ownership, marriage ties, and connections to state offices and officials. In the context of the anti-Soviet jihad, however, those mitigating factors diminished in importance. Increasingly, what mattered was connection to the Peshawar parties that controlled the weapons, money, ideological arguments, and legal system needed to sustain a prolonged guerilla war.

Another area in which the political parties invested heavily was education. Mujahidin parties managed schools in areas that they had liberated, and some commanders provided basic literacy classes to their mujahidin. Such efforts were especially focused on the refugee population in Pakistan, which in the mid-1980s was estimated at close to 3.5 million, many of them young children. The Islamic political parties recognized the importance of educating these children. Western donors were mainly interested in supplying weapons with which the mujahidin could fight the Soviets, and the parties were happy to receive this largesse. But beyond the immediate goal of defeating the Soviet Union, the parties were intent on reforming their country, and they realized that they needed to start that long-term process by educating children.

While conducting survey research in the Kachagarhi refugee camp outside Peshawar in 1984, I visited a number of party-run schools (*maktab*). Although these schools were not identified as madrasas, they provided an education strongly grounded in Islam. One example of this focus is a Pakhtu reading primer that I obtained. Like most primers, it begins with the alphabet, with each letter accompanied by a word that begins with that letter and a short sentence that includes that word. Of the forty-three letters in the Pakhtu alphabet, thirty-two are illustrated in the primer with words or sentences that relate directly to Islam or jihad. For example, the letter *tay* is illustrated with a picture of a sword (*turah*) and the text "Ahmad has a sword. He conducts jihad with the sword." The letter *fay* is illustrated with the word *firman* (edict or command) and is accompanied by these sentences: "The Holy Qur'an is God's command. We have accepted the command of God. Mujahidin accept the command of their Muslim leaders [*amir*]."

The primer also includes other moral pronouncements, including one on brushing your teeth: "Brushing teeth is the order [*sunat*] of the Prophet. Brushing teeth is good for health. Brushing teeth prevents disease. Those who don't brush their teeth have bad breath, people dislike them, and they get sick." Whether the subject is personal hygiene, greeting people with a respectful *salam,* visiting sick people in the hospital, or helping the needy, these pronouncements are all grounded in the language of religious belief. Jihad is referred to throughout the text, sometimes in the form of short essays: "Afghanistan is our dear country. . . . Our country has big cities and nice weather. . . . The Russians have occupied our country. The Muslims of

Afghanistan do jihad against the invaders." Sometimes it is invoked in exhortatory poems: "I am a young mujahid fighting for Islam.... I have a sword in my hand. I have a gun on my shoulder. I have a canteen at my side, full of clean water. I am going to the battlefield, fighting for my country. I never stay back. I am going to fight."

The tone of the primer is lightened by a handful of jokes: "A stupid man was walking by a village during the winter when he was attacked by dogs. He tried to pick up a stone. When he found that it was stuck to the ground, he shouted, 'What kind of a village is this—they unleash the dogs and tie down the stones!'" But the dominant theme throughout is jihad and the obligation, even for children, to support it, as in this short essay at the end of the booklet:

> Zalmai is the son of a mujahid. He asked his mother, "Where has my father gone?" His mother replied, "My son! Your father has gone to jihad." The son asked again, "With whom is he fighting?" His mother told him, "Your father is fighting the Russians and their servants." Zalmai asked, "Who are the servants of the Russians?" His mother told him, "The servants of the Russians are the Khalqis and Parchamis." Her son told her, "As the son of a father who has taken his head in his hands for the liberation of religion and the country, I must follow his example!"

It is impossible to assess with any certainty the effect of a primer on a child's worldview. My first exposure to reading was in the form of very large Dick and Jane books that the teacher propped on her desk, pointing at each word as we repeated the sentences after her. I loved those books. I loved the illustrations, and I loved decoding the words. But it never occurred to me until much later that I was learning a great deal more than words and simple stories. I was learning about why I should obey my parents and not take unnecessary risks, and how I should care for my pets and clean up after myself. I was also absorbing a particular view of what a family was supposed to look like and what sort of houses they were supposed to live in, what sort of behavior was expected of boys and girls, and how those expectations were different for each.

Similarly, I wonder just how influential that Pakhtu primer might have been for its intended audience, especially considering the straitened circumstances in which those children lived. Learning to read surrounded by suburban lawns in the U.S. Midwest in the 1950s accustomed me to a particular understanding of what the world was like and what I could expect from it. The possibility that such an understanding might be flawed, or partial, or not generally shared by everyone else on the planet only came later. After spending many hours in refugee schools, watching the children—that is, the boys—recite the words written on the blackboard, I have often wondered what it was they were absorbing and whether the recitation of those words—so many of which were religious in nature—inevitably drowned out alternative words and possibilities.

As much as I believe that those camp schools provided a refuge for Afghan children, I know that they did not open up worlds to them as my school opened up worlds to me. Reading Dick and Jane eventually enabled me to read on my own, but these children were less likely to become literate: most of them had to work when they were not in school, first in their own homes and later in whatever jobs they could find on the street, or else become mujahidin. The world they occupied was for the most part a closed one. For those with the talent, inclination, and opportunity, learning to read was less likely to lead them to read other kinds of books than it was to make possible reading the same kind of book in greater depth and detail.

In the context of the jihad, employment opportunities for top students were more plentiful for those with a religious mindset than for those with a more secular orientation. The political parties had offices to staff. They needed clerks, teachers, and editors for their growing publishing operations, and they needed commanders who could read and write as well as lead and fight. Schools and madrasas were set up to provide this manpower, but, more fundamentally, their role was to inculcate a worldview that would have been unfamiliar to tribal refugees for whom religious belief and practice were always an adjunct rather than a central concern. In this sense, the primer helped provide the groundwork for instilling a different way for children to view and be in the world. Its function was not just teaching the rudiments of literacy. It was introducing young people to a novel disposition to death. Sacrifice per se was not highlighted in the primer, but the text nevertheless helped to establish the foundation on which the ideal of self-sacrifice would become the natural expression and extension.

FOUR

Virtue and Vice

PICTURES AT AN EXECUTION

The U.S. invasion and occupation of Afghanistan were precipitated by the attacks of September 11, 2001, but the stage for the invasion was set several years earlier, when the feminist Revolutionary Association of the Women of Afghanistan (RAWA) released a video showing a group of Taliban unloading a woman covered in a blue burqa from the back of a pickup truck onto the field in Kabul's football stadium and forcing her to her knees, and then one of the men raising an AK-47 to the back of her head and firing (figure 15). One can find many gruesome images on the Internet, but this one, viewed by thousands, if not millions, of viewers on the RAWA website, sent shock waves around the world and helped to mobilize a worldwide awareness of and movement against the Taliban. In the United States, the Feminist Majority Foundation, led by Mavis Leno, the wife of the comedian and late-night television host Jay Leno, spearheaded a campaign to isolate the Taliban. The organization convinced UNOCAL, an oil development corporation, to halt its plans to build a gas pipeline through Afghanistan to Pakistan. The video clip continued circulating on the Internet, and it became a centerpiece of the documentary *Beneath the Veil,* featuring Saira Shah, which was broadcast for the first time shortly before the September 11 attacks and then rebroadcast continuously by CNN in the United States, Channel Four in the United Kingdom, and other channels in Europe in the days after the attacks.

Although it is impossible to assess precisely the impact of the widespread distribution of this video on public opinion, it certainly helped to eliminate any doubt that Americans might have had as to the evil of the Taliban and the rightness of U.S. efforts to eliminate them. Through the mediation of a

(c) www.rawa.org

FIGURE 15. Taliban execution, Kabul Stadium, Nov. 16, 1999. From Revolutionary Association of Afghan Women (RAWA) video.

sixty-one second video clip, the narrative shifted. Americans were no longer merely avengers: they were liberators. It was no longer just al-Qaeda that was the enemy: it was the Taliban as well, and this broadening of the focus had important consequences. The United States was not just looking for locations where Osama Bin Laden might be hiding out: it was also focusing on destroying the infrastructure of Taliban rule. As it turned out, this did not take long, but, once accomplished, it left the United States with the job of establishing a liberal democracy in which women would play a prominent role, as promised. Despite much carping during his presidential campaign about the previous administration's ill-advised efforts at nation-building abroad, now President George W. Bush found himself in the role of nation-builder-in-chief. The task did not at first appear hard to pull off. The Taliban deserted Kabul and the other cities in a matter of weeks, and things seemed to be going so well that the president quickly decided to expand his offensive to Iraq.

That's another story. In this chapter, I tell the story of why the Taliban executed that woman in Kabul. To be more exact, it is not this particular execution that I want to focus on.[1] What matters for the purposes of this book is what she represented and why the Taliban felt it necessary not just to execute her but to stage that execution as a spectacle in the biggest venue available, before a crowd of thousands—including a tightly packed group of heavily veiled RAWA activists shielding from view one of their members with a video camera, who preserved the moment for posterity.

This woman was the most infamous example of Taliban public violence, but she was far from alone. The following are news summaries of public punishments that I was able to cull from the Western press in 1998, the third year in which the Taliban was in more or less full control of the country:

February 10: Man convicted of treason, hung from a crane that was then driven slowly through streets of Kabul.

February 15: Taliban soldier convicted of theft, had face blackened with coal and then strapped to front of a truck and driven through streets of Kabul.

February 20: Amputation of right hand of thief performed in a school.

February 25: Three men convicted of sodomy buried under rubble for thirty minutes. Life of one spared when he was pulled out alive.

February 27: Woman receives one hundred lashes for walking on street with unrelated man. Man escapes. Two other men have hands amputated for theft. Hands displayed for edification of crowd.

March 14: Execution of a *talib* [religious student] convicted of murder. Execution carried out by victim's brother in Kabul Stadium. At same ceremony, man lashed for adultery.

April 1: Execution of murderer on the sports grounds in Spin Boldak, near Pakistani border.

May 1: Man executed by gunshot in Kabul Stadium. Execution performed by relatives of the victim. At same ceremony, two men flogged for drinking whiskey.

June 15: Two alleged Iranian spies hanged in Herat.

June 19: Thief has right hand and left foot amputated in Kabul Stadium.

August 6: Three men found guilty of banditry have right hands and left feet publicly amputated in Kandahar.

August 14: Murderer executed and hands of two robbers amputated in Kabul Stadium.

October 6: Saudi man executed in Kandahar for engaging in activities hostile to Osama Bin Laden.

October 6: Three talibs executed for sexual crimes and extortion during battle for Mazar-i-Sharif.

October 30: Three government officials convicted of taking bribes given thirty-six lashes in Kabul Stadium and sentenced to six months in prison.

November 12: Guests at wedding ceremony in Logar punished for listening to music (nature of the punishment not specified). In Pul-i Khumri bazaar, 250 audiotapes and 12 videocassettes reportedly burned. In Helmand, thirty-eight heroin and hashish addicts and gamblers and twelve music lovers punished according to shari'a.

November 27: Father of murder victim slits the throat of a convicted murderer in Kabul Stadium. In same ceremony, two men convicted of stealing $1,400 have hands amputated.

December 28: Convicted murderer executed, and right hands and left feet of two highway robbers cut off in Herat.

In addition to these reported cases of public punishment, there were undoubtedly others that escaped press attention, given how difficult the Taliban made it for journalists to work in Afghanistan. By 1998, the Taliban had solidified their rule and their agenda, as indicated by the upgrading of the Department for the Promotion of Virtue and Prevention of Vice (Amr Bil Maroof Wa Nahi An al-Munkar) to the status of a government ministry. The distinctive Datsun pickup trucks used by the morality police were regularly patrolling the streets of Kabul and other cities, and the campaign to cleanse the country of corruption was undertaken in earnest. This was also the year when the Taliban decided to close more than a hundred girls' schools in and around Kabul, and when the Taliban leader, Mullah Omar, ordered villages to appoint inspectors to ensure that people were saying their prayers properly.

In 1998, too, the Taliban decreed that tailors should no longer take women's measurements, barbers should no longer trim beards, and music should no longer be played at weddings. Hindus were ordered to wear yellow cloth badges on their garments to identify themselves as non-Muslims, and all male students at Kabul University were ordered to grow full beards and wear turbans. Flying kites and applauding at sporting events were banned. All buses carrying women in Kabul were required to be fully curtained, and all bus drivers were ordered to refrain from speaking with female passengers and from wearing "shiny clothes." In the same year, when pirated VHS copies of the movie *Titanic* covertly appeared in the bazaar, the morality police began to arrest young men wearing their hair in the *titanik* style, modeled on the floppy forelock of Leonardo DiCaprio's doomed character in the film.[2]

Would-be DiCaprios were not the only ones going to jail for their haircuts. An October 13 story in the *New York Times* reported that seventy-five men were serving ten-day sentences in Pul-i Charkhi prison for having trimmed their beards.[3] Small prisons were set up throughout the city to handle the overflow of taxi drivers, shopkeepers, and students picked up for violations related to their grooming, their dress, their music, and their imbibing of illegal substances (heroin and hashish use being more prevalent than alcohol, which was difficult to obtain and conceal). Women were less common offenders, partly because they were under the control of their families, which in most cases restricted their movement in public. In addition, the morality police had more difficulty detecting the clothing and makeup women might be were wearing under their burqas, but when one of the patrols spotted a woman on the street with bare ankles, they would reprimand her then and there, often beating her on the legs with the short whips and rubber hoses that many of them carried for this purpose.

GUNMEN

To understand how and why the Taliban became so interested in curbing public immorality, I need to go back three years to 1995 and the trip I took to eastern Afghanistan in company with my friend Shahmahmood Miakhel. This was the year when the Taliban first came to power, though they had not yet succeeded in conquering Kabul or Mashreqi ("the East"), as the region comprising the provinces of Ningrahar, Kunar, Laghman, and Nuristan is generally referred to by Afghans. At the time, the region was under the nominal control of what was known as the Eastern Shura, a council composed of commanders affiliated with the mujahidin parties. The government of President Mohammad Najibullah, which had been publicly and loudly declaring its independence from both the Soviet Union and communist ideology ever since the Soviets withdrew in 1989, had been replaced by a coalition government made up of the parties that had moved their bases of operation from Peshawar to Kabul.

Nominal does not even begin to describe the nature of this alliance, which involved continuous jockeying for power among the principal Peshawar parties. The long-standing animosities extended to other parties run by Shia Hazaras, whose base of support during the Soviet occupation had been in Iran, and by other ethnic groups (Tajik, Uzbek, and Turkoman in particular) whose interests had never been represented by the Peshawar parties during the years of the anti-Soviet jihad. Political skirmishing soon turned into full-scale street battles and artillery bombardments. Kabul, which had been spared destruction during the decade of Soviet control, now became the center of the worst violence, and whole neighborhoods, especially in the western part of the city, were reduced to rubble.

There were several vectors of conflict, but one of the most intense involved the rivalry that had long existed between the two Islamist parties, Hizb-i Islami and Jamiat-i Islami, and between their respective leaders, Gulbuddin Hekmatyar and Ahmad Shah Massoud.[4] Their mutual loathing had been tempered during the Soviet occupation by the fact that the Hindu Kush mountains lay between them, Massoud having decided to base his operations in the mountains of the Panjshir Valley whereas Hekmatyar was a principal in the power machinations of the Peshawar parties. But, once the parties relocated from Peshawar to Kabul, the animosity between these two men, which had first developed when they were students at Kabul University, blossomed into full-scale war.

In comparison to Kabul, Mashreqi was relatively peaceful, but Shahmahmood and I were reminded of the violence in the capital as we traveled from the Khyber Pass to Jalalabad and passed a huge camp spread over several miles along the road and stretching as far into the distance as we could see. It was occupied by IDPs (internally displaced peoples), refugees from the fighting in Kabul that had begun in 1992. In the eastern region, the absence of violence concealed a different sort of war. The party commanders in the east had come to something close to a truce, but they had done so in part because they were all busy carving out their own slices of the carcass of a country that had already endured nearly two decades of war.

By 1995, it could be said that war between the mujahidin and the Marxists had mutated into a war of the mujahidin against the people. After seventeen years of fighting, the fronts had no place to go, and the mujahidin had no other skills. Many had come of age during the war. Some had joined up as little more than children, carrying supplies to mujahidin bases. The fronts were their homes, their commanders more influential and relevant in their young lives than their fathers (assuming that their fathers were still alive). And many of the surviving fathers could no longer support their families. With the pipeline from Peshawar dried up, the mujahidin fronts were deprived of funds. Even for those who genuinely wanted to put down their weapons, it was not at all clear what they could or should do or even where they could go after the departure of the Soviet invaders.

Simply laying down arms and returning to the fields—turning swords into ploughshares—was not an easy option. Villages were depopulated. Ownership of land in many places was contested, as a large percentage of the population had become refugees. Those who stayed on to farm had new problems to deal with. Property boundaries were under dispute; tenants had taken over from owners who had moved to Kabul or sought refuge abroad; vast tracts of land had been strewn with land mines. Even where deeds were clear and uncontested, much of the land had lain fallow for years, and those who still knew how to farm and wanted to do so needed funds for equipment and seed. Most of all, they needed assurance that their investment of time, money, and energy would be secure.

We traveled through eastern Afghanistan in July, when the fields should have been lush and green; instead, we saw endless stretches of brown soil, untilled and untended. We also passed massive piles of cut timber at the base of the tributaries of the Kunar River, waiting by the road to be transported to Pakistan. In the past, the forests had been protected by the local tribes that owned the land, with the number of trees harvested each year strictly controlled. When those protections lapsed, armed factions within and outside the tribes began to fell trees indiscriminately, denuding centuries-old stretches of forest. It was not only the traditional tribal leaders who had been displaced. When we entered the village of Enzeri on the east bank of the Kunar River, searching for the tomb of Enzeri Mullah Sahib, a Sufi saint of the early twentieth century, we found that the tomb had been torn down and left as rubble. Members of the Wahhabi branch of Islam had destroyed the tomb because it violated their belief that there should be no veneration of saints in Islam and no memorial commemorating any being other than God.

The war had divided every village and town in this way. Every community had both supporters and enemies of the communist regime. Within each of these camps were further political and religious divisions: Khalqis and Parchamis, Hizbis and Jamiatis, Wahhabis and Sufis. And there were ethnic and personal animosities, some of which had preceded the war and then found expression through it. Some scenarios arose time and again: after the communists took power, an insignificant village man joined the party and was elevated to a position of authority. Taking revenge for all the years of perceived abuse by others, he used the power handed to him to expel people he disliked and to take land from his rivals. The rivals came back ten years later to reclaim their property and avenge themselves. Even if the communist was dead by then, his alleged misdeeds, particularly if they involved killing, still had to be avenged, perhaps against the man's son or brother.

In the postwar chaos, no one had the authority or jurisdiction to force the antagonists to come to terms. Tribal law, where it had existed, had often been superseded by Islamic shari'a law, which for its part had been politicized by the parties. Thus, even petty disputes that might have been easily resolved in the past through the intervention of tribal or religious authorities continued to simmer and spill over into sudden violence that made the original dispute all the more difficult to settle. Islam, which had long provided avenues for resolving conflicts, was now synonymous with violence and strife. In such circumstances, who could play the role of peacemaker, and what framework could be used for managing disagreements and disputes? Not only had Islam been compromised in its ideals, but society itself had been stripped of its mechanisms for righting itself and maintaining equilibrium. Those mechanisms, in any event, had never been pushed to the extremes encountered in the war years. Available mechanisms seized up and failed, and there was nothing at hand to replace them.

By 1992, no Afghan could hold onto the image of the mujahidin as heroic freedom fighters or Muslims in the mold of the Prophet's followers, the conceit propagated by the parties in the early years of the jihad. In eastern Afghanistan, those who called themselves mujahidin were called gunmen (*topakian*) by others. Although some mujahidin had certainly believed in the cause of jihad and were ready to disarm once the Soviets left, others had different motivations. Most fighters had sacrificed the opportunity for an education and career, and the front they had fought with became their family. Many felt more loyalty to their commander than to the party. Some of the commanders had been opportunistic from the start. Some had formed militias that fought for the government and then switched sides. Others had been in the resistance from the start but had changed party allegiances, some multiple times. As a result, the basic premise of the war—that this was a jihad to save Islam—had become discredited, and formerly respected mujahidin had increasingly come to be viewed simply as dangerous men with weapons in their hands.

Commanders faced an urgent need to feed and equip their fronts. Cut off from both Kabul and Peshawar, their only option was scavenging from the area around them. That meant preying on local shopkeepers, sometimes under the pretext of collecting Islamic *zakat* (religious tax), though this fiction was largely discredited, particularly when multiple fronts all claimed to be the legitimate collectors. Other measures included setting up roadblocks and demanding a "road tax" from every passing vehicle and a percentage of the farmers' harvest—in short, extorting the last sources of revenue from already impoverished communities, squeezing the lemon dry and then scraping the pulp.

In the face of these depredations, the story goes, Mullah Omar, the putative founder of the Taliban movement, was inspired to action. On one occasion, it is said, Mullah Omar came upon the mutilated bodies of an Afghan family by the roadside. The family had been stopped in their car by a local commander and his bodyguards, who had robbed the victims, raped the women, and then killed the whole family. After burying the family and reciting funeral prayers, Mullah Omar returned to the madrasa where he taught and asked his students and other mullahs to take a vow to do everything in their power to end the inequity and barbarism that was plaguing their country.[5]

Buud, na buud: it was and it wasn't. Who knows whether this story is true? But, in any case, the rise of the Taliban in the south and the speed with which they were able to mobilize a campaign to conquer the rest of the country is the stuff of legends. According to outside observers, they could not have accomplished what they did without the help of the Pakistani government. Though such assistance provides a partial explanation for the Taliban's success, it does not explain how they managed to steamroll their opposition in areas that were chock full of well-armed, battle-tested mujahidin groups that no previous force had been able to pacify. In many areas, the Taliban were welcomed as liberators, and this reception goes back to how they presented themselves to the people, beginning with their self-description as religious students (talibs), who traditionally are near the bottom of the status hierarchy.

The Taliban were not pretending. Many were, in fact, mullahs or mullahs-in-training. Though he later embraced the role of *amir al-mu'minin,* the commander of the faithful, early on Mullah Omar made no grand claims to authority. In marked contrast to the games played by the Peshawar parties in exaggerating their leadership credentials, the Taliban emphasized their humble origins. In so doing, they eschewed the cults of personality that characterized party politics in Peshawar. Likewise, where other parties had symbolically associated themselves with various institutions, whether the madrasa (clerics), the shrine (Sufis), or the tyrant's prison (Islamists), for the Taliban the symbolic center of gravity was the village mosque, and their politics were as simple as their symbolism. Their avowed goal was not to invent a new form of government or to elaborate a new vision of heaven on earth but simply to purify the country of the pollution and contagion with which it had been afflicted, not just by the communists but also by corrupt mujahidin. With these aspirations, they aligned their interests with those of the bulk of Afghanistan's population.

RITES OF VIOLENCE

The Peshawar parties were led by relatively educated men. Almost all had graduated from high school. Most had some university education. Some had advanced degrees, and a few were professors. Not surprisingly, their propaganda efforts focused on printed texts containing a great deal of ideological content; even with the inclusion of photographs, most of these texts would have been lost on the illiterate majority. The Taliban chose a simpler form of pedagogy that did not rely on print or images, a pedagogy of the street and the public square. Young talibs, all dressed alike in their Kandahari clothing and black turbans, roamed city streets in search of vice. They enacted a public spectacle in which the forces of good—the judges of the Ministry for the Promotion of Virtue and the Prevention of Vice—apprehended criminals whose bad behavior would be punished according to Islamic law before the largest possible crowd, thereby demonstrating to the onlookers what they could expect if they strayed from the path of virtue.

Under the Taliban, the pedagogy of print gave way to the pedagogy of public punishment, and its aim was different. The Peshawar parties had been concerned with forming a vanguard through which they could mobilize fighters to wage guerrilla war against the government and its Soviet backers. Now, fighting was still going on, and recruits were still needed to suppress anti-Taliban forces in the northern and central regions of the country, but most of the foot soldiers were recruited from the vast array of independent and party-run madrasas that had been set up in Pakistan during the jihad years, with additional manpower obtained by dragooning young men off the street. Between the supplies provided by their Pakistani patrons and their capture of Afghan government stores, the Taliban had what they needed to put their military enemies on the defensive. However, for the pacification of the population, weapons of war were not what was needed. For this purpose, the Taliban employed the machinery of public spectacle.

Punishment is a normal function of government, of course, and the Taliban performed this task in accordance with Islamic law, or at least in accordance with their interpretation of it. The only decision that needed to be made was whether the punishment would be conducted in private or in public, and, if in public, just how public it should be. Previous regimes had conducted most of their business in secret, with enemies of the state disappearing from view and executed without trial, appeal, or public notification. This choice appears to have been deliberate. Secrecy allowed the regimes to exercise both intimidation and deniability. The Taliban—as part of their campaign of reform—not only brought their administration of Islamic law into public view but also gathered the largest possible audience to witness it. Nowhere, however, did that law stipulate the use of stadiums for mass viewing of the dismemberment of bodies, the use of cranes as gallows, or the driving of the cranes through the streets to exhibit the hanged criminals' bodies even to those who did not attend the execution.

Significantly, one of the first acts undertaken by the Taliban after they had taken control of Kabul in 1995 was to enter the United Nations compound where the former communist president, Najibullah, had taken refuge when his government collapsed three years earlier. The Taliban forces castrated and shot both Najibullah and his brother and strung their bodies from a traffic control tower in a central intersection in downtown Kabul—an act that was photographed and reproduced in newspapers around the world. Although most outsiders probably viewed the photographs as evidence of Afghanistan's continuing crisis, and perhaps of Afghan cruelty, the public execution of Najibullah had a different meaning at home.

The Islamic party leaders in charge of the city had allowed Najibullah to remain under U.N. protection, even though he had been the author of many massacres, disappearances, and secret executions both as head of state and earlier, as director of KHAD, the Afghan intelligence service. It is doubtful that the parties were concerned with protecting U.N. neutrality. Rather, their thinking seems to have been that, whatever his crimes, the former president might play a useful role in a postcommunist government. As a Pakhtun and a prominent member of the important Ahmadzai tribe, he could be called on to secure the neutrality of fellow tribesmen. In addition, several of the most powerful Islamic party leaders had already shown their willingness to collude with high-ranking figures from the Marxist period. These included Gulbuddin Hekmatyar, the head of Hizb-i Islami, who at one point allied himself with the former defense minister, Shahnawaz Tanai. In publicly executing Najibullah and his brother and displaying their mutilated bodies, the Taliban appear to have wanted to send a message that no quarter would be given to

FIGURE 16. Taliban destruction of the second Bamiyan Buddha, Mar. 2001. From *The Destruction of the U.S.S. Cole* video, produced by al-Qaeda in June 2001.

those who had fought on the wrong side of the jihad or who violated the sanctity of that endeavor.[6] The Taliban intended to show that their administration would be guided by a consistent moral vision rooted in the Qur'an and the *hadith* (the stories of how the Prophet Muhammad governed his followers in Mecca and Medina). In keeping with this intention, the Taliban had patrols in pickup trucks sweeping through the streets of Kabul soon after their takeover, keeping an eye out for citizens violating tenets of Islamic law.

Perhaps the largest and most spectacular Taliban "execution" involved not human criminals or former heads of state but the two enormous statues of the Buddha, fifty-three and thirty-five meters in height, respectively, carved into the cliff face overlooking the town of Bamiyan in central Afghanistan (figure 16). From roughly the second to the seventh centuries C.E., what is now Afghanistan was one of the principal centers of Buddhist worship and study, and formal and informal excavations continue to turn up sites and artifacts associated with the long and prosperous years of Buddhist governance. Latter-day Afghan Muslims have long used destruction of Buddhist artifacts on their soil as a means of demonstrating Islam's dominance and historical supremacy. Many Sufi shrines, including that of the mullah of Hadda, were built on top of or within sight of remains of Buddhist stupas, and one of the Mullah of Hadda's deputies set up his center in the village of Butkhak, whose name can be translated as "idol dust."

If the Taliban destruction of the Buddhas in March 2001 was far from unprecedented, it was nevertheless unique in its scale and complexity. After standing for centuries, the massive structures had shown more damage from erosion than from human attack. The Taliban destruction was also unique in that it was undertaken in spite of intense international lobbying for the preservation of the statues, including appeals from Saudi Arabia, Pakistan, and other Islamic countries on which the Taliban depended for assistance. Ignoring these appeals, the Taliban filmed the event so that the moment of the statues' obliteration could be preserved and broadcast for the edification of Muslims everywhere.

The destruction of the Buddhas as an execution bears a striking similarity to the Taliban's execution of criminals. In both situations, the Ministry for the Promotion of Virtue and the Prevention of Vice was responsible for the decision and based the judgment on shari'a law. In both situations, destruction alone was not enough: executing criminals and blowing up Buddhas had to be turned into spectacles enacted before the widest possible audience. The responsible minister, in other words, took his job quite literally to be that of propagating virtue as well as of preventing vice. He had to make sure not only that wrongdoers were properly dealt with but also, and even more important, that other people were exposed to what was right and thereby deterred from doing wrong.

From the Taliban perspective, the existence of the Buddhas was less an affront than an opportunity. No Afghan had venerated these statues for centuries, and there was no danger of Afghans reverting to idol worship. But destroying the Buddhas allowed the Taliban to do something that no one had done before and to claim a connection to the deepest roots of Islamic history. In Katherine Verdery's words, tearing down a statue "not only removes that specific body from the landscape as if to excise it from history, but also proves that because it can be torn down, no god protects it. As it is deprived of its timelessness and sacred quality, the 'sacred' of the universe in which it had meaning becomes more 'profane.'"[7]

Purity and Danger

As the overthrow of President Daud in 1978 signaled the beginning of a new era of socialist society, so the killing of former president Najibullah and the public executions that followed were meant to demonstrate the government's commitment to realizing its own utopian ideal, based on the holy revelation and the Prophet's instructions and example. The morality squads of young soldiers that roamed the streets of Kabul and other cities under

Taliban control were the vanguard of this revolution, just as the Marxist cadres had been the vanguard of their revolution eighteen years earlier. The goal was to cleanse the streets of irreligious behavior left over from the previous regimes as well as of the violence that had permeated the city. Each flogging and execution thus could be seen as a ritual of purification, a scouring of the minds and bodies of the citizenry in service of God's will and the Taliban state's efforts to erase the contamination of the preceding decades and revive a prophetic legacy that had lain dormant for fourteen hundred years.

To understand the Taliban concern with purity, one has to keep in mind where they were coming from. Most of the Taliban were just what they called themselves—religious students—and their idea of order came from what they had read in their madrasas in Pakistan and rural Afghanistan. When they arrived in Kabul, they confronted a society totally different from any they had known. There had always been a stark divide between Kabul and the rest of the country, especially the rural areas. An American anthropologist who conducted fieldwork in Ghazni in the mid-1970s noted that the rural Pakhtuns he was working with referred to the contrast between their way of life and the life of the city in binary terms: we are rough, they are smooth; we are hard, they are soft; we are straight, they are crooked.[8] In a similar fashion, the poet Rafiq Jan expressed shock in some of his verses at the immorality he had witnessed on a visit to Kabul after it had fallen to the communists:

> The youth of Kabul have become scattered and the girls independent.
>   I saw in the city many different women.
> Straight, straight, they were looking at everyone,
>   And, by the Qur'an, they were not ashamed.

In *Purity and Danger,* her masterful study of the human quest for symbolic order, Mary Douglas notes that "ideas about separating, purifying, demarcating and punishing transgressions have as their main function to impose system on an inherently untidy experience. It is only by exaggerating the difference between within and without, above and below, male and female, with and against, that a semblance of order is created."[9] On taking power, the Taliban were confronted with various kinds of disorder. One was the disorder of a country ravaged by war and predatory commanders, which was the kind of military problem they knew how to deal with. Kabul represented a problem that they were less prepared to confront. The pizzerias, discotheques, and miniskirts of the 1970s were long gone, but the people of Kabul had their own distinct habits and customs; they even carried themselves differently from the people of the countryside. The Taliban recognized this difference and dealt with it in the only way they knew how, which was to try to ferret out the disruptive elements in the city, to name them and punish the perpetrators, according to the tenets of their faith, before they could spread a more general disorder through the social body.

Punishment of the representatives of disorder was not enough, though. Containing the disease required a kind of ritual sterilization that demonstrated to those who might be inclined to error what awaited them should they act on their sinful thoughts. Again quoting Douglas, "Holiness is exemplified by completeness. Holiness requires that individuals shall conform to the class to which they belong. And holiness requires that different classes of things shall not be confused."[10] In Islam, one of the greatest moral problems is associated with *fitna,* which can be defined as a state of political disorder in which people are unable to fulfill their duties as Muslims. The Taliban saw it as their holy duty to eliminate the fitna affecting Afghanistan, and their punishments were a way of ensuring not only that people obeyed the law but also that "different classes of things" would be kept separate and distinct.

Another useful and related way to view the Taliban's use of public violence is as a ritual intended to reclaim sacrifice from its debasement at the hands of the Peshawar parties. The disparity between verbal protestations of piety and material demonstrations of self-interest and ambition had rendered suspect all words coming from the mouths of party leaders, even those praising martyrs. Any sense of moral order that had existed under Soviet occupation and Marxist rule had evaporated. Muslims were killing Muslims. Former heroes of the resistance were held responsible for massacring the mujahidin of other parties as well as civilians. Local commanders kept dancing boys as ornaments and sex slaves. Mujahidin raped and pillaged. The tribal honor that had given meaning to the first stage of the jihad had given way to Islamic piety, but now both had been replaced by a predatory lawlessness. The moral disorder of this era represented the gravest threat that an Islamic society could face—worse even than the threat of infidel attack, because it was a cancer that was destroying the social body from within. In Islamic tradition, better an unjust tyrant than fitna. A tyrant is one man and can eventually be deposed, but fitna permeates the whole society like a disease, and it cannot be eradicated by political or military means alone.

The Taliban's public rites of punishment effectively replaced the martyr—whose value as a symbol had been largely debased—with the criminal defiler, whose destruction could provide a different sort of lesson. The martyr sacrificed himself to save society. The criminal was sacrificed by society to save itself. And just as the martyr necessitated continued struggle on the part of the living to ensure that his sacrifice would not be in vain, so the punishment of the criminal necessitated continued vigilance and surveillance by the guardians of moral order to ensure that the public lesson had been learned. Standing on the far side of both these ritual acts was a mythic image of fulfillment: Paradise promised and attained for those who followed the martyr's path, and the certainty of punishment in the afterlife for those who disobeyed God's commandments on Earth.

When juxtaposed with the martyr, the criminal brings to mind Giorgio Agamben's *homo sacer,* the person "who can be killed but not sacrificed" and whose subjugation to the arbitrary power of the state demonstrates the state's sovereignty. Conversely, it can be said that the martyr is the one who cannot be killed because he has sacrificed. During the Soviet occupation, the least established of the political parties—those led by ex-university students—used the credentialing of martyrs as their avenue to power, as a means of differentiating between legitimate and illegitimate violence. Similarly, when the Taliban formed a state out of the chaos of the post-Soviet civil war, they found in the public repudiation and punishment of those they judged and punished as criminals a way to demonstrate their sovereignty by demarcating "the threshold on which violence passes over into law and law passes over into violence." [11]

In *The Political Lives of Dead Bodies,* Katherine Verdery notes that dead bodies are "excellent means for accumulating something essential to political transformation: symbolic capital. . . . Dead bodies, in short, can be a site of political profit," particularly in regard to "establishing political legitimacy." [12] The Islamist parties in Peshawar had exploited this potential in their use of martyrs as a foundation for their claim of political authority, but, over time, as these parties and their leaders lost credibility because of their abuses of power, martyrs ceased to function as a source of political legitimacy. The Taliban, however, struck on a new (old) way to revive the power of dead bodies as political symbols through the use of spectacles of punishment whose efficacy lay in the association between collective violence and purification. In Verdery's words, "Punishment purifies a public space that the guilty had made impure." [13]

This insight echoes and builds on the analysis of Henri Hubert and Marcel Mauss, who demonstrated that the pure and the impure are not "mutually exclusive opposites; they are two aspects of religious reality."[14] Likewise, the criminal and the martyr can both be thought of as "sacred beings," whose sacrality is mediated by the terms of sacrifice (whether retroactively inferred or ritually carried out). The vector of sacrifice can be directed toward either sanctification or purification, and the Taliban rite of sacrifice represents an attempt at social purification through the public destruction of victims.

The association seems clear, but the question remains: How can killing someone judged to be a criminal serve the function of purifying public space and protecting society? That is, what sorts of killing, or what conditions under which killing occurs, change it from something socially destructive to something socially beneficial? Verdery does not answer these questions directly, noting only that "the feelings of awe aroused by contact with death—seems clearly part of their symbolic efficacy," and that "because all people have bodies, any manipulation of a corpse directly enables one's identification with it through one's own body, thereby tapping into one's reservoirs of feeling."[15] These observations still fail to explain how the act of killing a human being in front of an audience of many other human beings can make that act socially and politically efficacious.

René Girard's discussion of collective violence helps shed light on the efficacy of what I have been calling the sacrificial machine. Sacrificial rituals are a response to conditions of disorder, or what Girard refers to as the "sacrificial crisis," which is brought about when the distinctions on which societies depend disappear.[16] In such a crisis, society takes on the character of an undifferentiated mob in which violence may break out anywhere, against everyone, as people all want the same things and pursue them at each other's expense. The result is the outbreak of "mimetic violence," in which an act of force by one individual against another is met with a retaliatory act, which in turn calls forth additional acts of violence, and on and on it goes. In such situations, the group loses its ability to exert control over its members, and society falls into an endless, expanding, and unstoppable cycle of revenge killings.

Words are not enough to end this cycle, according to Girard. Uncontrolled violence can be stopped and order reasserted only through violence itself—but it must be violence of a different kind from the mimetic violence that characterizes the stage of sacrificial crisis. Specifically, the conclusive act of violence must be an act of collective killing by which the energies unleashed in the stage of crisis are deflected onto a surrogate victim, whose death acts to cauterize the potentially fatal wound inflicted by reciprocal violence on society.

One analogy for this process is the technique that oil-field workers use to control a wellhead that has caught fire and is burning uncontrollably. In such situations, water does no good, and it is impossible to get close enough to cap the well. The solution is the counterintuitive one of setting off a powerful explosion close to the flames. If it is done properly, the explosion sucks the oxygen away from the well, suffocating the fire and giving the crew time to cap the wellhead. In a similar way, an act of collective violence captures for itself all available energy and denies that energy to those inclined to continue the pursuit of personal vendettas.

Sacrifice, as Girard conceives of it, is thus an act of violence that forecloses the risk of retaliatory violence by involving everyone simultaneously and collectively. We are all there, we all participate, we are all collectively implicated and could be accused of a crime were it not for the fact that *we all did it together*. The fact of totality negates the possibility of retaliation and collectivizes the guilt. The logic here goes something like this: The killing was authorized and necessary. It had to be done. The law said so, and the victim deserved what he got. Now life can return to normal. The "new normal," however, is not the normal that characterized the earlier period of reciprocal violence. Through the act of collective violence, society as a whole (or the authority that claims to represent it) has asserted its right to direct violence in lawful ways, and the members of society, through their participation, have demonstrated their acquiescence to and acceptance of this authority.

The effectiveness of such an act of collective violence depends on the identity of the victim. Between the victim and the community there must be both commonality and difference. The victim must be someone with whom other members of society identify, but in relation to whom there is a crucial social link missing. Without commonality, the act of violence would lose all meaning and potency. (Sacrificing a sheep might work just fine in certain contexts, but, in times of crisis, something greater and more intimately related to the group at large must be offered up.) Without difference, society would be exposed to the threat of retaliatory violence from those with a connection to the victim. The selection of the sacrificial victim necessitates a degree of willful misunderstanding: the ability of sacrifice to overcome the crisis of mimetic violence depends on its ability to conceal the displacement that the rite embodies. In other words, the collective guilt of killing a possibly blameless victim must be masked in order for ritual to succeed in expelling violence from the community.

One way to ensure these elements of commonality and difference is by selecting the victim from among members of minority groups within the community who are distinguishably different from the majority and relatively powerless to go against them, as has happened repeatedly through European history to Jews and Gypsies. Another way is by so degrading the victim that the group assembled to carry out and witness the sacrifice no longer recognizes the victim as one of them (as has happened, for example, when groups have used tar and feathers or other symbolic means to effectively dehumanize the victim, who thereby becomes easier to strike down without either remorse or the likelihood of retribution).[17]

Applying Girard's analysis of sacrifice to events in Afghanistan is fairly straightforward. Having suffered through years of discord, Afghanistan was beset by an unprecedented sacrificial crisis, characterized by a loss of critical social distinctions and a plague of reciprocal violence and revenge killings that extended from the top ranks of the government in Kabul to the smallest village. The capital itself, which had been insulated from violence through the years of communist control, had been shelled by a former prime minister. Ethnic groups fought street battles for control of formerly mixed neighborhoods. In the provinces, former heroes of jihad had become scavengers preying on the populations they had once protected. In response to this situation, the Taliban initiated a campaign to purify what had been contaminated. In calling themselves talibs, the movement self-consciously identified itself with a class of society that had given up land, property, and any larger ambition in pursuit of religious knowledge. The focus of the Taliban campaign of purification was eliminating corruption from the major cities and principally Kabul, which was always considered the most immoral of cities and the worst offender against Islamic norms and laws.

The Taliban use of public punishment can thus be seen as part of its attempt to open up the exercise of government power to public scrutiny, but it can also be seen as a way of involving the public in the sacrificial act and, through their participation, making them complicit as well. Seen from a distance, these executions might be recognized as scapegoating rituals, and maybe some of the people present in the stadium saw them that way too, but their presence at the ritual also made it more likely that, to expunge their own guilt for being witnesses to what they realized on some level to be an illegitimate and unfair exercise of violence, they defuse their guilt by recognizing the actions of the authority as warranted and correct. This judgment would be reinforced by the knowledge that the victim had been tried in an Islamic court of law and that the penalty exacted was determined by shari'a law. The act of witnessing is as important as the killing itself and can be experienced variously and simultaneously as terrifying (he could be me), thrilling (he isn't me), shaming (he doesn't deserve what he's getting), and pacifying (I don't want it to be me next time). These contradictory feelings are ultimately resolved by the readily available and socially encouraged rationalization that the act was carried out according to the law and by the passage of time, which blurs disturbing memories.

The Taliban's embedding of its regime in Islamic law insulated it from accusations of arbitrary abuse of power. Its containment of the exercise of collective violence in public ritual channeled the diffuse violence percolating through society into a single stream directed at one selected victim. These rituals, in this sense, were not just the normal, everyday exercise of judicial responsibility. They became the means by which the government demonstrated its power to the people, reclaimed and re-legitimated the use of violence as an instrument of rule, and claimed a monopoly on the use of violence by attempting to enforce the notion that revenge was the province not of the people but of the government alone.

One modification to Girard's theory seems to be required, and that concerns his description of collective violence as all against one, which is to say, society as a whole engaging in violence against a selected victim and thereby sharing equally in the responsibility for the action. The genius of the Taliban—or, more accurately, the genius of early Islam—was to enmesh in one ritual act the energies of both collective and retributive violence. *Qisas* is a category of crimes for which Islamic law allows retaliation to be incorporated in the punishment: in the case of a murder, for example, one of the close family members of the victim can act as executioner, allowing the family to discharge its obligation to retaliate against the murderer or the murderer's family. In this way, the problem of revenge killings is overcome, as Girard contends, but not by a collective act of violence. Rather, the authority sanctions an act of individual revenge but retains for itself the right to make the judgment of guilt or innocence, and to arrange the circumstances of the retribution. Making the execution of the sentence a public event effectively implicates the whole community in both the process of arriving at the judgment and the execution of the sentence. Likewise, these practices preclude the family's taking justice into its own hands and thereby prolonging the cycle of vengeance. The state thus maintains its authority while also recognizing longstanding social norms and expectations for retribution.

One important question is whether the punishments performed by the Taliban warrant the label of *sacrifice*. They certainly qualify as such in the abstract terms set forth by theorists like Girard, but they would not be termed sacrifice by the Taliban themselves. By their lights, they were *hudud,* punishments stipulated and authorized under Islamic law—nothing more, nothing less. Nevertheless, sacrifice encompasses a broad range of actions and contexts. Afghans who went into battle against the Soviets knew that they might be killed, and they steeled themselves to this possibility by framing their actions through ritual. For their part, the Afghan political parties used the terminology of sacrifice ex post facto to commemorate their dead and, indirectly at least, to encourage others to follow in the footsteps of the martyrs. There is nothing inherently ritualistic in these acts of killing and dying. What turns them into sacrifice is that they are socially constructed as such before and after the fact.

The Taliban did not at any point consider what they were doing as an act of sacrifice, even if they did invoke a ritual frame for their actions, offering prayers and in other ways indicating that they were engaging in these acts of destruction in obedience to God's orders. In characterizing the Taliban rites as acts of sacrifice, I go back to the assertion of Hubert and Mauss that "the same mechanisms of sacrifice can satisfy religious needs the difference between which is extreme. . . . It can tend to both good and evil; the victim represents death as well as life, illness as well as health, sin as well as virtue, falsity as well as truth." [18] Sacrifice, they note, is "the means of concentration of religious feeling; it expresses it, it incarnates it, it carries it along. By acting upon the victim one acts upon religious feeling, directs it either by attracting and absorbing it, or by expelling and eliminating it. Thus in the same way is explained the fact that by suitable procedures these two forms of religious feeling can be transformed into each other, and that rites which in certain cases appear contradictory are sometimes almost indistinguishable." [19]

One amendment I would offer to this statement is to substitute "sacred feelings" for "religious feelings," the point being that sacrifice is not inherently or necessarily religious (in this case, Islamic) in orientation. The "feelings" that are concentrated in sacrifice can often, maybe mostly, be described as "religious" in nature, but they can also relate to other domains to which humans attribute sacrality, including the domains of honor, patriotism, and even perhaps good manners. Humans delineate for themselves their own conceptions of what matters most. Often they attach some supernatural component to that conception, but not always.

A second question that must remain unanswered is how long the Taliban could have maintained its regimen of public punishments. Collective violence might be the solution, as Girard contends, to a crisis of civil disorder, but bringing violence out into the public square runs two risks: first, that the violence will spill out of its ritual vessel, and second, that it will lose its efficacy over time, thus weakening and delegitimizing the government. There is certainly evidence that the Taliban overplayed their hand. The combination of draconian moral policing, selective violence against non-Pashtun minorities, and the inability to solve the economic and social problems of an impoverished and broken society might have led the Taliban to ruin. That possibility was forestalled, however, by the September 11 attacks on New York City and the Pentagon and the subsequent American intervention on the side of the Taliban's great enemy, the Northern Alliance. Would the Taliban have fallen if left to their own devices? We cannot say for sure, but it is clear that the Taliban that reemerged after their defeat in 2001 is a very different creature from the Taliban of the 1990s and one that has found new ways to reengineer the sacrificial machine for its own purposes. However, before we can get to that part of the story, we must turn our attention to the Arab influence on developments in Afghanistan and the reengineering of sacrifice brought about by the attacks of September 11, 2001.

FIVE

Fedayeen

TO THIS POINT, MY FOCUS has been on the transformation of sacrifice within Afghanistan and among Afghans. Here I turn my attention to the role of non-Afghans in this process, specifically two key figures who came to fight in the Afghan jihad and who individually and collectively changed the conception and practice of sacrifice in Afghanistan, by Afghans, and ultimately in many more places by many more people. The two figures are Abdullah 'Azzam, the founder of al-Qaeda, who set in motion the influx of foreign fighters into Afghanistan and gave the movement much of its early ideological focus and collective luster, and Osama Bin Laden, who initially focused on giving organizational and logistical coherence to al-Qaeda and later redefined its mission from helping Afghanistan to spearheading a global jihad.

I have titled this chapter "Fedayeen" because it is a term the Arabs used for themselves. It is not a term that Afghans tended to use for themselves or for the Arabs. The terminology is important in that many of the Arabs who came to Afghanistan did so specifically "to sacrifice themselves," which is the root meaning of the Arabic term *fedayeen*. Their goal was not the liberation of Afghanistan from the Soviet Union or to defeat communism. For many, if not most, it was to die in battle, to go from fedayeen to shahidan: from those willing to sacrifice themselves to those who have succeeded and become martyrs.

Afghanistan is the context within which a larger process of change took place related to the ideology and structure of sacrifice, but it was not just Afghans who contributed to this process, and, in the end, it has not just been Afghans and Afghanistan who have been affected by the change brought about on Afghan soil. In examining the complex and dynamic interaction of internal and external forces operating in Afghanistan, my goal has been to understand the "structure of the conjuncture," which is to say, how these forces came together to give birth to something new and terrible.

The principal external stimulus for that transformative process was the invasion by the Soviets, whose mode of conducting warfare outstripped existing ways both of fighting and of contesting government power. In the process, it also eroded deep-seated Afghan ideals of honor. In their espousal of communist ideology, the Soviets and their Afghan allies provided a symbol of infidelity that fit the Manichean binaries of the Islamic political parties, enabling them to portray themselves as the proper and necessary champions of all that was godly and good in the eternal battle with evil. Those who died in that battle received the parties' benediction for having sacrificed themselves in that ultimate and divinely ordained struggle.

Midway through the decade-long Soviet occupation, Arabs began to arrive in Afghanistan to fight alongside the Afghans. Though they were far fewer in number, the effect of this second invasion was ultimately as significant as the first, and perhaps in the end it will prove more far-reaching. The Soviet impact was effected from without. The impact of those often referred to as the "Afghan Arabs"—the Arabs who came to Afghanistan to participate in the Afghan jihad both during the Soviet occupation and its aftermath and under the Taliban—was effected from within.[1]

'Azzam and Bin Laden have both been the subjects of intensive study, so I focus here on one particular aspect of their careers that has been less fully discussed: how they helped to transform sacrifice into the conceptual hub and practical pivot around which jihad is now conducted. If, in the early poetry of jihad, the martyr's body was viewed as the passive object of the enemy's violence (in the poet Gauhar's words, made "a sieve from the bullets"), the martyr's body now became the chief weapon for inflicting violence on the enemy. If, before, martyrdom was the unfortunate consequence of battle, it became, through the efforts of the Afghan Arabs, the sought-after goal.

ABDULLAH 'AZZAM

Although Abdullah 'Azzam's ideas were less influential than those of predecessors like the Egyptian Sayyid Qutb (1906–66) and the Pakistani Abu Ala Maududi (1903–79), and he himself was far less famous than his protégé, 'Azzam was a crucial figure in transforming the Afghan jihad into a global conflict (figure 17).[2] Indeed, it is difficult to imagine that the September 11

Why not? And the Quran was revealed
to him from above the seven heavens.
AL MUJAHID SHEIKH ABDULLAH AZZAM

FIGURE 17. Abdullah 'Azzam. From *The Destruction of the U.S.S. Cole* video, produced by al-Qaeda in June 2001.

attacks could have taken place if 'Azzam had not laid the groundwork for them years earlier.[3] He provided not only organizational ability but also inspiration. Central to his vision of jihad was a mystical understanding of the role of sacrifice.

If the Peshawar parties found a way to instrumentalize martyrdom, making the dead do service to the party beyond the grave, 'Azzam managed to make them a source of inspiration to Muslims throughout the world who might be contemplating leading a different sort of life. Under the twin assaults of modernity and Islamism, the mystical traditions that for centuries had been institutionalized in the Sufi orders had begun to erode, with many of the orders themselves becoming calcified and corrupt as they were taken over by hereditary leaders more interested in preserving their family position than pursuing mystical practice. 'Azzam in effect appropriated mysticism from the precincts of Sufism and transferred it to the realm of jihad, and he did so through the figure of the Martyr.

'Azzam was among the first Arabs to arrive in Peshawar in the mid-1980s. A Palestinian by birth, he had made his initial forays into jihadi politics by opposing the Israeli occupation of Palestinian territories, but he reportedly was disillusioned by the secular foundation of Palestinian nationalism and left to teach theology in Saudi Arabia before eventually relocating to Peshawar, where he found his calling. 'Azzam established an organization—the so-called Maktab al-Khedamat (Service Bureau)—to provide financial and logistical support to the mujahidin. He also traveled widely, including to the United States and other Western countries, to meet with groups of young Muslim men whom he hoped to recruit to fight in the Afghan struggle.

His efforts drew Arabs to Peshawar in sufficient numbers to form their own units, which became famous among the Afghans for their often-reckless disregard for personal safety—motivated less by their desire to defeat the enemy than by their pursuit of martyrdom. 'Azzam was largely responsible for instilling this attitude, which he cultivated through numerous speeches, sermons, and publications. Three of his texts in particular stand out as essential in establishing the bases on which the jihad was redefined and restructured following the end of the Soviet occupation and the loss of its original raison d'être.

Join the Caravan

The first of 'Azzam's most influential texts was *Join the Caravan*—the caravan of the title being the caravan of martyrs.[4] Martyrdom, however, is less central to the text than jihad itself, whose scriptural basis 'Azzam develops through voluminous references to the Qur'an and the traditions of the Prophet. As a theologian, 'Azzam could substantiate and legitimize his concept of jihad with a scholarly grounding that few if any Afghans could emulate. The jihad that emerges from *Join the Caravan* is not a course of action that depends on context or circumstances (e.g., an invasion of your home country by an infidel army) but one that can and should be chosen on its own merits (i.e., a Muslim should fight to defend Islam whether or not he himself, his family, or his home country is immediately threatened).

For 'Azzam, jihad is not an option but a requirement of faith, and a requirement that is not satisfied by distant support of those doing the fighting but only by direct participation. This was not a new feature of Islamist thought: it goes back to earlier Islamic reformers, Sayyid Qutb in particular, who insisted that jihad was a central tenet of faith that could not be evaded because of distance or extenuating circumstances. 'Azzam embraced this precept and applied it specifically to the jihad in Afghanistan, telling potential recruits in the Middle East, Europe, and North America that despite the distance and differences in custom and language, the Afghan struggle was equally their struggle. This argument appealed to young men from a diverse array of countries, and it was an approach that Bin Laden continued after he took over leadership of the Service Bureau.

A second element in ʿAzzam's conception of jihad that had far-reaching consequences was his assertion that struggle should not be inhibited by the likelihood of civilian casualties. Regrettable deaths would occur in combat, but this consequence was legally acceptable according to his interpretation of scriptural texts, even if the casualties were Muslims. Both this belief and the acceptability of offensive jihad would come to matter a great deal, especially when Bin Laden and his associates began to imagine what might come after the Soviet withdrawal. An engineer by training, Bin Laden did not have the knowledge and the Islamic scholarly credentials to issue directives of the sort that ʿAzzam assembles in *Join the Caravan,* but he inherited from ʿAzzam the theological arguments he would need to justify operations like the embassy bombings in East Africa in 1998, the strike against the USS *Cole* in 2000, and the September 11 attacks in 2001.

Signs of Allah the Most Merciful in the Jihad of Afghanistan

ʿAzzam was not the only theoretician and cheerleader of jihad. Many others have provided a scriptural basis for defining, delimiting, continuing, and extending the struggle. What separated ʿAzzam from these other scholars was the extensive time he spent traveling to fronts in different parts of Afghanistan, observing jihad in practice, and listening to and chronicling the stories of the mujahidin. In a sense, ʿAzzam was a journalist of jihad, but his perspective was not that of a modern journalist, intent on telling a factual story, based on empirical evidence, that fits within a more general chronology of events. ʿAzzam was more like a medieval chronicler—part annalist, part hagiographer, whose focus was not on chronology or the relationship between events but rather on the ecstatic truth hidden beneath the mundane details of death and dying. *Signs of Allah the Most Merciful in the Jihad of Afghanistan* is a compilation of stories collected in his travels from various mujahidin he met, who told him of miracles (*karamat*) associated with martyrs, as well as other signs of the umbrella of protection God had placed over the mujahidin, allowing them to defeat their enemies in the face of overwhelming odds.

For 'Azzam, scripture rather than science mattered, and the text thus begins, as one might expect from a scholar, with scriptural evidence for miracles and an extensive discussion of the nature of miracles, who performs them, and under what circumstances. Admitting that the stories he is about to recount still stretch the bounds of credibility and might appear more like fairytales than real events, 'Azzam reassures his readers of the reliability of his account, having "personally heard them with my own ears; and [I] have written them with my own hands from those Mujahideen who themselves were present. I have heard these miracles from such men who are trustworthy and reliable, and who have been constantly on the battlefield. The miracles are many, so much so that . . . [their] large number does not entertain the possibility of fabrication."[5]

Many of the miracles involve divine assistance to mujahidin in the midst of fighting: enemy bombs that fail to explode; birds that hover over mujahidin informing them of an imminent attack by enemy forces; the appearance of angels on horseback (often visible to the enemy, though not to the mujahidin themselves) who turn the tide of a battle; bullets that strike but do not pierce the body; tanks that run over mujahidin but do not crush them; and so forth.[6] The majority of the miracles 'Azzam recounts, however, and the ones that inspire his most fervent interest, involve martyrs. The most commonly repeated story, told in multiple variations, involves the incorruptibility of the martyr's body: the sweet, musk-like odor that emanates from the ground where the martyr is buried; the wounds—like stigmata—that continue to bleed long after the martyr's death; and the shafts of light that shine from his grave up into the sky. In order to affirm the truth of these stories, one of 'Azzam's more industrious and empirically minded informants—a front commander—is said to have opened up a number of the graves of mujahidin, sometimes years after their deaths, and found the bodies of his former comrades still intact.[7]

For all of its acknowledgment of the importance of empirical proof, the book does not purport to be a scientific treatise; the focus throughout is on the miracles themselves and the implicit evidence they provide not only of the existence of God but also of his active interest in and support for those of his creatures who recognize him and follow the teachings of his Prophet. With this approach, 'Azzam appropriates to himself the domain of martyrs and, through them, the cause of jihad, a phenomenological discourse that was previously associated (at least in Afghanistan) mainly with saints.[8] Some of those saints themselves engaged in violent jihad, but their lives were not defined by it. Rather, they were defined by the mystical practices associated with "the greater jihad" (*jihad al-akbar*)—the struggle to defeat the carnal self. The goal of this nonmaterial jihad was to get close to God, to become one of his "friends" (*awliya*). Its practices centered on the chanting of names of God (*zikr*), prayer, fasting, and extended periods of seclusion (*chilla*), during which the saint confronted and defeated the temptations of the material world and the tricks of Satan. 'Azzam effectively takes the DNA of these stories and injects it into the body of the martyr, who hereafter is to be seen as the true saint. 'Azzam's preliminary exegesis of the different kinds of miracles establishes the theological basis for this transference. Thus, though the kind of saints found in old stories might have disappeared, and the mystical practices they perfected are no longer widely followed, the qualities represented and the mystical bonds with the divine they achieved are alive and well, albeit transplanted into the person of the shahid (martyr), with Sufism as a form of mystical practice being effectively replaced by shahadat (martyrdom).

The Lovers of the Maidens of Paradise

Much of the content of 'Azzam's *The Lovers of the Maidens of Paradise* is similar to *The Signs of Allah,* and many of the same miracle stories are repeated. The difference is that, rather than concentrating on the miracles as phenomena in themselves, 'Azzam turns his attention to specific martyrs and the characteristics that made each unique and exemplary. The miracles associated with each martyr are recounted, but they are secondary to the portrait of the martyr himself. Most of those profiled in the book are Arabs martyred in the Afghan conflict. A number are young men recruited by 'Azzam himself, and they represent many of the countries of the Middle East. 'Azzam's accounts are different from the biographical accounts that appear in the Afghan martyr magazines; their almost ecstatic language combines direct address, narrative, and poetry, as evidenced in his profile of Yahya Senyor from Jeddah, the first Arab martyred in Afghanistan:

> It was the Night of Arafat, and the Russians had pounced on you from above and from below. Hearts had reached to the throats; you rose with your brothers for Suhoor to fast the Day of Arafat in the land of the battle, for if the fasting of Arafat expiates two years' sins, how great is fasting Arafat under lava sprinkled from the sky as if it was a shower of rain! This, no doubt, has a reward which is much greater, and in an authentic hadith, it is stated that whoever fasted a day for the sake of Allah, Allah will make the distance between him and the Fire the length of seventy trenches.

So your brothers said to you, "O Yahya, let us eat Suhoor."

You replied, "I am going to perform ablution." Then you clarified yourself, saying, "By Allah, I am not in a state of Janaba [ritual impurity], rather I am bathing to meet the Hoor which I saw in my dream. I have never seen a woman in my dream, but tonight she came to me with her clothes, her flirtatiousness, her beauty, her purity, and the blackness of her eyes—she is the Hoor!"

The battle of Jaji ended, but you were not lucky, O Yahya, in attaining Martyrdom. Thus, your brothers began to joke with you, saying, "Where did the Hoor go, the one that you insisted would arrive?!"

One of the Arab brothers told me, "Yahya stood at the graves of the three Arab Martyrs which lay at the peak of Jaji and he started to address them saying, 'Soon I will be joining you, with the permission of Allah.'"

The 7 of Muharram 1405 [September 23, 1985] arrived and on that day you had an appointment with Martyrdom, the Martyrdom which you had not refrained from asking for day and night. It was at the hands of a group of Communist agents, who opened fire on you at the gates of Jaji, that you attained it and you sealed the sale (of your soul)—insha Allah.[9]

'Azzam's Influence

'Azzam's assassination in 1989 remains unexplained: those who planted the high-powered explosive that blew up his car have never been positively identified. Some speculation places the blame on Western agents, some on Jordanians controlled or manipulated by Israel. Another possibility is that it was the work of one or another of the Peshawar parties struggling in the wake of the Soviet withdrawal for supremacy in the jihad. Other speculation has fallen on Bin Laden and his close associate, Ayman al-Zawahiri, both of whom were advocating strategies for the post-Soviet period that differed from 'Azzam's.

The identity of his killers will probably always remain in doubt, but there is no question of his importance in nurturing global jihad. Though his formulation of jihadi doctrine was significant, others could have made the same arguments he did, and they probably would have done so when the need arose. His greater contribution, and the one that it is difficult imagining that anyone else could have made, was the artful way in which he elaborated martyrdom as a source of personal fulfillment. Others had referred to the "luck" of the dead in achieving the status of martyr; 'Azzam set out to provide the empirical evidence for the glory of martyrdom. The Peshawar parties had had the same intention, but the obituaries they published of even the most important figures in their party are perfunctory in comparison to the elegiac evocations that 'Azzam produced.

'Azzam better understood the propagandistic uses to which martyrdom could be put through the poetic invocation of the stories of the dead and the elaborate description of the moment of death. Recognizing that death itself could be turned to advantage, he embraced it and exalted death as the test of true faith and the passageway to eternal bliss. In this regard, the miracle stories he annotated and compiled were probably even more important than the hagiographies in *The Lovers of the Maidens of Paradise*. As Daryl Li notes, *Signs of Allah* was "immensely popular, going through multiple editions and printings in Lahore, Jidda, Amman, Beirut, Alexandria, and translations into English, Turkish, Bahasa, and Serbo-Croatian."[10]

In the same way that 'Azzam animated the figure of the Martyr, he infused another mythic figure—that of the houri—with new life, taking vague and enigmatic scriptural references to a being who exists in the mythological domain of djinns and other obscure, half-believed creatures and using these images to create an essential actor in the drama of Islamist self-fashioning. This was fundamentally different from the self-fashioning of the young tribesman who imagined himself a hero and could anticipate enjoying the reward for his risk and his daring in this life. Such a young man had a source of both inspiration and potential disgrace in the figure of the young woman who observed him from a distance, who would either admire or rebuke the young man through the composition of landai poems. Everyone who mattered would know who was being either lionized or laughed at in the recitation of a specific landai at a particular time and in a particular circumstance, and the imagination of a woman's eye aflame with desire or narrowing in judgment was sufficient to ensure a young man that his name would achieve positive immortality.

I cannot put myself in the position of the Yemeni or Egyptian boy who read 'Azzam's hagiographies; I can somewhat better imagine that, for Afghans, houris might have provided a positive alternative to the unseen girl making up verses in her head to try out on her friends as they filled water jugs at the well. The figure of the living girl personifies potential fulfillment but also the threat of mockery and of loss to a rival. The houri represents no such threat. She is a beauty who can be enjoyed without fear that she might someday be taken away or leave of her own accord. She is the martyr's eternal reward who will neither rebuke nor age and whose desire and fidelity are assured.

In animating the figure of the houri, 'Azzam found in sexual desire an untapped source of energy to fuel the sacrifice machine. The houri had always been available as a latent resource, but, as with her companion the shahid, the potential of the figure had not been realized in the course of the war. 'Azzam, more than anyone else, brought the houri to life, making her a figure toward whom the would-be martyr could channel all of the desire that hormones awaken in young men and that society seeks to control. In animating the houri and making her real to the mujahid, 'Azzam effectively bypassed societal restrictions on sexuality (in the same way that jihad bypasses restrictions on violence) and offered to young recruits a path to fulfillment in all the ways that young men desire.

Extending the machine analogy, I would argue that 'Azzam's innovation on the original sacrificial design was, first, to reinfuse it with meaning. The meaning was not new. People had always believed that those who sacrificed themselves in the path of jihad went to heaven after they died. For many Afghans, however, this understanding had been tarnished by the self-serving actions of the Peshawar parties through the ten years of Soviet occupation. Many casualties during that occupation had resulted not from fighting the communists but from battles between rival factions representing different political parties. 'Azzam not only endeavored to mediate some of the bitterest of these disputes but also sought to remind people of what it was they were fighting for, why it mattered, and what the rewards would be for those who fulfilled God's commandments. Faith might have been tarnished, but 'Azzam provided assurance that martyrdom endured as the path of redemption. That message found its most immediate and receptive audience among the Afghan Arab guests rather than among 'Azzam's Afghan hosts, but his efforts ensured that it reached and endured in both communities.

A second development relates to 'Azzam's animation of the miraculous amid the depressing realities of a society at war. The claim here is not that 'Azzam discovered miracles or that he somehow singlehandedly made them relevant to the war. It is rather that he consolidated myriad stories into a consistent narrative that amplified the message. Hearsay and anecdote became evidence and affirmation that many small things were tied together into one great thing. The main audience for these stories was not in Afghanistan: Afghans were the material of 'Azzam's stories. 'Azzam wrote in Arabic, and the principal audience for his miracle stories and hagiographies was primarily in the Arab world but also in other countries and in many other languages.

Through 'Azzam's efforts, Afghanistan was transformed into a mythical world of enduring possibility that transcended the political circumstances of the Soviet occupation. Through his stories, Afghanistan morphed from a place of death, dislocation, and suffering into an enchanted realm in which the original spirit of Islam had come back to life. When Afghans first took up arms against the Soviets, propagandists in the United States were quick to associate Afghan freedom fighters with the backwoodsmen who fought against British tyranny at the time of the American Revolution. 'Azzam accomplished something similar, though far more potent and long-lived. Before 'Azzam, the Afghan story was of a small, backward nation taking on and defeating a modern superpower. 'Azzam's Afghanistan, however, was not a nation in the traditional geopolitical sense but the Prophet's Arabia reawakened, a place where disenchanted Muslims could experience the mythic time of the Prophet and, through that experience, renew their faith and become something different from anything they had ever thought possible. Afghanistan became, in effect, a real-life movie set in which young Muslims could become heroes, with 'Azzam himself as the scriptwriter and producer. His imaginative inducements and practical assistance enabled at first dozens and later hundreds of foreign fighters to come to Afghanistan to fulfill their newly imagined destiny.

'Azzam's final and most important contribution—the contribution that gave meaning to all the others—was to turn martyrdom from something that *might* happen to a believer into something that *should* happen: a fate that should not simply be aspired to in the abstract but actively pursued. The foreign fighters 'Azzam brought to Afghanistan became famous for their pursuit of death and their disappointment if they did not die as a result of their heroics. Afghans did not share this attitude. As one familiar joke had it, "Afghans want to be both martyr and *ghazi*, and then return safely home" (*Afghanan ghuwari chi ham shaheed wee, ham ghazi aw ham kor ta sahe salamat kor ta rashee*).

The difference is distilled in the distinction between fearlessness and fear. Afghans traditionally admired those who demonstrated fearlessness through their actions. The risk of death made survival sweeter, but the point was always to survive. Fearlessness was rewarded by the admiration of the living. 'Azzam's foreign fighters operated with a different set of assumptions. They were far from home, and for them, all virtue emanated from fear of God. The only true proof of that fearlessness was the death of the believer. Earning the admiration of the living was desirable only in that it might inspire others to emulate the believer's example. All that mattered to the believer was what God's judgment of him would be, and that judgment was far more likely to be a positive one if the believer's action led to his death. Such action was not sacrifice by accident or by retrospective certification by some political party but sacrifice by design and through intent (niyat).

OSAMA BIN LADEN

According to Mustafa Hamid, one of the early Afghan Arabs who came to Peshawar to support the jihad, the focus of the training regime established under 'Azzam's direction was "on the spiritual and moral side, rather than the military side."[11] For all the inspiration he provided and the enthusiasm he engendered, 'Azzam's emphasis on martyrdom over military success was an obstacle to victory:

> 'Azzam was a very good speaker.... But this was not sufficient at that time, and in fact may have been misused in some places.... Because these speeches put the youth in the mood of loving to die; to go to paradise and not to care about anything else. Although training was given on how to use the weapons alongside this religious training, there was no training on tactics, or more importantly on the political side of the military work and the implications of this regionally and internationally.[12]

Under the sway of 'Azzam's rhetoric, many Arab recruits disdained the notion of training altogether, seeing it as "a 'secular' tendency, which contradicted the principle of 'putting our trust in God.'"[13] Experience and expertise were beside the point. 'Azzam's recruits "wanted to participate immediately in combat, believing they were following the example of the Prophet Muhammad and his Companions."[14] The objectives of combat meant less to these men than the experience, and if they were not going to die right away, they at least wanted validation of the promises they had read about and that formed the basis of their dreams of bloody sacrifice: "I remember during the jihad against the Soviets, the youth would come back to Peshawar angrily shouting, 'Where are the miracles?' They had read about miracles in the magazines that were being published about the jihad and then when they got to the fronts they did not see any miracles."[15]

Unlike 'Azzam, who was more interested in right thinking than in fighting, Bin Laden pictured himself as a warrior, and he was not content to sit in

FIGURE 18. Osama Bin Laden. From *The Destruction of the U.S.S. Cole* video, produced by al-Qaeda in June 2001.

Peshawar and support the jihad behind the scenes (figure 18). He wanted to be directly involved, even if it meant defying 'Azzam's authority. Bin Laden began his career in jihad as one of 'Azzam's principal confederates and financial backers. However, from the start, there were differences of approach and temperament that would eventually cause them to part ways. In 1986, Bin Laden withdrew funding from the Maktab al-Khadamat. Nominally, he disagreed with the way the organization was being administered, but the conflict might have had more to do with philosophical disagreements about the role of the organization in supporting the jihad. Bin Laden's differences with his mentor came to the fore during a trip to Paktia Province, when Bin Laden saw for the first time the primitive conditions in which mujahidin were living. "When he saw the conditions Abu Abdullah [the name by which Bin Laden was known to his fellow Arabs] said he felt guilty for taking so long to visit, and he felt it was a big sin that he had not come earlier; he found himself wanting to be martyred there."[16]

Unlike many of the youthful recruits that 'Azzam had inspired, however, Bin Laden was willing to put his own martyrdom on hold for the sake of the jihad. He offered practical support in the best ways he knew how: by using his considerable wealth to directly finance the mujahidin in their fight with the Soviets and his engineering background to fortify bases inside Afghanistan. One such base was Zhawar, in a dry riverbed in the southern part of Paktia Province, which I visited in 1984. Even to my unpracticed eye, it did not appear that the mujahidin stationed there were taking its defense very seriously. Many of them were, in fact, army deserters and captured soldiers. Although they had been conscripted to dig tunnels in the cliff walls, their efforts did not appear especially energetic, and they had little in the way of heavy equipment to aid their work.

The inadequacies of the training and fortifications were demonstrated over the next two years as the Soviets mounted major offensives to gain control of Zhawar and the surrounding area. In the process, they rendered the base useless as a transit station for moving men and supplies into Afghanistan. Although the mujahidin of Maulavi Jalaluddin Haqqani's Hizb-i Islami party were ultimately able to dislodge the Soviet paratroopers and government troops who had taken the base, the offensive revealed the limitations both of the bases themselves and of the troops manning them, including one group of Arab fighters who were so ineffectual that they gained the sobriquet "Brigade of the Humorous."[17]

A few months after the Soviets withdrew from Zhawar, Bin Laden established his own base, which he called al-Masadah (Lion's Den), in the northern Jaji region of Paktia Province. In April 1987, a year after the end of the Zhawar campaign, the defenders repelled a Soviet attack on the Jaji base, in large part because of improved training and defensive fortification. Although relatively unimportant in military terms, the battle afforded new status to Bin Laden, allowing him to portray himself not only as a military leader but also as a hero who, in Hamid's words, "could come like the musketeer on his horse, and win the battle by himself. Later, this behaviour became even bigger when he declared war on America thinking he could liberate the Ummah [Muslim community] by himself."[18] More immediately, the battle helped Bin Laden to emerge from the shadow of 'Azzam, who was thereafter regarded as a preacher rather than a military strategist, and to raise Bin Laden's standing among the young Afghan Arabs as "the leader who would help them see combat, and possibly attain martyrdom."[19]

In attracting these new foreign recruits, however, Bin Laden and his followers became increasingly detached from the Afghans. The forces at the numerous training camps he established were always composed solely of Arabs and other foreign fighters who had little contact or communication with Afghans, and this division only deepened as the Arabs became more assertive and confident fighters. Afghans recognized the value of Arab support for their jihad, and as fellow Muslims they felt some constraint in how much they could object, but they nevertheless complained, often bitterly, about Arab arrogance.[20] This sentiment was exacerbated by doctrinal differences between the strict Wahhabi and Salafi orientations of the Arabs and the more tolerant Hanafi faith of the Afghans.

One specific area of discord centered on the Afghan custom of raising flags over the graves of their martyrs, a practice that the Arabs viewed as *shirk* (polytheism) and therefore unlawful. On at least one occasion, Arabs removed such flags, setting off a serious enough dispute that Maulavi Khales, the leader of one of the Peshawar parties, had to travel to Kandahar to mediate it.[21] Given the moral calculus of sacrifice, in which the living owed a continuing debt to those who had died in battle, the Wahhabi interdiction against prayers and flags at the graves of martyrs can be seen from the Afghan perspective as both sacrilege and immorality, as well as a violation of the mujahidin's loving memories of the friends of their youth, their brothers from the sangar.

In 1989, two years after the battle of Jaji, the Soviets withdrew their forces in a ceremonial procession of tanks that crossed the Amu Darya River back into Soviet Central Asia. The faux solemnity of that event contrasted with the furious combat that immediately followed their departure centered on the eastern city of Jalalabad, where the Hizb-i Islami party of Hekmatyar and the Ettihad-i Islami party of Abdul Rab Rasul Sayyaf were staging a major offensive not only to dislodge the communist regime left behind after the Soviet retreat but also to gain the upper hand in what was assumed would be the ensuing race to control Kabul. The Afghan Arabs were quick to join the fray, in no small part due to the efforts of 'Azzam, who "was shouting about it very loudly. . . . In his *Al-Jihad* magazine, he made pages about the *shuhada*—those who were killed in battle. He was supporting the campaign very heavily and bringing attention to it and this attracted people from outside Afghanistan to come and join. They didn't read anything about the weapons or the battle even, they only read about the martyrs, and they came to join to be martyrs."[22]

The siege of Jalalabad turned into a major defeat for the mujahidin, who were unprepared to mount a frontal assault on a major fortified city. The failure of the operation set the stage for the bitter civil war that followed and dented the prestige of the Afghan Arab leaders who had so vociferously encouraged their followers to join the battle. The stalemate that followed the siege left the Arabs marooned. With the Soviets out of the picture, many hesitated to join in the internecine war between the mujahidin parties that was no longer a clearly defined jihad. Over time, many of the foreign fighters departed to join the conflicts in Bosnia and Chechnya. Others, notably the mujahidin from Algeria, returned home to initiate bloody campaigns against their own governments. The absence of clear direction and the diminished prestige of established leaders like 'Azzam and Bin Laden also led to the development of new splinter groups, not so much concrete political parties as "free radicals"— floating groups of undisciplined militants who attacked established leaders and strove to outdo each other in their fiery promotion of jihad.

Hamid has termed this group the Jalalabad School, in recognition of the role that the failed battle of Jalalabad played in their formation, and he characterizes them as lacking "any leadership, strategy, or political thoughts; without belonging to a nation or a homeland." More often called *takfiris* (referring to the act of declaring a fellow Muslim or a Muslim ruler a *kafir*, or infidel), these were students of a school without teachers, "impetuous youth with extreme Salafi thoughts and a careless approach; they did not care or did not think about the consequences of their actions. This Jalalabad School . . . spread and infiltrated . . . the School of al-Qaeda, when [Bin Laden] was encouraged by the kind of shiny operations that had no strategy and no political vision and the peak of all of that was the operation of 9/11."[23] But September 11 was still a long way off. Bin Laden himself would have been in no position to establish a base from which to mount such an operation, even if it had occurred to him to do so. Instead, he chose this moment to desert Afghanistan, first for Saudi Arabia and later for Sudan. It would be six years before he would return and begin to build the machine that would initiate a new epoch of world history.

The Declaration

In the summer of 2002, a large and battered box arrived at my office. I knew it was coming, but it was bigger than I expected. Inside were more than 1,500 audiocassettes, with their containers tossed in as though they had been extracted from a landfill. In fact, they had belonged to Bin Laden and been spirited away from his home in Kandahar shortly after the Taliban deserted the city following the fall of their regime in 2001. The story I was told is that they were found by a CNN stringer in a Kandahar shop, where they were being used to record the Bollywood music long outlawed by the Taliban. The tapes were not blank but filled with sermons and speeches, some by Bin Laden himself, and the stringer quickly realized that they might be significant. For CNN, audio-only tapes had limited value, but one of the producers, who knew I had archived other audiovisual material from Afghanistan, asked if I wanted to provide a repository for them. Certain intelligence agencies might have exercised their right to confiscate this material, but they apparently did not want it. I was not sure that I wanted it either, but I agreed to take it.

I enlisted the aid of an anthropology colleague who was a skilled Arab linguist to help me make sense of what was in that box.[24] The bulk of the material consisted of formal lectures and speeches by dozens of Islamic scholars, clerics, and political activists, the vast majority of them in Arabic. Many of the cassettes featured 'Azzam, and twenty-four cassettes featured Bin Laden himself. One of these tapes, recorded in 1996, contains the speech that became known as "The Declaration of War against the United States Occupying the Two Holy Places." It provides an extraordinary glimpse into Bin Laden's ambitious plans at what might be described as the nadir of his political career. Shortly before, he had been stripped of his Saudi citizenship and forced to leave his refuge in Sudan; his financial accounts had been frozen and one of his closest associates accused of embezzlement. After the Soviets had pulled out and the mujahidin had begun attacking each other, the jihad leaders were divided over what should come next. Bin Laden still had a small cohort of followers who had accompanied him to Sudan and eventually back to Afghanistan, but he had encountered increasing difficulties in rallying recruits to his cause, in part because no one any longer—himself included—was quite sure what the cause was or should be.

At this unpromising moment, Bin Laden took an extraordinary step, redirecting militant action away from armed struggle in Muslim nations and toward global jihad. In 1996, Bin Laden needed, more than anything else, a place to live, which was proving difficult to find despite his still-extensive wealth. Though respected by many for his reported bravery and his ascetic disavowal of the privilege he had inherited, Bin Laden had burned many bridges through his public attacks on Arab regimes, and Afghanistan was one of the few places where he could land his plane and make a home for his family and a base of operations for his political ambitions.

The "Declaration" was first released to world audiences in summary form by the Arabic-language newspaper *Al-Quds al-Araby* on August 30, 1996. An English-language version of the Arabic summary was produced by the Associated Press and duly noted by newspapers around the world.[25] However, the complete text never appeared in any major papers, and the significance of the statement continued to be overlooked even after the September 11 attacks made Bin Laden arguably the world's most famous man. The speech is a good deal more than a declaration of war, and it had several intended audiences. One was the world's press, and, for them, the snippets that were reproduced as headlines were adequate. But the audience Bin Laden was most interested in was young Arab men, already sufficiently alienated from the world around them that—if properly motivated—they would consider leaving their homes and traveling to Afghanistan to join a movement that badly needed new recruits and direction.

It was not an easy sell. The victory over the Soviet Union was already a distant memory. Most of the youth 'Azzam and Bin Laden had originally inspired had achieved their desired martyrdom, drifted off to other battles, or left the jihad altogether. In any case, those still alive were no longer all that young, and Bin Laden needed to inspire and attract a new generation of Muslims with concerns other than the threat of communism. Afghanistan had been enmeshed in a bloody and demoralizing civil war during the time he had been away, and the Taliban were still new and untested. Indeed, it was not at all certain how receptive the new government would be to Bin Laden's agenda, which was implicitly threatening attacks against the United States that would be launched from Afghan soil. However disaffected his potential recruits might be, Bin Laden was asking them to give up everything they had, travel to a primitive country, and live without any of the amenities they were used to.

Had Bin Laden still been living a comfortable life in Saudi Arabia, his words would have lacked sincerity and power, but his listeners presumably knew that the speech they were hearing on tape cassette had been delivered in a sparsely furnished room in a new base he was building at Tora Bora, just a few miles from his old base in Jaji. For these young men, Bin Laden would have seemed something like a modern-day Sufi, living a life of ascetic self-denial and devoting himself to the spiritual and worldly jihad first declared by the Prophet himself. The fact that Bin Laden situated himself in "Khorasan . . . on the summits of the Hindu Kush," as he tells his listeners, would also have reminded them of his role in the battle of Jaji, the one unvarnished success of the Afghan Arab efforts, and it might also have evoked the hadith that the End Time would be announced by the appearance of black banners arising in the eastern region of the Islamic caliphate, encompassing parts of present-day Iran and Afghanistan, that was known to early Muslims as Khorasan.

The aspect of the speech that has drawn the most attention is the declaration of war itself, but this is arguably the least important part of Bin Laden's message. It was the pretext by which he sought to reawaken interest in jihad. The declaration of war against the United States rebranded the struggle, making the endeavor both grander and more ambitious than it had ever been imagined before. It also effectively provided a solution to the nihilism of the takfiris who were attacking their fellow Muslims and finding fault with all established leaders. America offered a bigger target that pushed local disputes into the background and turned jihad into a global enterprise.

Just as important, however, Bin Laden was hoping to reawaken the spirit of sacrifice. The assassination of 'Azzam in 1989 had left a vacuum less of leadership than of inspiration, a vacuum that Bin Laden now sought to fill. He was not looking to start a mass movement but rather seeking "a few good men" who were prepared to endure the hardships of training in Afghanistan and to sacrifice themselves when called upon. Such men would be not only devout Muslims but also sufficiently alienated from the world that they would be more than willing to leave it.

The speech is studded with references to "youth" who "struggle," who "vie," who "advance," and especially who "believe":

> These youth believe in what they have been told by God and His Messenger, God's blessings and salutations upon him, with regard to the magnificence of the reward for the struggler and martyr. Exalted God says: "But those who are slain in the way of God, He will never let their deeds be lost. Soon will He guide them, and improve their condition, and admit them to the Garden which He has announced for them." The Exalted also says: "And say not of those who are slain in the way of God, 'They are dead.' Nay, they are living, though ye perceive it not."[26]

Bin Laden follows 'Azzam's example in filling the "Declaration" with numerous evocations of the rewards awaiting those who die as martyrs:

> The most favored martyrs are those who meet the battlefront without turning their faces until they are killed. Those are the ones who prance in the highest chambers of paradise. Your Lord sends them his laughter, and should your Lord laugh to his servant while he remains in the world, no final reckoning need be made.

> The pain that a martyr discovers in death is merely like a pinch felt by any one of you.

> For God, the martyr is endowed with a special characteristic: he is to be forgiven at the first gush of his blood, shown his seat in paradise, festooned with the jewels of his faith, married to heaven's dark-eyed beauties, exempted

from the tribulations of the grave, given protection from the terrifying Day of Judgment, adorned with a crown of dignity upon his head—a single ruby of which is better than the world and anything in it—married to seventy-two of heaven's dark-eyed beauties, and given the right to intercede on behalf of seventy relatives [on Judgment Day].[27]

This is all standard Islamic martyrology that could have come from 'Azzam's pen. Bin Laden's more original and surprising rhetorical move is the invocation of the pre-Islamic age, the *jahiliyya*. For most militant Muslims, radicals and clerics alike, the jahiliyya was the Age of Ignorance. But Bin Laden, well versed in the poetic traditions of his ancestral home of Yemen and a poet himself, loved the poetry composed before the coming of Islam, especially its glorification of men on horseback who rush into battle with swords raised and ready to strike. He believed that God had a reason for choosing an Arab as the recipient of his revelation and the Arab Bedouin as the first to hear that message. He found much to admire in the culture of the jahiliyya, including the ethos of honor and bravery in battle.

One of the great attractions of Afghanistan for Bin Laden, in fact, was that the centuries-old poetic traditions he admired from the Arab world were still alive there. The poems of Rafiq Jan, quoted in chapter 2, are in the spirit both of the pre-Islamic verse Bin Laden quoted and of his own compositions. Like Rafiq Jan's early poems, especially his mocking depictions of the communist leader Nur Muhammad Taraki, Bin Laden's "Declaration" has a strong satirical element, in this case directed at William Perry, the secretary of defense under President Bill Clinton, who is addressed in the speech by his first name:

I say to you, William: these youths love death as you love life. They have inherited dignity, pride, courage, generosity, sincerity, daring, and the will to make sacrifices, from father to father. They are steadfast at war, and sincere in the encounter. They have inherited these qualities from their ancestors from the time of the pre-Islamic Age of Ignorance [*jahiliyya*]. Islam came and firmly established these praiseworthy morals, and perfected them.[28]

Rather than ignore or denounce what came before Muhammad's prophecy, as most Islamists had done, Bin Laden sought to capture the spirit and ethos of pre-Islamic ideals and harness them to his radical Islamist agenda. This proved a novel way to reach young men who sought glory in the here and now as much as they worried about the judgment of God in the afterlife. Many in the Arab world, notably the Saudi royals, had used images and symbols, as well as Arab poetry, for their own purposes, but Bin Laden saw these royal appropriations as profane abominations by hypocritical and illegitimate leaders. In his hands, he believed, the tribal traditions of independence, martial valor, and obedience could help to overcome the pusillanimity that had taken hold of Muslims and kept them in bondage to corrupt rulers and Western imperialism.[29] Bin Laden longed for a reawakening of the martial glory of tribal culture, a glory that had been lost in part because of the suffocation imposed by the rigid, unimaginative orthodoxy of a clerical class principally intent on preserving its own power.

In his pioneering tract *Milestones,* published in the mid-1960s, Sayyid Qutb divided the world into two kinds of societies, Islamic and *jahili,* with the jahili societies being defined by their embrace of materialism and sensual instinct over moral value. Bin Laden's insight was to recognize the utility of referring back to the original notion of jahiliyya and highlighting the deeds and values of those times that could inspire a new generation of warriors. In the "Declaration," he alludes to two kinds of immortality: the eternal life in Paradise achieved through God's favor, and the immortality achieved in this world through the recognition of one's actions. Although most commentators ascribe more weight to the former in the jihadist worldview, Bin Laden increasingly emphasizes the latter forms of immortality—the commemoration of the deeds of those who die in battle—in his vision of combat against America.

The poetry recited in the "Declaration" is redolent of mythic struggle undertaken with sword and lance rather than truck bombs and AK-47s. Supernatural heroes on horseback gallop beside mortal warriors transformed into fierce beasts. Such imagery provides listeners attuned to its language with much the same sense of exultation that fans of fantasy films experience when they see brave knights join swords with evil demons (and one should not assume for a moment that such films were any less familiar to Arab than to American youth):

> A youth, who plunges into the smoke of war, smiling
>> He hunches forth, staining the blades of lances red.
> May God not let my eye stray from the most eminent
>> Humans, should they fall, Genies, should they ride
>> [And] lions of the jungle, whose only fangs
>> [Are their] lances and short Indian swords.
>> As the stallion bears my witness that I hold them back
> [My] stabbing is like the cinders of fire that explode into flame
>> On the day of the stallions' expulsion, how war-cries attest to me
> As do stabbing, striking, pens, and books.[30]

For Western readers, this is the stuff of myth—the Riders of Rohan fighting orcs—but for those who contemplate committing themselves to a path of militancy that could very well result in their own death, such language provided a heroic model that connected their own imagined destinies with those of the mythic heroes of the past. 'Azzam had promised recruits the pleasures of Paradise. Bin Laden added to these benefits the prospect of being honored by the living and having their stories joined to those of the Prophet and his companions.

HOLY TUESDAY

Numerous books have been written on the planning and organization of the September 11, 2001, operation and on its geopolitical significance.[31] However, relatively little has been written on the cultural and religious dimensions of the operation. The general trend in terrorism studies is to view motivation through the reductionist lens of psychology while ignoring the cultural context within which a decision to act is sown, fertilized, and finally brought into being. In the case of September 11, one text in particular stands out as especially relevant and useful in making sense both of what happened and of the place of sacrifice in the fulfillment of Bin Laden's plan. Given my notion of a sacrifice machine, I follow Hans Kippenberg in referring to this document as a *spiritual manual* in order to emphasize that the attack launched against the United States was undertaken in the guise of a ritual act as much as a military operation.[32]

Three copies of the document, discovered in three different locations, were found among the personal effects of the hijackers. A translation from the original Arabic was posted on the FBI's website a few weeks after the attack. One copy belonged to Muhammad Atta, the leader of the hijackers who piloted American Airlines Flight 11 into the North Tower of the World Trade Center. It was found in his suitcase, which was not on the plane with him only because his flight out of Portland was delayed; though he made the connection in Boston, his luggage did not. A second copy was found in the bag of one of the hijackers whose mission to attack the White House ended in a field in Pennsylvania. The third copy was left in a car parked at Dulles Airport outside Washington, D.C. Given Atta's movements in the weeks before the attacks, it is likely that he was responsible for distributing the text to the four groups of hijackers as each prepared to launch its attack from hotel rooms on the East Coast.

From the distribution of the surviving copies, we can infer that the document was composed while at least three of the four groups were still in communication ahead of the attacks, but many questions remain unanswered. Did the fourth group have a copy? Was it read aloud to each group in their hotel room by the leader? Was it passed from hand to hand so that each person could read it quietly to himself? Or did each person have his own copy to read whenever he wanted reassurance or a reminder of what to do next? Clearly, two of the three copies were intended for incineration along with the hijackers, but what about the one left at Dulles? Was it an accident that it was found, an oversight on the part of a nervous reader? Or was it left intentionally, perhaps as a way to demonstrate the singleness of purpose and the religious inspiration of the hijackers to reporters and analysts who might try to demean and desecrate the sacred nature of the undertaking? We do not know and presumably will never know the answers to these questions. But here I assume that this document was intended for private use and that any dissemination was unintentional. From the point of view of historical understanding, however, it was a fortuitous accident, in that the existence of this document tells us a great deal about what was going on in the minds of the hijackers, or at least about what those who dispatched them wanted them to be thinking and doing in the hours leading up to their deaths.

According to Yosri Fouda and Nick Fielding, the author was probably Abdul Aziz al-Omari, who was one of the youngest of the hijackers but "recognized by the rest as having an exceptional knowledge of Islam" and—they add—the possessor of "a neat hand," a fact that apparently excludes Atta from consideration because he had terrible handwriting.[33] I have not seen this assertion confirmed through any official source. But it certainly makes sense that the author would be one of the hijackers, since it is unlikely that Bin Laden, Khalid Sheikh Muhammad, or any of the other al-Qaeda leaders would have wanted a document of this sort to be transmitted or transported any distance, given the chance of interception.

Although it has internal headings, the five-page document has no title—which is logical if it was not intended for reproduction or use beyond a small circle of committed men. The text is divided chronologically into sections. It begins with the "Last Night," which details a series of ritual actions for the hijackers to perform the night before the attack; it continues with "The Second Step," which provides guidance for the morning of the attacks (leaving the place where they had spent the night, traveling by taxi to the airport, passing through the security checkpoint, boarding the plane, and

FIGURE 19. Abdul Aziz Al-Omari and Muhammad Atta passing through security check-point at Portland, Maine, airport on the morning of Sept. 11, 2001. TSA surveillance photograph.

finding their seats); and it concludes with "The Third Phase," which gives instructions for what is to take place once the operation has been initiated (figure 19).

One of the most striking features of the manual is what is absent from it. There are no operational instructions in the text, no logistical details or rehearsal of "the game plan" as one might expect for a complex and risky maneuver of the sort the hijackers were trying to carry out. This is instead a spiritual guide, and many of the instructions it provides relate to the recitation of specific scriptural passages at precise points in the process. As much as anything, it seems that the text is focused on transforming the ominously empty time before the beginning of the mission into a series of ritualized actions and obligations. This is the period when doubts and regrets are most likely to loom and when those facing the unknowns of death are most likely to turn back toward the familiar routines of their previous lives.

As Henri Hubert and Marcel Mauss note, sacrificial rites convert profane time and space into sacred time and space. This conversion requires the creation of the proper conditions for the performance of the rite. Prior to the ceremony, "neither sacrifier nor sacrifice, nor place, instruments, or victim, possess this [sacred] characteristic to a suitable degree. The first phase of the sacrifice is intended to impart it to them. They are profane; their condition must be changed."[34] So, too, the hijackers' manual is given over not to operational instructions but to liturgical observances that will strip away the profane elements of everyday life and ensure that the act will be carried out under proper conditions and with the appropriate attention and respect. In Hubert and Mauss's words, "The place of the ceremony must itself be sacred: outside a holy place immolation is mere murder."[35] The manual attempts to ensure that all the spaces of the mission, from the hotel rooms through the airports to the cockpits of the planes, are rendered sacred.

Ritual imposes prescribed words and actions that make the situation fit a predetermined mold. The deeds and words of the Prophet, as described in the Qur'an, are considered beyond reproach. So the writer of the manual wants the reader to model his words and actions as closely as possible on the words and actions handed down to believers through the Qur'an and the Traditions of the Prophet. Ritual words and actions also serve to banish external or emotional distractions and concentrate the actor's focus on the task at hand. In this case, the writer demands complete attention for a practical reason as well: anything less might lead to disastrous consequences for their mission. Much of the document centers on turning the mundane actions to be undertaken—hanging out in the hotel room, showering and shaving, taking a taxi to the airport, getting on the plane—into a sequence of ritual actions that must be accompanied by appropriate words, leading to the final, explosive act of sacrificial violence.

Certain complications present themselves in applying Hubert and Mauss's analysis to September 11. One is the difficulty of disentangling the roles of sacrifier, sacrificer, and victim. The hijackers seem to embody all three of these roles. It also might be said that the position of sacrifier was shared with Bin Laden, who set the ritual in motion:

> In sacrifice ... the consecration extends beyond the thing consecrated; among other objects, it touches the moral person who bears the expenses of the ceremony. The devotee who provides the victim which is the object of the consecration is not, at the completion of the operation, the same as he was at the beginning. He has acquired a religious character which he did not have before, or has rid himself of an unfavorable character with which he was affected; he has raised himself to a state of grace or has emerged from a state of sin. In either case he has been religiously transformed.[36]

September 11 effected just such a religious transformation for Bin Laden. The hijackers were dispatched to whatever rewards awaited them, but Bin Laden remained behind to experience the results of the sacrifice: enhanced prestige among those sympathetic to his cause as well as the hatred and anger of those whose fellow citizens had become the victims.

These complications do not diminish the relevance of Hubert and Mauss's analysis. To the contrary, they make more apparent the demonic brilliance of the attack and how its construction as an act of sacrifice magnified its impact, which exceeded even what Bin Laden himself could have hoped for. This outcome, too, is anticipated by Hubert and Mauss's analysis:

> Once the victim has been set apart, [the sacrificial act] has a certain autonomy, no matter what may be done. It is a focus of energy from which are released effects that surpass the narrow purpose that the sacrifier has assigned to the rite. . . . Thus sacrifice naturally exceeds the narrow aims that the most elementary theologies assign to it. This is because it is not made up solely of a series of individual actions. The rite sets in motion the whole complex of sacred things to which it is addressed.[37]

In order to make sense of this "whole complex of sacred things," it is important to keep in mind that, for all its apparent simplicity, sacrifice can be directed toward a variety of ends. As I have argued throughout, the act of killing involves a straightforward conversion of one kind of energy into another, but that energy can be channeled in many directions.

Reading the 9/11 manual, one can forget the horror that is about to be inflicted by the hijackers on innocent people. The repetitive and by-now familiar language of ritual supplication and historical allusion dulls the mind to what is being contemplated and prepared for. But then one is reawakened to the perverse distortion of the document in the eleventh paragraph of "The Third Stage," when the writer advises the hijacker what to do on the airplane if someone tries to stop him, an instruction that is evocative more of liturgy than of hand-to-hand combat:

> And when God grants any of you a slaughter, you should dedicate it to father and mother because they have a claim on you. Do not disagree among one another and be absolutely obedient. If you slaughter, rob those you have killed as this is a custom of Muhammad's, on condition that you don't rob if there is danger of neglecting something more important, such as paying attention to the enemy, his deceptions and attacks.[38]

In their analysis of the text, Makiya and Mneimneh demonstrate that the author is drawing on a template for ritual sacrifice, the sort of sacrifice that is made each year during what Arabs generally refer to as the Eid al-Adha and Afghans call Eid-i Qurban, the feast of the sacrifice that marks the willingness of Ibrahim to sacrifice his son, Ismail. The language used in this paragraph of the document is the language not of combat but of sacrificial ritual:

> The Arabic word used for "grant" is *manna,* as in the biblical manna; it connotes the idea of a bounty or an act of grace conferred by God upon a person who has not asked for it. The Arabic for "slaughter" is *dhabaha.* The author has pointedly chosen it over the more common *qatala,* which means, simply, to kill. The classical dictionaries tell us the primary meaning of *dhabaha* is to cleave, slit, or rip something open. This is the word used for slitting the two external jugular veins in the throat of an animal. It is quick, direct, and always physically intimate; one does not slaughter with a gun, or a bomb, from afar. . . . *Dhabaha* in the context of the hijackers' document is such a ritual act, one that is normally performed to make an offering to God. *Dhabh* in this sense is an act prescribed in great detail by Muslim religious law.[39]

Makiya and Mneimneh go on to note that the author of the text is telling his readers that acts of resistance against them should be viewed not in the practical terms of combat but as "a gift bestowed by God upon the man chosen to kill him." The act of sacrifice is viewed as a ritual of remembrance for the gifts that God has bestowed: first and foremost the gift of life itself, which is signified in the sacrificer's dedicating the sacrifice to his parents (we assume that an illegible word in the text is the word for mother): "Between God's generosity in providing an occasion for slaughter and the obligation of filial devotion (greatly stressed in the Koran) is the act of slitting a passenger's throat with a box-cutter."[40]

The act of murder is here overlaid by a ritual apparatus that obscures the humanity of the victim. In essence, the victim is no more than a beast of slaughter, whose death should be as painless as possible but whose identity and rights as a human being are negated. The author seems to recognize the possibility that, when faced with the reality of killing another person—in other words, when seeing a flight attendant in front of him with blood spurting from her neck—he might have second thoughts, might even be horrified by what he has done. To forestall this possibility, the author immediately warns the future hijacker to temper any inclination toward mercy. To value compassion over accomplishment of the mission would be an act of "treason." Mercy is thus reduced to a nicety that must be abandoned if it in any way compromises the higher ethical responsibility to fulfill one's duty to God— which is to say, to kill an infinitely larger number of people.

Defining the act as a ritual sacrifice conveys the obligation that it be properly conceived and carried out. Proper performance of the ritual requires remembering that a sacrifice is an offering, and the offering itself is the acknowledgment of a debt owed. The sacrifice is made to God, who is responsible for all life and to whom all debts are ultimately due, but it is to be made on behalf of, and in repayment of the lesser debt owed to, the hijacker's parents, who are responsible for his particular life. It is telling that the author advises the hijacker to clear the debt to his parents just at the moment before he is to repay the larger debt he owes to God.

The 9/11 manual advises that, when taking control of the airplane, the hijacker must not act out of a spirit of revenge ("Do not seek revenge for yourself. Strike for God's sake"). It goes on to recount the story of how the Prophet's cousin and son-in-law, 'Ali, retreated from battle after a nonbeliever spat on him; he killed the man only later, after he had renewed his vow to God and assured himself that he was acting not out of vengeance for this humiliation but out of a desire to worship God. However, the invocation of this story can be misleading, because revenge is at the core of these attacks. Whatever was going on in the minds of the hijackers themselves is impossible to know, but we have a clearer sense of what motivated their patron, Bin Laden, who repeatedly used the terminology of vengeance in his public pronouncements (such as the video produced in early 2001 celebrating the attack on the USS *Cole* in Aden Harbor). From Bin Laden's perspective, the effrontery of the United States' "occupying the Land of the Two Holy Mosques" called for retaliation. This occupation was an act of religious desecration and also, for Bin Laden, an act of dishonoring and humiliation, the equivalent on a global scale to the act of the infidel who spat on 'Ali.

The attacks on New York City and the Pentagon have been generally, and rightfully, viewed as attacks on the centers of U.S. financial and military power, but they should also be seen as a form of more visceral, tit-for-tat revenge for a greater affront: the desecration of what Muslims view as the most sacred place on Earth. In essence, Bin Laden was responding to the challenge posed by this violation by violating, in turn, what he saw as most precious to the United States. For him, the act was not a matter of taking human lives, to which he ascribed no transcendent value. Whereas Westerners enshrined "human rights" and condemned those who put a greater value on divine law, for Bin Laden what mattered was obedience to God, and he pursued that end heedless of the material and human cost. The repeated invocations of sacrificial terminology in the instructions can thus be seen as transforming the intended murders of hundreds or thousands of people into offertory sacrifices, intended to avenge a community (the Muslim ummah) aggrieved by prior acts of infamy.

The manual may also have had a further purpose. In feud, sacrifices sometimes serve not to institute peace but to provide cover for later acts of violence against one's enemies. Parties to a feud sometimes violate sacred oaths and obligations even before the blood of a sacrificial animal has fully congealed. Nor do they necessarily hold back from striking their enemies in the sacred confines of a mosque or while they are at prayer. Bin Laden undoubtedly conceived of the September 11 attacks in mystical and spiritual terms, but he was also contemplating revenge for the desecration of Muslim lands as well as ambitions to build a new Islamic polity on the ruins of the American empire. Returning to the story of 'Ali contained in the 9/11 manual, it will be recalled that 'Ali's response after being spat on was not to forgo vengeance. The man who offended 'Ali is duly struck down. The point was to make sure that he had the right intention and to remind himself that it was not for himself alone that he sought revenge but for God as well. In this way, vengeance is turned into sacrifice, and, so with Bin Laden, revenge against America is turned into an act of worship.

Sacrifices are undertaken for various reasons, one of which is as a group response to a major affliction for which there is no known pragmatic solution. Thus, when a community is beset by plague or drought, there might be no other recourse but to turn to supernatural beings for assistance. In doing so, the community recognizes divine dominion as well as its own responsibility for the injury that has befallen it, and it accepts that, in order to be relieved of this affliction, it must give up something in return. In chapter 4, I discussed the way in which the Taliban turned public executions into rituals of purification, the affliction visited on Afghanistan being the epidemic of wanton violence and corruption unleashed by two decades of war. The September 11 attacks can also be seen as purificatory rituals in the sense of offering a sacrifice in order to cleanse a space that has been rendered impure and whose impurity is causing harm to the community.

In *Formations of Violence,* his study of sectarian politics in Belfast, Northern Ireland, Allen Feldman describes how the evolution of the conflict in Belfast was reflected in changes in spatial relations between Protestants and Catholics. Over time, formerly mixed neighborhoods were turned into segregated, defended neighborhoods through acts of "sacrificial violence" that were both compensatory and purificatory in nature. Most attacks happened along the partitions dividing the two communities, but paramilitaries also performed more complicated raids into the territory of their enemies. These raids were all the more effective for both their audacity and their outrage. One tactic was to leave the bodies of murdered enemies on their own doorsteps for their relatives to discover. Feldman refers to such acts, intended to maximize the symbolic effect of desecration, as "sacrificial transfers."[41] In other words, by killing members of the enemy's community and leaving the dead bodies at symbolically significant locations in the enemy's own territory, the attackers were simultaneously purifying their own space and polluting the space of the enemy. In a complement to Girard's theory that sacrifice can be used to bring a halt to revenge killings, these acts of sacrificial violence polarized the communities implicated by that violence and made peace all the more difficult to achieve.

The September 11 attacks can be seen as involving a form of Feldman's "sacrificial transfer." From Bin Laden's point of view, one goal of the attacks was to lift from the shoulders of Muslims and transfer to his enemies the humiliation and dishonor brought about by the U.S. presence on holy soil. Muslim territory was purified by depositing the dead bodies of enemy citizens on the symbolic thresholds of American capitalism (the World Trade Center), American military strength (the Pentagon), and American political power (the unsuccessful attempt of Flight 93 to attack either the White House or the Capitol). These acts massively raised the stakes of the conflict and increased the likelihood of further suffering for Muslims, but that outcome would help to reveal the cosmic nature of the conflict between the Muslim world and the West and would expedite that conflict's ultimate, inevitable resolution in the End-Time battle that Bin Laden anticipated and longed for.

. . .

For the most part, Americans have been fixated on the ways in which September 11 has altered their way of life, but in his book *Landscapes of Jihad*, Faisal Devji reminds his readers that the institutions undergirding Islamic faith and practice have been fundamentally transformed as well and that "Al-Qaeda's jihad may already have done more than any previous movement, secular or religious, liberal or conservative, to throw open the world of Islam to new ways of conceiving the future . . . not only by breaking down the old-fashioned narratives of clerical, mystical and even fundamentalist authority, along with their respective forms of organization, but also by recombining these dispersed elements in extraordinary novel ways."[42]

Devji is right in this assertion, but he could have also mentioned that it was not only traditional Muslim institutions that were undermined by

September 11. So, too, was al-Qaeda itself. With America intent on avenging the attacks, al-Qaeda was forced into hiding, limiting the ability of its leaders to exert much more than symbolic leadership over subsequent events. In the vacuum al-Qaeda itself created, new organizations like the so-called Islamic State have formed, and older groups like the Taliban have had to adapt to the changed circumstances that active American intervention in the region has brought about. Among the key changes has been the adoption of new forms of violence or, rather, the appropriation of forms of violence that had previously been restricted in their use. Of particular importance has been the development of an unprecedented regimen of suicide bombing that has taken the ethos and practice of sacrificial killing to a new extreme.

September 11 taught groups like the Taliban and, later, the Islamic State that violence, staged as spectacle, could have a variety of strategic effects, at least some of which could be useful to their organizations. In the next chapter, I examine the development of suicide bombing, but I do so not in relation to the strategic objectives of suicide bombing or to the individual psychology of those who accept the role of suicide bomber. These have been the primary foci of most analysts of the practice. My own focus is, first, on the ways in which suicide bombing relates to Afghan culture, particularly to the Pakhtun variant of Afghan culture of the eastern borderland with Pakistan, which has become perhaps the primary location from which suicide bombers have been drawn, where most have been trained, and where many acts of suicide bombing have taken place. My second focus is on how suicide bombing relates to and extends the ethos and ritual practice of sacrificial violence.

In approaching this topic, I begin with a brief discussion of suicide bombing as it first developed among Palestinians. It is difficult to assess how the technique and technology of suicide bombing spread from Palestine to other countries or even if there was a specific courier or connection. For my purposes, Palestine is less important as a place of origin than as a paradigm and point of contrast. There are commonalities in the practice of suicide bombing across cultures. There are shared grievances and ideological influences that come into play, and the organizations that sponsor the practice and train and dispatch the suicide bombers are motivated by similar strategic considerations. However, such commonalities have tended to overshadow the particular ways in which practice relates to culture and place, and, in the case of suicide bombing, how it has both affected and been affected by the culture in which it is now embedded.

SIX

Suicide Bombing

PROTOTYPE

In an article published in the *New Yorker* in the fall of 2001, Nasra Hassan reported on interviews she had conducted in the West Bank with Palestinians involved in the first "martyrdom operations" conducted against Israeli targets in the early 1990s.[1] If suicide attacks began elsewhere, the specific practice of strapping explosives to one's body probably began here. Remarkably, one of the suicide bombers Hassan spoke with, referred to as S., was able to provide her with a firsthand account of his experience. On his mission, his explosive vest failed to detonate, and he was shot in the head. He lay comatose in a hospital for two months before he was declared brain-dead and his body was turned over to his family. Yet he miraculously survived, and five years later—married and the father of three sons (all named after "martyr heroes")—he spoke with Hassan about his motivations for "martyrdom." He refers to the "high, impenetrable wall" separating the believer from Paradise and Hell. "Allah has promised one or the other to his creatures. So, by pressing the detonator, you can immediately open the door to Paradise—it is the shortest path to Heaven." In describing his preparations, S. notes that he and his fellow recruits "were in a constant state of worship. . . . We told each other that if the Israelis only knew how joyful we were they would whip us to death! Those were the happiest days of my life. . . . We were floating, swimming, in the feeling that we were about to enter eternity. We had no doubts. . . . All martyrdom operations, if done for Allah's sake, hurt less than a gnat's bite."[2]

In the course of her research, which was allowed by her interlocutors in order to counter negative publicity about martyrdom operations, Hassan met with others in the category of "living martyr" (*al shaheed al hayy*) preparing to go on suicide missions—a term they disparage, preferring instead to call them "sacred explosions." The young men she met ranged in age from eighteen to thirty-eight, and all, she notes, seemed to be what one might call ordinary:

> None of them were uneducated, desperately poor, simple minded, or depressed. Many were middle class and, unless they were fugitives, held paying jobs. More than half of them were refugees from what is now Israel. Two were the sons of millionaires. They all seemed to be entirely normal members of their families. They were polite and serious, and in their communities they were considered to be model youths.[3]

According to her informants, Hamas and Islamic Jihad, the two organizations that sponsored martyrdom operations, relied solely on volunteers at least age eighteen. They rejected those who were the sole wage earners in their families or who were married and had family responsibilities. Once the volunteers were selected (from what is described as a horde of applicants), trainers kept a close eye on their self-discipline, discretion, and piety. Their motives were questioned, on the assumption that someone who had volunteered for personal glory or for revenge alone would waver at the last moment and thereby corrupt the purity of the sacrifice and the success of the mission.

The training required intense spiritual exercises, including prayers, recitations of the Qur'an, and attending up to four hours a day of religious lectures. The living martyr drafted a will and usually left a ritualized video replete with costumes, props, and background emblems and signifiers testifying to his resolve and determination. These videos were held until after a successful operation and then distributed as evidence of the pure intent of the martyr and inspiration to other young men: "The young man repeatedly watches the video of himself, as well as the videos of his predecessors. 'These videos encourage him to confront death, not fear it.... He becomes intimately familiar with what he is about to do. Then he can greet death like an old friend.'"[4]

On the day of the operation, the living martyr was expected to perform ritual ablutions, put on clean clothes, and pray with other Muslims in a mosque. Like the September 11 hijackers, the would-be martyr was expected to offer prayers as he traveled to his final destination and to utter the phrase "Allahu akbar" (God is great) at the moment of detonation. Following his death, copies of the video were distributed to the media and to shops for sale. Posters with the martyr's face were posted on walls. The operation became the basis for sermons, and the martyr himself was immortalized in songs and chants in which his name and that of other martyrs were praised as examples of bravery and devotion. Despite the grief of losing their loved one, family members were expected to mark his martyrdom by holding a celebration on the scale of a wedding, with female family members ululating in expression of the honor the martyr had bestowed on the family through his sacrifice.

Hassan's article presents an idealized account of the practice of killing oneself in order to kill others. The informants, who agreed to talk with her mainly so that both Muslims and non-Muslims would know their side of the story, minimized the brutality of the act and emphasized the spirituality and idealism of those willing to die for their faith. Their accounts reminded me of the training engaged in by Sufi disciples in Afghanistan. The disciple, like the living martyr, devotes his life to eliminating the separation between himself and God in the hope of extinguishing his material self in the nonmaterial Divine. The Sufi path to this state of being is through *zikr,* a practice variously conceived and observed by different Sufi orders but which generally involves repetitive chanting of the names of God, in a circle with other devotees and under the supervision of an enlightened leader (*pir*). In all orders, the path of devotion requires absolute submission to the pir, the representative of God, in relation to whom the disciple imagines himself as servant, slave, or "dead body."

Martyrdom operations follow a similar sort of rhetoric and process, but they provide a shortcut to the ultimate, joyful fusion of the self with God. Sufi training is long and arduous, and there are no guarantees that all that effort will end in the desired ecstatic union with God. Failure is always a possibility for the martyr, too, but in the end, pushing a detonator is far easier than following the path of mystical devotion. Barring technical glitches, discovery by the enemy, or a last-minute failure of nerve, the result is guaranteed. Believing in that guarantee is a requirement, in fact, of enjoying the ultimate reward. The failure of a mission is taken as evidence of the weak faith of the person who undertook it.

Over the past half-century, Sufi orders have gradually diminished in importance in many countries, including Afghanistan. They have been marginalized in large part by other Muslims who reject and sometimes harshly suppress the mystical beliefs and practices associated with Sufism, such as the veneration of pirs as near godlike, pilgrimages to and worship at the shrines of saints, and the purchase of amulets sold by descendants of those saints. Zikr is still practiced, but the institutions dedicated to it exert less influence than they did before the rise of Islamic radicalism. Yet the desire for spiritual transcendence abides, and it can be argued that martyrdom operations have provided an alternative path to that end, one that is better suited to our impatient, embattled times.

Sufism was adapted to a slower, more forgiving world that allowed for gradual fulfillment of spiritual ambition and accepted the idea that there might be multiple paths to the same spiritual end. In that vanished world, becoming a Sufi was a life path, with progress marked by degrees of achievement and offering attendant satisfaction. Martyrdom operations lend themselves to a world of inflamed political passions, a world in which political power is in dispute, the weapons to combat oppression are easily acquired, and the circulation of media images creates a global stage on which any actor can have his moment of glory. Martyrdom operations likewise reflect in an oblique but tangible way a transnational consumer society in which young people seek instant gratification of their desires and in which the greatest danger to faith for many is not the government repression but personal anomie, the enervating loss of meaning and hope in the world as it is and a concomitant lack of interest in the world as it should be.[5]

. . .

The picture one gets of martyrdom operations in Afghanistan is very different from the Palestinian model Hassan presents. This is partly because of the more chaotic situation in Afghanistan. Whereas Palestinian suicide bombing developed in the tightly controlled confines of the West Bank and within a culturally homogenous population with clear political goals, the war in Afghanistan is a more sprawling affair, involving a greater geographical area, a more diverse set of actors, ethnicities, and nationalities, and an often-difficult-to-discern set of interests, agendas, and priorities on the part of those engaged in the practice.

I begin this discussion by presenting representative examples of suicide-bomb attacks as reported in the Afghan press. On this basis, I go on to consider the role of Pakistani madrasas, where many of the suicide bombers are recruited and trained. These institutions have to be factored into any analysis of how suicide bombing has become institutionalized to the degree that it has. However, focusing on madrasas can also lead to an overemphasis on the role of Islamic ideology and of Muslim clerics in recruiting and indoctrinating potential suicide bombers. Such recruitment and indoctrination happens and is an important element in the suicide-bombing phenomenon. However, it is also necessary to understand the cultural context that gives rise to people willing to give up their lives and to consider factors that are not directly related to religion.

Most analyses of motivation focus either on the mind of the attacker or on the organization that sponsors the attack; relatively few consider the cultural context of these attacks. In attempting to dissect and make sense of the practice of suicide bombing, there are strategic and psychological reasons that must be taken into consideration, of course, but analysts have largely ignored the cultural matrix out of which this practice has arisen, and much of what follows in this chapter is devoted to laying out a framework for understanding why, given the circumstances that now exist in Afghanistan, suicide bombing is a "logical" response—the logic here being not of an objective, rational character but one determined by the cultural understandings that provide the coordinates by which people orient themselves to the world around them.

The final section of the chapter takes up the case of Humam Khalil Abu-Mulal al-Balawi, a suicide bomber responsible for the attack at Camp Chapman in eastern Afghanistan in 2009. Al-Balawi was a Jordanian who spent only the last few hours of his life in Afghanistan, but his story is nevertheless relevant for understanding the transformation of sacrificial violence in Afghanistan, which has never been a story just about Afghans. Abdullah 'Azzam gave to sacrifice both the aura of the miraculous and the promise of future paradisiacal reward. Osama Bin Laden reawakened the mythic past, allowing potential recruits to imagine themselves wielding swords and riding stallions to glorious death. His confederate Khalid Sheikh Muhammad unlocked the potential of sacrifice as a mass spectacle with the attacks of September 11. For his part, al-Balawi fashioned for himself, and vicariously for others, a new identity rooted in the mythic realm of Khorasan but fabricated in the borderless world of the Internet, which has become the latest and perhaps most dangerous battleground of jihad.

CONFESSIONS

Between late 2001, when the United States launched its invasion of Afghanistan, through late 2015, by which point it had substantially reduced its troop commitment and decreased its aid to the Afghan government, the United States had spent close to $1 trillion. In the judgment of most observers, however, these funds have made little difference in the lives of most Afghans, who still struggle to earn a living and face the same hardships as they did before the Americans arrived. The promises of democratic reform have also been disappointing: many of the jihadi leaders remain in positions of power, and the elected government has proved ineffective at improving the basic health, security, and employment needs of the people.

Meanwhile, after its initial setbacks, the Taliban has gradually regained much of its strength, recruiting a new generation of fighters and asserting authority in many parts of the country from which it had previously been expelled. The Taliban success derives in large part from its having learned to pinpoint and exploit the weaknesses in the American military machine. At first, its tactics principally involved the use of improvised explosive devices (IEDs) to attack the vehicles used by the United States and its coalition partners in the International Security Assistance Force (ISAF). Later, and partly in response to changes in tactics by the Americans, the Taliban developed the technique of deploying suicide bombers to attack military, government, and civilian targets.

In contrast to Hassan, who was given direct access to Palestinian suicide bombers, I have had to rely on second-hand sources, and most of what I have been able to discover comes from people who were either captured by the government or lost heart and turned themselves in. My information on the topic comes primarily from my collaboration with Danish Karokhel, the editor of the Pajhwok News Agency in Kabul, who gave me access to interviews his reporters have conducted with captured suicide bombers as well as other materials related to suicide bombing, including videotaped testimonies of captured suicide bombers.

It must be admitted that some of these testimonies resemble taped confessions from the 1980s that were distributed by the communist government of captured mujahidin admitting their "crimes," and this resemblance is probably not coincidental. The individual placed before the camera or who tells his story to a group of reporters is—we must assume—either reciting what he has been ordered to say or adapting his story to fit a narrative he believes his audience wants to hear. (Otherwise, presumably, the interview would not have been made available for public consumption.) Even keeping this caveat in mind, it is worth reviewing some of these stories to see what threads emerge. Here, then, is a representative sample, all published by the Pajhwok News Agency in recent years (and, in some cases, slightly edited by me for readability):

Akhtar Nawaz, 14, a resident of the Darbakhel area of Miranshah, the capital of North Waziristan, told reporters he learned to use weapons from two Pakistani trainers at the Qari Jamat Madrasa in Miranshah. "We were told Americans have occupied Afghanistan and a jihad is going on there. Anyone who launches suicide attack directly goes to heaven," he said. He sneaked into Khost Province from the Ghulam Khan area with the help of two Pakistanis—Yaro and Qahar—to conduct an attack against the Afghan army.[6]

. . .

Ghamai, alias Janan, a resident of Deh Khwaja village in the ninth district of southern Kandahar City, said he was forced to carry out a suicide blast. "A suicide attack organizer named Mirwais invited me to join a Taliban group." After some days, Mirwais phoned him to come to Spin Boldak. "When I met him and another man named Naeem, they blindfolded me and took me to Mullah Ahmad, their group leader, in the Chaman border town of Pakistan," Ghamai recalled. He quoted Mullah Ahmad as telling him: "Be ready for a suicide attack. Your family will be given 500,000 rupees, and you will go to heaven. If you refuse, we will kill you and all your family members."[7]

. . .

Khalid Rahman, a Pakistani militant who surrendered to Afghan forces in eastern Ningrahar Province, told reporters that his brother, Gul Rahman, a student at a religious school in Miranshah, had gone missing from his school two years ago. After a month, five gunmen arrived in a car and told his family that Gul Rahman had embraced martyrdom. Khalid Rahman then launched a search for his missing brother and visited the madrasa where his brother was studying. He also went to a religious school run by the Haqqani network, but he was told that his brother was no longer alive. During the search, he was kidnapped by gunmen and taken to a militant training centre in Hangu. Rahman said he was among hundreds of young men getting military training at the camp. "We learned different suicide bombing techniques at the training centre," the twenty-year-old said. "I did not want to shed the blood of innocent Afghan people, so I surrendered to security forces."[8]

. . .

A man arrested on charges of planting bombs has alleged children are sexually abused in Pakistani seminaries, the National Directorate of Security said on Wednesday. The bomb maker was arrested while planting an explosive device on a road leading to the Al Biruni University in the Kohistan district of central Parwan Province. An NDS press release said that the detainee from Kapisa Province, Mayel Agha, had confessed to making and planting bombs. He received religious education at the Ahya ul Ulum Madrasa in Peshawar. Madrasa director, Shah Hakim Mazhar, sexually abused children and planned to abuse him as well, Agha alleged. Mazhar offered him money, but the student escaped and learned to make mines in Waziristan.[9]

. . .

A dozen children were rescued and their kidnapper was detained by security officials in the eastern province of Laghman. Security officials showed the twelve children and the alleged abductor to media representatives at the provincial intelligence office. The children were kidnapped from Noorgram District of neighbouring Nuristan Province and the kidnapper wanted to transfer them to Pakistan, officials said. The children and their kidnapper were captured in the Tirgari area on the outskirts of the provincial capital, Mehtarlam, late on Saturday night. The minors were reunited with their families. But the detainee, Obaidullah, denied abducting the children, saying he wanted to take them to the religious seminary of his brother in Pakistan. The father of a child, Abdul Qadir, a resident of Noorgram, said Obaidullah had deceived him by saying his son would get education in Pakistan. He asked the government to enroll the children in religious schools in Afghanistan.[10]

. . .

A resident of Kohat district, Saifullah is being held at police headquarters. He joined the Taliban in Kohat after he left home due to a dispute with his brother. "I met a Talib at a centre in Kohat and I told him that I wanted to go for jihad in Afghanistan. The Talib blindfolded me and took me to Haji Zahir," Saifullah said. . . . He said he was taken to a car, which reached a house after a long journey. The house had nine rooms and a garden. He was told that it was in the Koshlagh area.

"Pakistani mullahs preached to us about the benefits of the jihad. Within two days, my mind changed. I started regretting my past life. I think they gave us something in the food that may have changed my mind," Saifullah said. He said a number of mullahs would visit them and would tell them that Americans had occupied Afghanistan and there should be a jihad against them. "I was among eight others willing to carrying out suicide attacks and another 32 boys receiving training for attacks."

He said a mullah named Qasim blindfolded them and took them to the Chaman border crossing. "I along with 14 others reached Tirinkot City in a car. I and two others remained with Mullah Qasim and the rest were sent to different parts of the city," he said. Saifullah said he and the two others were kept in a house. He said they spent at least two months wandering around the city to select a proper time and place for an attack. "Many times we encountered foreigners, but Mullah Qasim would escape after seeing foreigners and finally we were arrested without carrying out any attack," he said. Saifullah urged the Afghan government not to hand him over to Pakistani intelligence. He said if he was handed over to Pakistan, he would be killed. He said it was his last wish to see his mother. He also thanked the Uruzgan police for their good behaviour.[11]

. . .

His young son resorted to a suicide attack as his demand for marriage could not be met due to poverty, says Rehmat Gul, a resident of Kabul. Gul has been living in a refugee camp in the Akora Khattak town of Pakistan's northwestern Khyber Pashtunkhwa province for the last 30 years. His son, Muhammad Yasin, 17, dropped out of a camp school as a result of penury. He has been a fruit cart vendor for the last two years, said Gul, a resident of Deh Sabz district in Kabul. "Yasin told his mother six months ago that he will carry out a suicide attack if his marriage was not arranged. Later, the demand was shared with me too, but I declined for reasons of poverty," Gul added.

One day, the boy left his cart in the bazaar and disappeared. A few days later, the man came to Afghanistan in search of his son. He searched for his child in Kabul and Maidan Wardak before returning to Pakistan, Gul said. "Three months later, I came back to Afghanistan and asked police and Afghan National Army officials in different areas about my son, but in vain." A month back Gul saw his son along with 20 other children on television, meeting President Karzai. The boys were arrested for attempting suicide attacks. But Karzai ordered their release on humanitarian grounds. He thanked the president but said his son was yet to be freed, and that he had no information about his whereabouts. Gul urged the authorities to release Yasin and thereby alleviate his plight.[12]

MADRASAS

The question that haunts this and every other study of people who willingly strap explosives to their bodies and blow themselves up is, Why? Questions of when, where, and how are all empirical in nature and accessible to comparison and generalization. The why question stands apart. The tendency of Western observers from the beginning has been to blame Islam. In considering religious motivations, it is important to bracket the notion that the prospect of reward in Paradise provides sufficient incentive for self-destruction. It is easy, for example, to overemphasize the "seventy virgins" motif, which accords so well with preconceptions of Muslim fanaticism and irrationality. Some recruits are drawn from the madrasa to suicide bombing, but it is also possible that some are drawn to the madrasa—or to the Taliban more generally—because of their desire to engage in suicide bombing, for reasons that have little to do with religious belief.[13]

The point here is that analysts of suicide attacks have tended to assume and overstate the importance of religion and the popularity and influence of the Taliban. As the 2007 U.N. Assistance Mission to Afghanistan (UNAMA) report on suicide attacks notes, failed suicide bombers who were captured and interviewed expressed considerable ambivalence toward the Taliban, and many of those associated with the Taliban suicide-bombing campaign are not voluntary recruits but have been either coerced or tricked into participating.[14] This is particularly the case with children, who cannot be presumed to have made an informed decision, and who have been subjected to a variety of threats and inducements (e.g., the promise to teach a young boy how to ride a motorcycle) whose implications they cannot be expected to comprehend.[15] Young children who become suicide attackers in Afghanistan are also likely to be seeking money for their families. Moreover, some have been orphaned or separated from their parents, caregiver, or community and join armed groups to gain security and food.[16]

Even when Taliban recruiters invoked the ideals of martyrdom and the rewards that accrued to the shahid, it was not always the promise of Paradise that closed the deal, as evidenced by an interview conducted by a UNAMA researcher with a sixteen-year-old boy who had been captured before completing his mission. When pressed about his beliefs about "shahadat," the boy said that he was told by his handlers that "Islam says you must kill foreigners because they do not respect God. If you kill them, you win God. I was not thinking of jannat (paradise). I did it because they would give me 10,000 Pakistan rupees. No question of paradise."[17]

At the same time, Islam clearly does matter, and it matters most concretely through the institution of the madrasa. Although no precise statistics exist, many Afghan analysts believe that madrasa students carry out roughly 70 percent of suicide attacks. Even when the attack is carried out by nonstudents, they have often received training at one of the unregistered madrasas that have sprung up throughout the tribal areas along the Afghan-Pakistan border.[18]

Madrasas have always provided an option in a society short on options. In the old world, the madrasa coexisted with the Sufi center (*khanaqah*) and shrine (*ziarat*) as places where the dispossessed and otherwise detached could find refuge and sometimes a channel for their genuine spiritual and scriptural aspirations. Over time, however, the Sufi institutions declined, leaving behind only madrasas, which have become increasingly extreme in their orientation. Madrasas compete for both students and financial support from wealthy donors, especially Arabs, who have pushed their own hardline Wahhabi and Salafi agendas.[19] Madrasas have continually grown in importance since the start of the refugee crisis in 1979, in response to the displacement of millions of Afghans deprived of their homes and livelihoods. An institution that originally prepared mullahs to shoulder the responsibility of overseeing mosques, supervise the education of children in basic religious principles and practices, and manage the ritual life of their communities thus has come to function as a safety net for families that cannot feed their children. The political possibilities of this situation were not lost on the Afghan Islamic political parties during the 1980s or the Taliban leaders who came to power after them.

My first encounter with Pakistani madrasas was in the refugee camp where I conducted research in the mid-1980s. At the time, little attention was paid to these schools, but it was already noticeable that parents who had the choice opted to send their sons to madrasas run by the Afghan political parties rather than to secular schools run by the Pakistani refugee authorities. They did so in part because religious education was subsidized and in part because the choice seemed not only ideologically appropriate but also a more reliable career path, given the preponderance of jobs provided by the parties to madrasa graduates. When I visited these schools and observed the classes, I was struck by the interweaving of jihad themes even into the elementary level of reading instruction, as noted in chapter 3. Older students received instruction in the use of weapons, and the curriculum mixed elements of Islamic theology with practical lessons that would prepare students to participate in the jihad when they had completed their studies (figure 20).

Pakistan, Saudi Arabia, and other Muslim countries actively supported the expansion of the madrasa system into freestanding institutions enrolling both Afghan and Pakistani students. This was a significant development in that the camp schools were day schools, with students returning each evening to their homes. The freestanding madrasas were often boarding schools that could have a far greater influence on the students' education and outlook. In the years since the Soviet jihad, madrasas in both Pakistan and Afghanistan have rapidly increased in number, but apparently still not fast enough, as parents complain that many boys cannot enroll because there are not enough places available.[20]

A brief portrait of what these schools were like circa 2000 is provided by Jeffrey Goldberg in his *New York Times Magazine* article "Inside Jihad

FIGURE 20. Afghan madrasa, ca. 1984. Author's photograph.

U: The Education of a Holy Warrior." He wrote about the Haqqania madrasa, where many of the Taliban leaders then ruling Afghanistan received their education. As with the Hamas and Islamic Jihad leaders who invited Nasra Hassan to observed their operations, the director of the madrasa had an agenda in allowing an American reporter access to the school: to prove to the world that his madrasa was a legitimate educational institution. This was before September 11 and the rise of suicide bombing, but even then stories were reaching the Western press that madrasas such as his were training centers for terrorists. During the Taliban offensive against the Northern Alliance, the director had closed the madrasa for a time to enable his students to take up arms in support of the Taliban, so there was no doubt where their sympathies and priorities lay. Yet he appeared intent on assuring the world that the training received at the school was strictly religious in nature.

There were 2,800 registered students at the time of Goldberg's visit, ranging in age from eight to thirty. Their numbers were drawn from "the dire poor," who were attracted to schools such as this one because of the free room and board, subsidized by wealthy Pakistanis and foreign Muslims. Younger students memorized the Qur'an; older students were enrolled in an eight-year course of study that included theology, scriptural interpretation, rhetoric, jurisprudence, Arabic language, and other subjects required of those seeking to become clerics and attain the title of mullah, *maulavi,* or *maulana.* Graduates of the eight-year program were eligible to continue with their studies toward the goal of becoming muftis, which would entitle them to make the binding declarations on religious matters known as *fatwas.*

Although students at the school shared the general Pakistani enthusiasm for cricket (an interest that had spread to Afghans as well) and were given the opportunity in the late afternoon to play the sport, there were few other extracurricular activities visible to the reporter. There were also no women present in any capacity. The youngest students lived in a locked dormitory under the supervision of older students. Despite the restrictions placed on them, all the students appeared glad to have access to regular meals, a place to sleep, and no requirement that they work mixing cement or carrying heavy loads at construction sites, as even young boys in poor families are often required to do to help make ends meet.

Goldberg does not dig deeply into the inner world of the madrasa; most of his time was spent debating ethics and defending the American campaign against Bin Laden, who was beloved by faculty and students alike. The impression the students had of Americans, according to Goldberg, was mostly that they were sexually omnivorous: "Many of them were convinced that Westerners will engage in sex with anything, anywhere, all the time. I was asked to describe the dominant masturbation style of Americans, and whether American men were allowed by law to keep boyfriends and girl-friends at the same time."[21]

Having attended an all-boy boarding school myself for four years, I find the preoccupation with sex among these mostly adolescent boys less surprising than the openness of its expression, especially regarding homosexuality. Many Afghans familiar with the culture of madrasas are aware of the contradiction between Islam's stated opposition to homosexuality and the ubiquity of the practice within madrasas, and some tie the phenomenon to the rise of suicide bombing. This connection is developed in an article by Muhammad Muhaq, who argues that the vigorous repression of the natural desires of adolescent males—even at the level of imagination—leads boys in these environments to seek release in homosexual relations, despite their taboo status in Islam.[22]

Muhaq's article begins with a consideration of the effect on adolescent boys not only of restricting contact with women but also, and more impor-tant, of teaching them that women are fundamentally different from men—men being fundamentally reasonable creatures, while women are ruled by desire. Consequently, women represent a continual threat to male reason and self-control, to such a degree that a brief glimpse of a woman's face, or even the sound her shoes make as she walks by, can lead a man to sinful thoughts and moral ruin. Male and female domains are generally segregated in Afghan society, but this practice is concentrated into a particularly poisonous distillate in the all-male madrasa.

What makes the madrasa environment especially pernicious and predatory, according to Muhaq, is the wide age range of the students and the absence of any adult supervision within the dormitories, along with the expectation that younger students will be respectful and obedient to those older than themselves. This combination of factors leads to the exploitation of younger students by older students: "Competitions sometimes take place over attractive prey among the powerful. . . . These competitions sometimes lead [to the] transfer of [an] attractive victim from one group to the other." Muhaq contends that young men cannot reconcile the contradiction between the Islamic injunction against homosexuality and their own involvement in the practice, however involuntary their own participation might be. Volunteering for a suicide mission is a way to cleanse themselves of the shame and guilt they feel: "On one hand, they feel heroic with such action, because they stand against important forces and on the other hand they get rid of the constant mental suffering."[23]

Although Muhaq's argument is speculative, and it is difficult to assess its empirical grounding, it accords at least in a general way with tensions associated with other, same-sex institutions, such as Catholic seminaries. Muhaq's claim regarding the contradiction between the moral precepts upheld by the institution and the actual behavior that goes on within its walls, as well as the deep psychological distress this contradiction creates in the minds of adolescents, also accords with the stories of post-traumatic stress suffered by victims of sexual abuse at the hands of Catholic priests. The difference, of course, is that in Muhaq's view this contradiction in the madrasa setting leads to purification through martyrdom, whereas in the seminary setting the desire for purification is more likely to lead to acts of self-mortification. Either way, the internal psychological ambivalence finds resolution—in one case permanent, in the other temporary—in violence against the self, violence that for the Muslim martyr avoids the label of suicide (a sinful act for both Muslim and Catholic) by being placed under the rubric of jihad.

A second factor that may link the act of martyrdom with the institution of the madrasa is the nature of the education itself. My thoughts in this regard derive from having spent my career teaching in a liberal arts college that prides itself on avoiding dogma and pushing students toward questioning received truths and learning how to find answers for themselves through critical thinking and problem solving. The educational experience in a madrasa (or seminary or yeshiva) is based on a different proposition—that the problem solving one learns to engage in is undertaken from a vantage of permanent and unchanging truth—and that the goal of the student is to learn how to find in the particularities of contemporary problems the essential issue that can be illuminated and answered through reference to scripture and prophetic traditions. These provide the foundation and model for answering all questions, now and forever after. Madrasa study involves gaining a deep familiarity with pertinent texts and sharpening one's capacity for logical reasoning, but all of this occurs within a fixed and immutable constellation of beliefs.

The mantras of a liberal arts education—"Question authority" and "Think outside the box"—can lead to another form of self-righteousness and a blindness to hidden orthodoxies. The orthodoxies of the madrasa education are explicit and recognized, and most of the curriculum is intended to help the student develop defenses against heresies he might encounter after he has graduated and moved into the ranks of practicing clerics. Before the war, scriptural truths had to compete with other orthodoxies, from the mystical beliefs associated with Sufism to the traditional value system of the tribe and then the new models introduced through the growth and increasing power of the state and its educational system. During the war, scriptural truth gradually vanquished its competition, with Sufism pushed to the margins, modern ideologies like socialism eliminated, and democracy put on the defensive for its association with Western liberalism and permissiveness. There are, of course, conflicts and competition within the ranks of mullahs and maulavis, sometimes all the more bitter because of the relatively small differences involved. But the madrasa student has the certainty that his vantage on the world is the correct one, and the momentum of history as he perceives it demonstrates that it is only a matter of time before this truth is fulfilled.

In this environment, with its emphasis on the fixity of truth, submission to discipline, and obedience to authority, one imagines that it takes less effort to convince students to martyr themselves, especially given the attractions of the Qur'an's promises for the afterlife. Given that madrasa students begin their classes at a young age, that they are never given access to any other way of viewing the world, and that they are separated from the potentially moderating views of parents and other family members who might hold contrary opinions or who might take their physical safety more seriously than the students do themselves, it seems hardly surprising that Taliban leaders would look to madrasas to provide the raw material for the exercise of regaining power by terrorizing the government and people of Afghanistan.

More surprising, perhaps, is the leaders' cynical treatment of the estimated 15 percent of suicide bombers without a madrasa connection who are influenced by Taliban propaganda or are coerced into participating.[24] When the Taliban formally launched their suicide-bombing campaign in January 2004, they announced their intention to send waves of bombers, presumably on the assumption that a few isolated attacks would be quickly forgotten, especially in a nation as inured to violence as Afghanistan.[25] Initiating such a campaign required bodies, and ultimately it was probably not in the Taliban's interest to rely for these sacrifices on madrasa students who could fulfill other functions and be of longer-term use to its organization. The impoverished streets and refugee camps of Afghanistan and Pakistan offered an abundance of bodies that had no better utility than to serve as explosive delivery systems.

Exploiting this resource meant treating these people not as people but as instruments. Their acquiescence was more important than their intent, which could be manufactured through the combined effects of propaganda (particularly sensationalist videos), lies ("There are no Muslims living in Afghanistan"), repetition, and prolonged isolation from family, friends, and the outside world in general. Thus, according to a form filled out and signed by a madrasa student who had completed six years of education, the would-be bomber agreed at the beginning of his training to forgo communicating with anyone other than his trainers. To ensure compliance with this rule, the trainee was obliged to turn over his cell phone and all his luggage, which of course might contain photographs, letters from family members, and other personal effects.[26] It has also been reported, though never to my knowledge confirmed, that the Taliban use drugs as a way of disorienting some recruits and ensuring their compliance.

THE DEBT OF HONOR

Though guilt, indoctrination, and intimidation explain some percentage of cases, it would be a mistake to believe that these factors are adequate in themselves or that the madrasa is the key to answering the question of why individuals become suicide bombers. Madrasas have undoubtedly played a vital role in recruiting and influencing potential suicide bombers. Yet even when madrasa students decide to sacrifice their lives, it is not self-evident that their motivation is religious. Belief and obedience might influence the decision, but it seems equally likely that the emotional vector leading to this violent way of death might originate elsewhere.

What has generally been missing in discussions of suicide bombers' motivation has been any substantial consideration of cultural factors. Those writing on the topic have tended to come from disciplines such as political science and psychology that downplay or ignore the importance of culture in favor of theoretical paradigms that highlight political or psychological factors.[27] The political science analyses have focused on the strategic logic, rational calculation, and organizational structure of terrorist groups rather than on individual motivation.[28] Although psychologists focus on individual motivation, many psychological studies neglect the cultural basis out of which motivation arises. Psychologists tend to posit the rationality of suicide attackers, arguing that they should not be viewed as crazed fanatics but rather as people who feel psychologically compelled to commit terrorist acts, often because of defects in the family unit that result in some sense of marginalization or yearning for social acceptance.

In the words of Jerrold Post, one of the most influential of these theorists, "Hatred is bred in the bone": those who resort to terrorist violence are either "carrying on the mission of their parents" or "rebelling against the generation of their parents."[29] In a similar vein, John Lackhar has argued that terrorists "suffer from defective bonding and dependency needs, fear of abandonment and existential anxiety. They are plagued by feelings of shame and use defense mechanisms that enable them to cast blame on others. Due to their disturbed sense of judgement, they are apt to distort reality, perceive it in a defective manner and act impulsively under the influence of this sentiment." Lackhar adopts a quasi-sociological slant to his analysis of the family as well, arguing that fathers are often a missing element in the upbringing of future terrorists, who are raised by mothers, "an oppressed figure in patriarchal and conservative societies . . . who transfer a great deal of the pain they feel onto their sons and create much frustration in them. These childhood experiences cause these young boys to become introverted and shy in comparison to their peers and foster in them the tendency to be attracted to charismatic figures. These are the type of youths that recruiters from terrorist organizations are looking for."[30]

Jessica Stern points to a quartet of what are essentially emotions—hopelessness, deprivation, envy, and humiliation—as the factors that "make death, and paradise, seem more appealing."[31] She examines a wide range of cases from around the world in order to elucidate common elements. However, in seeking breadth, she sacrifices depth, as her analysis rests on the assumption that what is signified by the "feelings" she distills from her interviews can be captured in English words and that what those words mean in English is what they also mean in the broad range of societies she surveys. One can say, for example, that many Afghans who decide to participate in suicide missions do so from a sense of "humiliation," but this assertion does not account for the factors that evoke this humiliation or ask how humiliation is constituted and why it leads to a particular set of responses and not to others.

Many of those who are knowledgeable about Afghan culture have discounted the importance of culture because of the opprobrium Afghans attach to suicide.[32] By this logic, because Pakhtunwali does not countenance suicide and because Pakhtunwali is thought to be the moral code of at least that subset of Afghans who produce the majority of the Taliban, then the motivation for suicide bombing must spring from some other source. However, as I noted in my discussion of the Dog Feud in chapter 2, is is better to conceptualize the role of culture not as a code but as a form of action, what Afghans refer to as "doing Pakhtu," which centers on working out contradictory moral imperatives through specific deeds, with sacrifice serving as an important component of the process of managing these conflicts. Here I delve more deeply into the constitution of honor as a background to understanding how participation in a suicide mission might come to be perceived as an obligation rather than a cause of shame.

Self-determination is embodied in the term *ghairat.* A man demonstrates ghairat when he follows his own course of action rather than following the dictates of others. Ghairat is also exhibited by someone who takes risks and accepts challenges, often in the context of personal rivalries. In Afghanistan as in other cultures, young people are more likely to engage in risky endeavors that promise adventure and glory than are their elders. Rivalry between paternal first cousins is particularly acute among young men, who can make a name for themselves by showing themselves to be braver and more self-assured than their immediate peers.

What most often brings Afghans into conflict are assaults on what is referred to as *namus,* those extensions of a man's person and status that are subject to violation by others. Wives, sisters, and other female patrilineal relatives are a man's primary namus; then come his residence and land and the land of the extended patrilineal family and tribe (which is to say, the property of all of those obliged by kinship to defend one another). Other symbolically charged assets, such as a man's gun (or even, as in the Dog Feud, his dog) can also be subsumed under the category of namus. To lose control of any of these possessions is to forfeit one's status as a man of honor. Thus, it could be said that a man's ability to defend his namus from violation constitutes the primary criterion of his worth in the tribe.[33]

A man who is incapable of defending his namus is referred to as *daus,* which can be translated as "cuckold," though that term captures only one dimension of its meaning and loses much of its affective power as well as many of its additional meanings, such as a man who spends too much of his time in the company of women, who is nagged and scolded by his wife, or who is too much under the control of his father-in-law. More powerfully, the term implies that a man is unable to protect the sexual honor of his female kin, even potentially offering them to other men, and that he lacks the power to defend his home, his lands, or his women. The term *dala* is frequently used as a synonym for daus, but it carries the added meaning of a "lightweight," though this translation again fails to capture the extent of its meaning or the depth of the insult. It implies that the person has debased his honor by inaction, cowardice, or selfish action.[34]

A man who fails to protect his namus is considered the most ignoble of creatures. He is *luchak,* which translates as "naked" but could almost be equated with someone in Western culture who exposes himself in front of others. A Pakhtun who gives up his land sacrifices his claim to social identity and membership in councils of the tribe. Such a man is referred to as *be ghairati* (cowardly, lacking in integrity), and it is said of such a man that he has "sold the bones of his forefathers" (*de plar au nikah hudunah-ye khartz kral*), implying that he has given up the very basis of his identity. To allow such trespasses to go unchallenged would be to admit one's own weakness. The appearance of weakness can usually be dispelled only by acts of violence.[35]

In one respect, namus is an absolute value. Once it is gone, it cannot be retrieved. In another respect, however, namus is a relative concept, attached most closely to the ability to defend the honor of one's personal possessions and, more broadly, to protect the honor of the Afghan homeland (*watan*). The Soviet Union's invasion of Afghanistan was judged as a violation not merely of national sovereignty but also of the namus of the country. Forcing the Soviets to withdraw allowed Afghans to reclaim their collective honor; by contrast, the loss of one's personal honor could not be regained if, for example, the chastity of one's sister or daughter was compromised.

The ideal of self-determination, or ghairat, figures in here because men are expected, in the first instance, to prevent assaults on their namus and, in the second, to do everything in their power either to restore their honor, where that is an option, or to take compensatory actions to demonstrate their obedience to the moral code when reclamation is not possible. Thus, for example, when the Soviets invaded and occupied Afghanistan, honor was not forfeited but merely placed in limbo until redressive action could remove the offense (in a similar fashion to how one's honor is jeopardized and placed in suspension, though not lost, when a family member is killed in a feud). When a female relative's chastity is violated, however, such redressive action is not available. Once lost, virginity cannot be restored as a border or boundary can. In such cases, the only action that will go partway toward healing the damage done is erasing the shame incurred by killing the parties involved. Such violence can be thought of as an act of ritual sacrifice in which the female relative and her paramour (or rapist—the distinction is largely moot) are served up as a burnt offering on the altar of honor itself.[36]

OCCUPATION

The American occupation of Afghanistan always felt different from the Soviet occupation, and the difference might be the level of intimacy and penetration involved. The Soviet occupation was managed from a distance. The occupiers were largely confined to the cities, and when they were in the villages and countryside, it seems that they never got too close. That may be partly an illusion, but it is largely confirmed by Soviet on-the-ground accounts.[37] The weapons of war employed by the Soviets were also blunt instruments, lobbed from a distance and aimed in a general way toward an elusive enemy. The Americans and their European allies got much closer. They used intelligence to find out what their enemy looked like, where he resided, where he was keeping his weapons, and who might be aiding him in his efforts. Seeking out this intelligence necessitated piercing the shell that surrounds the Afghan home, that zone of separation and invisibility on which honor depends.

Because of this intrusion, ultimately the offenses committed by the Americans seemed more like sexual assault than territorial invasion. The American way of war, based on metrics and intelligence, depends on being able to see into places and uncover people's secrets. Honor, in contrast, depends on keeping some things out of sight. For the most part, the Afghan government understood and respected this reticence, but their clumsy partner often did not. President Hamid Karzai, who came to power in 2002 through the machinations of the Americans, understood the danger of being associated with allies who violated Afghan codes. The name of Shah Shuja, the mid-nineteenth-century Afghan ruler who allied himself with the British in their occupation of Kabul, has become synonymous with "puppet"; the same epithet was applied to Babrak Karmal, the president brought to power by the Soviets.

Under the regimes of both Karmal and Karzai, the power of the state came to be associated with moral laxity, particularly with respect to the city of Kabul. Whereas the Americans saw themselves as bringing "freedom" to Afghanistan, many Afghans came to associate their presence with the indiscriminate mixing of men and women and the general turbulence that erodes the fine distinctions on which honor depends.

On the most basic level, visibility and invisibility were delineated by walls. Kabul has always been a walled city, marked today by the ruined fragments of fortress walls that snake up the sides of the mountains that dominate the city. Walls surround every house and provide privacy and autonomy to all but the poorest families, those who are consigned to living on the streets. Afghans maintain the right to dictate the terms of visibility and invisibility for their own families—to determine who may and may not see inside those walls. Certainly protecting the honor of women is at the center of this concern, but it extends beyond sex and gender to involve family honor and autonomy. If women are expected to be hidden from public sight by walls and burqas, men are expected to spend most of their time in public—even at home, where they are expected to entertain visitors in the guest room. Afghans have always been lauded for their hospitality. But, as much as that hospitality is a way to demonstrate generosity, it is also a system for managing social relationships and controlling the space within which the dynamics of visibility are performed.

Home and Away

Things got off to a bad start for the Americans and their coalition partners for two reasons related to these dynamics. One is that they insisted on building walls around themselves. There were understandable reasons for doing so, but the effect was to undermine the ideals and demands of visibility and the system of reciprocity underlying it. Americans strictly controlled who could enter their spaces, and they likewise restricted movements of American officials outside these perimeters. So Americans demanded that Afghans come and see them, and then they enacted a variety of humiliating rituals to which Afghans were subject every time they entered American restricted spaces. It was likewise almost impossible for even well-meaning and culturally sensitive Americans to engage in the reciprocal exchanges of hospitality that are central to Afghan culture. They were not permitted to assume the role of either host or guest to Afghans. Unlike the Afghan home, which, despite its forbidding appearance, is open to guests and visits, the walled compounds of the internationals were designed to keep outsiders out and insiders in.

These walls, literal and figurative, extended to the convoys of armored vehicles and tinted-glass SUVs used by diplomats and officials and the barricades that closed off roads when they moved through the city; they included the body armor and tinted sunglasses that the soldiers wore, as distinctive a feature of American identity as the burqa was of Afghan identity. For each side, this identifying garb summarized all that was alien, uncomfortable, and finally repugnant about the other. To the Americans, the burqa was a defiant and obstinate gesture in the face of the occupiers' insistence on visibility. For Afghans, the burqa symbolized their omnipresent concern for family honor and the right to self-determination, even in the public sphere. For the Americans, what mattered most was maintaining the maximum degree of bodily security—thus the up-armored Humvees and Kevlar (bulletproof) vests. For Afghans, what mattered more even than the safety of their bodies was the integrity of their honor—thus the burqa as a symbol of the inviolability of namus and the right to maintain privacy even in public.

Although those walls and Kevlar undoubtedly saved lives, they also made the American presence in Afghanistan a daily affront to Afghan honor. The American insistence on visibility also, ironically, blinded them to the people among whom they were living and on whose support they depended. The proliferation of walls contributed to the distrust and distortion that corroded virtually every cross-cultural relationship and helped destroy the dynamic of reciprocity within Afghan society as well.

The most damaging feature of the early American occupation centered on the practice of house searches. In the name of security, Americans invaded Afghan homes when they believed occupants might be involved or complicit with Coalition enemies. Never mind that U.S. intelligence was often accurate; what mattered more was that they reserved for themselves the right to dictate the terms of their relationship with Afghans, not only choosing how they would make themselves visible but also controlling the visibility of those whose homeland they were occupying. Nothing provided better fodder for

Taliban propaganda than stories of armed American soldiers smashing through compound doors and bursting their way into people's homes in the middle of the night, forcing women in their nightclothes to undergo inspection. The UNAMA report mentions several such incidents and their connection to suicide bombing:

> One 33-year-old Dari speaker from Baghlan, who received the death penalty for being a member of Al Qaeda and organizing suicide attacks at Dyncorp and Chicken Street in Kabul, complained about abuses perpetrated by U.S. troops and recalled his outrage when he "heard on the radio about the Americans' taking a woman from her home and her family in Baghlan and keeping her in detention at Bagram air base." He was also dismayed by the "American soldiers standing watch as Afghan security forces conduct house searches."

. . .

> One 26-year-old Pashtun from Zabul (who received ten years for preparing three cars for suicide attacks), recounted how his "home in Zabul was raided by Afghan forces as the Americans watched and encouraged them."

. . .

> One attacker "explained to UNAMA staff that the first time he saw a foreigner in Afghanistan, he was pointing a gun at him. He asked of the UNAMA interviewer, 'What do you expect us to think of them when they abuse us like this in front of people in our own community?'"[38]

Many of the stories of what motivated suicide bombers relate directly to the humiliation that arises from being confronted by strangers wielding weapons and entering homes uninvited, and the inability to challenge them as equals. The feelings they report of anger, outrage, and frustration stem from the helplessness at being confronted by men who are obtuse in the ways of honor, adamant in pursuit of their own objectives, and unwilling to acknowledge in even a cursory fashion the honor of those they command. The Afghan ideal of self-determination demands a response to such affronts to maintain self-respect and honor in the eyes of peers. For a man to fail to respond is to forfeit his identity as a man. Until the affront is reciprocated, the individual exists in a state of liminal suspension.

Here, it is worth referring again to the story of Sultan Muhammad Khan, recounted in chapter 2. Near death after being shot by rivals, his father pleaded with Sultan Muhammad not to seek vengeance for his killing but instead to allow the father to die a martyr's death. The son replied, "If I do not have the force and power in me to take revenge on one person for every bullet that has struck your body, then I would not be your son."[39] Every Afghan understands the moral logic at the heart of this story, even if they would not choose the same course of action. But some do choose to act, and they do so because they feel that failing to do so would be to forfeit their self-respect and sacrifice their identity—to lose their name, to become nothing.

Encouraged by the Taliban and given the required tools, some find that the way they can recover their honor and identity is by killing themselves in the process of killing those who have defiled their honor or who are in some way associated with and representative of those who have defiled their honor. The act of blowing oneself up redresses wrongs in three domains: personal honor, Islam, and governance. The bomber reclaims lost honor and standing in the community, he does his duty (*farz 'ain*) according to Islam (as interpreted by Taliban clerics), and he performs the political act of striking an unjust oppressor. If you feel that your identity has been jeopardized and that that identity can never be rehabilitated because of the asymmetry of power, then it becomes more imaginable to consider killing yourself, if in so doing you will kill one or more representatives of the force that has denied your identity in the first place. Islam can cement this plan of action, but it is not necessarily the case that religion is the determining factor. The notion that killing infidels is a religious duty simply reinforces and gives weight to the decision and can help quell doubts as to whether or not this course of action is justified and legitimate.

Drones

House searches were not the only American tactics that Afghans perceived as dishonoring and dishonorable. Air attacks also provoked outrage, for example, when faulty intelligence led to aerial attacks on wedding processions wrongly identified as Taliban convoys. But the use of drones in the later period of American engagement (from 2005 onward) was even more damaging to the Afghan perception of Americans. This was also about the same time that the number of suicide-bombing attacks began to increase exponentially.

From the American perspective, the shift to drones represented a retreat from direct involvement in counterinsurgency in which the goal was to win hearts and minds to the more straightforward, less messy business of identifying and eliminating terrorists one-by-one. From an Afghan perspective, however, drone strikes were not combat but cowardice. When American troops were present on the ground, Afghans could imagine that they were engaged in a battle with an honorable foe, despite the imbalance of power. Drones represented something different and unprecedented, because the operators of these unmanned aircraft fought without any risk to themselves. To the Americans, that was their beauty; to the Afghans, that was their shame. As discussed in chapter 2, risk and daring are important aspects of tribal combat. And the surveillance capacities of the drones—specifically, the ability to see inside the walls of people's homes at any time of night or day—were a further affront to Afghan honor.[40]

During the administration of President Barack Obama, drones became an increasingly important component of the American campaign in Afghanistan, until, by 2015, drone strikes accounted for a greater percentage of weapons fired than manned aircraft.[41] According to the Bureau of Investigative Journalism, drone strikes have resulted in a total of between 989 and 1,441 deaths, including 60–81 civilians.[42] A larger number of drone strikes have been carried out in neighboring Pakistan, which we know more about because of the relative freedom afforded to journalists and investigators there to conduct independent research. The situation in the two countries is, of course, closely related. The vast majority of drone strikes conducted in Pakistan have taken place in the Federally Administered Tribal Area (FATA) along the Afghan frontier, whose residents share close linguistic, cultural, and often personal ties with Afghans over the border. Most of the suicide-bomb attacks that occur in Afghanistan are initiated from Pakistan, and so in a sense the chief beneficiary of these strikes has been the people of Afghanistan, who have fewer terrorists to contend with when a drone strike is successful. However, the equation of costs and benefits is not quite so simple.

Despite claims by the U.S. government as to the "surgical precision" of its attacks and the limited number of civilian casualties, American drone strikes have killed hundreds of civilians who were either misidentified as insurgents or collateral casualties.[43] Drone strikes also exact a terrible psychological and social toll on the populations who live under the threat of attack. David Rohde, a *New York Times* reporter who was kidnapped and held by the Taliban, describes the experience of drone surveillance: "From the ground, it is impossible to determine who or what they are tracking as they circle overhead. The buzz of a distant propeller is a constant reminder of imminent death."[44] Safdar Dawar, president of the Tribal Union of Journalists in Pakistan, writes about his response to the presence of drones:

If I am walking in the market, I have this fear that maybe the person walking next to me is going to be a target of the drone. If I'm shopping, I'm really careful and scared. If I'm standing on the road and there is a car parked next to me, I never know if that is going to be the target. Maybe they will target the car in front of me or behind me. Even in mosques, if we're praying, we're worried that maybe one person who is standing with us praying is wanted. So, wherever we are, we have this fear of drones.[45]

One resident described the "wave of terror" that comes over a village whenever drones are flying: "Children, grown-up people, women, they are terrified. . . . They scream in terror." Another resident noted, "Before the drone attacks, it was as if everyone was young. After the drone attacks, it is as if everyone is ill. Every person is afraid of the drones."[46] A third who had been injured from flying shrapnel in a 2011 attack on a tribal assembly reported that "I can't sleep at night because when the drones are there . . . I hear them making that sound, that noise. The drones are all over my brain, I can't sleep. When I hear the drones making that drone sound, I just turn on the light and sit there looking at the light. Whenever the drones are hovering over us, it just makes me so scared."[47] This is not combat, at least as Afghans define the term, but a form of "psychic imprisonment within a perimeter no longer defined by bars, barriers, and walls, but by the endless circling of flying watchtowers up above."[48]

Beyond the individual psychological damage inflicted by drone strikes, communities suffer in a variety of ways. Because people are afraid of being in large groups, they keep their children at home rather than send them to schools, and they avoid tribal jirgas, which are the main mechanism for resolving local disputes. The normal routine of visiting has also been affected. Hospitality, as much as feud, is reciprocal; without the possibility of exchanging visits, social life breaks down. Likewise, important social rituals are impeded, notably funerals and the attendant rites of grieving that are so important for the relief of psychological distress (though funerals of drone victims are in any case fraught occasions, given the mutilated, incinerated, and often unidentifiable condition of the bodies).[49] Drone strikes have also fomented suspicion and distrust based on rumors that locals, attracted by the substantial bounties promised to those who help locate wanted insurgents, are planting signaling devices in homes and vehicles. Whether warranted or not, such rumors have drawn the attention of militants, who seek out and kill suspected informants.[50]

From the American perspective, drones have the great advantage of saving American lives, but the exercise of killing by remotely controlled machines and the concomitant distancing of Americans from combat have substantial repercussions. As Grégoire Chamayou notes in his study of drone warfare, it is not only the drone operator who is distant from the "battlespace"; the *person* being targeted has also been displaced. Drone operators and intelligence analysts use "the all-seeing eye . . . [to] find out who is important in a network, where they live, where they get their support from, where their friends are."[51] "The focus is on understanding 'patterns of life,' and deviations from those patterns. . . . '[You're] now getting into a culture study,' says the analyst. . . . '[You're] looking at people's lives.'"[52]

The basis for this form of "culture study" is not person-to-person interviews as in anthropology but the collection and analysis of SIM-card and biometric data and the gradual development of social-network graphs that allow circumstantial identification of terrorist networks. Positive identification of known terrorists is best, of course, but where such identification is not possible, the likelihood of an individual's involvement in terrorism can be assessed through the tabulation of his or her associations. This approach to combating terrorism represents more than simply the development of a new toolkit. It also constitutes a fundamental shift in philosophy and policy away from "hearts and minds" counterinsurgency to remote control counterterrorism.

It needs to be emphasized that drone strikes are not part of a long-term strategy whose ends are conceived and rationalized from the beginning and whose means are accommodated to those ends. Drone strikes are, rather, a tactical solution to an immediate problem, an approach that fails to take into account its long-term consequences. In this respect, the ascendancy of drone strikes is a natural and perhaps inevitable response to the original offense perpetrated by the September 11 attackers, for just as al-Qaeda's jihad is "globalized as a series of effects that have lost sight of their own causes,"[53] the same can be said of drone strikes, which are not only a globally deployed series of effects that have lost sight of their causes but also a series of effects that have neither a strategic logic nor any discernible endpoint in mind. More than anything else, drone strikes resemble extrajudicial executions, sometimes based on little more than statistical analysis and probability, in which the executed include many who are innocent of any crime other than being in proximity to a target.[54]

Dealing out death in this impersonal way has consequences. American technology may inspire shock and awe, but neither of these responses lasts long, and recent history has demonstrated that cowed compliance is a less likely response than nihilistic outrage, with those harmed by state violence seeking opportunities for revenge. The real losers here are not the Taliban but the tribal elders, the keepers of the traditions that have served people so well for so long. With the elders' voices mute, their institutions ineffective, and their authority suspended, individuals affected by drone strikes and intent on revenge must decide on a course of action with few options to choose from.

This problem is not just tactical or strategic: it is also profoundly personal, even existential. With those responsible for their suffering holed up securely in their walled compounds or executing their strikes from distant bases in the United States, individuals intent on regaining their honor have few options, the most salient and available of which is the path of becoming a suicide bomber. The cost of this decision is that the individual also gives up his autonomy. Regaining his honor may be his goal, but achieving that goal requires obedience to a political organization that might be nearly as disagreeable to him as the United States military.

Without more supporting evidence, connecting suicide bombing to honor as I have done is conjectural. Easier to prove perhaps is that the immediate consequence of drone strikes has been an increase in the number of people willing and sometimes eager to become suicide bombers. Baitullah Mehsud, a former leader of the Pakistani Taliban, is quoted as saying, "I spent three months trying to recruit [suicide bombers] and only got 10–15 persons. One US [drone] attack and I got 150 volunteers."[55] Mehsud himself became the victim of a drone strike in August 2009, but, before that successful attack, the United States had made four other attempts on his life, killing dozens of civilians in the process, including a sleeping eight-year-old boy.[56] Revenge for these killings would come from an unexpected source: a Jordanian doctor named Humam Khalil Abu-Mulal al-Balawi, who, four months after Baitullah Mehsud's assassination and in response to it, blew himself up inside the CIA headquarters at Forward Operating Base Chapman, near the city of Khost in eastern Afghanistan (figure 21).

With al-Balawi, we introduce another Arab to the story of sacrifice. The roles of 'Azzam and Bin Laden are more clearly manifest, and their influence is easier to assess. Al-Balawi is significant less for the influence he exerted than for the testimony he provides to the process I document in this book, a process of embracing sacrifice as the point of life and of combining in the act elements that make it the supreme expression of political and personal self-assertion against the efforts of the state to reduce the individual to the

FIGURE 21. Humam Khalil Abu-Mulal al-Balawi. From martyrdom video, 2009.

conditions of what Giorgio Agamben called "bare life." Understanding the significance of the act requires consideration as well of how it relates to the larger political context and the shaping of that context by drones. Al-Balawi's act, I will argue, can best be understood in terms provided by Agamben in his discussion of homo sacer, the man who can be killed but not sacrificed.[57] Al-Balawi reverses that equation, and he does so by once again reengineering the machinery of sacrifice, in the process bringing it into the digital domain.

THE REVENGE OF *HOMO SACER*

Al-Balawi's profile differs radically from that of the "average" suicide bomber. He was a medical doctor and did not attend a madrasa. He was relatively well-off. He was married and had two children. His pathway to martyrdom was not through any familiar form of indoctrination: he came to his jihadist beliefs via late-night Internet surfing, where he first gained fame under the pseudonym Abu Dujaanah al-Khorasani. Al-Balawi's incendiary postings brought him to the attention of Jordanian intelligence officials, who arrested him and turned him into an agent for their side—or so they thought. Given some rudimentary training in intelligence procedures, al-Balawi was dispatched to Pakistan with the assignment of infiltrating the upper reaches of the Taliban leadership. His handlers believed that his history of radical postings, along with his training in medicine, would make him a plausible and useful asset for the Taliban and would allow him to gain access to their inner circles. His medical expertise brought him to the attention of Ayman al-Zawahiri, Bin Laden's second-in-command, who had a history of medical problems. That, at least, was the story that Jordanian intelligence and the CIA came to believe and the basis on which they invited al-Balawi to a secret meeting at Camp Chapman, where he was to be given the equipment that would enable the CIA to zero in on al-Zawahiri's location when al-Balawi treated him for his various ailments.

In their excitement over this unique opportunity, intelligence officials let down their guard sufficiently to admit al-Balawi to the inner precincts of their base without any of the usual security checks. Once inside the base, he detonated the C4 explosives that encased his body, killing seven CIA officers and contractors, a top Jordanian intelligence official, and an Afghan CIA employee. The attack was one of the worst disasters in CIA history—as well as a public embarrassment once the rudiments of the story were revealed. Not only had the officers present violated the most basic security procedures in allowing a dubiously vetted agent into their base without being properly checked, but they had bought the implausible story of al-Balawi's overnight conversion from avid Internet supporter of jihad to trustworthy CIA asset.

All of this has led to much speculation by Western analysts: Was al-Balawi playing the Jordanian and CIA intelligence officials from the beginning, or did he have second thoughts and recommit himself to the jihadist cause once he got to Pakistan? Was he a wily triple agent or merely a pretender who felt compelled, once he was among the Taliban, to make good on all the radical posturing his Internet avatar had so long presented to the world? In jihadist circles, however, al-Balawi's motivations are seen as unequivocal and demonstrated by one of several video statements he produced in the weeks before his departure for Camp Chapman.

The video, titled *An Interview with the Shaheed Abu Dujaanah al-Khorasani (May Allah Have Mercy on Him), Hero of the Raid of the Shaheed Amir Baytullah Mehsud (May Allah Have Mercy on Him)*, takes the form of a question-and-answer interview in which al-Balawi describes his background and motivations for undertaking his suicide mission.[58] In both the interview and the labeling on the transcript published by as-Sahab, al-Qaeda's media arm, al-Balawi is referred to as "the poor slave Abu Dujaanah al-Khorasani," the persona he adopted for his Internet posting, indicating perhaps that he chose to leave behind the identity into which he was born in favor of the person he invented and wanted to become.

In the interview, al-Balawi says little about his earlier life and nothing about the wife and child he was leaving behind. He focuses on his actions in support of the jihad and the planning that had gone into his martyrdom mission. He recounts his many unsuccessful attempts to join the jihad in Iraq, which in hindsight he believes were meant to fail because "Allah decreed something else for me." This is a refrain throughout the video: Man proposes, but God disposes. He lists three decisive moments that changed him from a doctor, late-night "jihobbyist," and passive observer to active jihadist. The first came about as a result of the situation in Israel:

> When I witnessed the events of Gaza—and very painful events they were—I can't forget the scene I saw on al-Jazirah channel, in which the daughters of Zion were watching Gaza as it was being bombed by F-16 fighter jets. They were using binoculars and watching the Muslims get killed, and it was as if they were just observing some natural phenomenon, or as if they were watching a theatrical film or something similar. So I wrote an article, the last of my articles, entitled "When Will My Words Drink from My Blood?" And all praise is due to Allah, the idea of mobilizing began to get stronger.

The second event was a dream "decreed" by Allah, in which he saw Abu Musab al-Zarqawi, the head of al-Qaeda in Iraq. So vivid was the dream that "it was as if he was in my house. I asked him, 'Aren't you dead?' He replied, 'I was killed, but I am as you see me, alive.' His face was like a full moon, and he was busy, as if he was getting ready for an operation. I wished I could take him to a secure place, and take him out in my car, and I also wished that we could be bombed so we could be killed together. Glory be to Allah, it seems that the secure place means martyrdom in Allah's path."

The dream had so powerful an effect on al-Balawi that he sought out dream interpreters, one of whom told him that "'the security organs will enter your house.' And I think that the vision has now been fulfilled and that its interpretation—with Allah's permission—is that I will mobilize in Allah's path, and the security forces will enter my house, leading to a martyrdom operation which will be revenge for the killing of Abu Mus'ab al-Zarqawi and the killing of many of our brothers by the spy drones in Waziristan. So Allah willing, this is the meaning of the vision." The third decisive event was the visit by Jordanian security foretold by the dream interpreter, which came about as a result of his growing renown, or that of his Internet avatar.

Al-Balawi acknowledges that, had the security forces not arrived and arrested him, he most likely would never have overcome his inertia to become anything other than a frustrated doctor/late-night militant. In his telling, he had prayed that he would not endanger the lives of others with whom he had come into contact on the Internet under the pressure of interrogation. God responded to this prayer by sending Ali Bin Zeid, a cousin of King Abdullah, security official, and later one of the victims of the Camp Chapman attack, who proposed that al-Balawi go to Waziristan as their agent: "But the amazing thing which I could hardly believe is that I had been trying to mobilize to Jihad in Allah's path but had been unsuccessful, then this idiotic man comes along and proposes that I go to the fields of jihad. All praise is due to Allah, Lord of the worlds: it was a dream come true!"

Al-Balawi goes on at length to belittle Jordanian intelligence, portraying the "weak arguments, *absurd* arguments" used to convince him, such as reminding him that King Abdullah was in the line of descent from the Prophet Muhammad and that his efforts on their behalf would make the Jordanians look good in the eyes of the Americans. More than anything, they tried to persuade him with financial incentives:

> So they think that if a man is offered money, it is possible for him to abandon his creed. They think that we worship wealth and lusts just like them. How amazing! How amazing that you propose [such things] to a man whose last article just a short while ago was called "When Will My Words Drink from My Blood?," a man who burns with desire for martyrdom and who motivates the Ummah to jihad!

In al-Balawi's account, all the while that Jordanian security officers were preparing him for undercover intelligence work, he was laying the foundations for his mission, even if the details of that mission were as yet unclear to him. He gave false impressions to his Jordanian controller, such as "the impression that I'm reluctant to go [to Pakistan] due to my fear of dying, so that he thinks I'm a believer in his religion, which is money; or like getting up and asking him for money and asking him about the rewards and gifts they're promising me."

Once he arrived in Pakistan, he continued to use "the same tactics the intelligence services use" to entrap their informants, at one point breaking communications for four months "in order for Jordanian intelligence to stew in its own juices thinking that this guy had abandoned it, so that if he came back to them and told them that conditions were difficult, they would buy his story quickly." When he did reestablish communications, he set the trap with a fabricated cell phone video of Atiyah Abd al-Rahman, a senior al-Qaeda official in Pakistan, to demonstrate to the Jordanians and the CIA that al-Balawi was getting close to the top echelons of the al-Qaeda and Taliban leadership.

Having sought for years to penetrate the inner councils of al-Qaeda, American and Jordanian security agents pounced on the bait and began pressing al-Balawi to meet with them so that they could pinpoint the location of senior al-Qaeda leaders. Initially, al-Balawi tried to convince Bin Zeid to come to Peshawar, but the Jordanian came back with what amounted to an even more propitious opportunity, "a bigger gift, a gift from Allah": a meeting with CIA officers in Afghanistan. The initial plan al-Balawi devised with Taliban leaders had been for al-Balawi to meet with Bin Zeid and for this cousin of the Jordanian king to be taken prisoner and thereby humiliate the whole Jordanian security apparatus. But the CIA's insistence on personally meeting with al-Balawi offered an even better opportunity: "When the Shura council would meet, I would discuss with the brothers how to inflict the largest possible defeat and slaughter with the least possible losses, and we agreed that this always manifests itself in the martyrdom operation." Al-Balawi describes this turn of events not simply as an opportunity but as "a blessing":

> It is a blessing from above seven heavens that I be given the opportunity to have my severed limbs be turned into shrapnel, to have my bones be turned into shrapnel, to have my teeth be turned into shrapnel which will kill these American and Jordanian infidels from the intelligence apparatuses. How could I possibly refuse?! This is truly an offer which is a gift from Allah, so how could I forfeit it?

Al-Balawi states that he alone was in a position to successfully undertake this operation. He alone had the connection with Bin Zeid, who would be present at Camp Chapman. Since Allah had provided him personally with this blessing "ready-to-eat," he was not going to allow anyone else to claim his reward. Besides, al-Balawi had another message to send:

When they think that this man is a spy, but then this man turns into a bomb, turns into a missile, turns into an explosive, this weakens the enemy's resolve and makes him understand that the sons of this religion have never bargained and will never bargain over this religion, and that this religion is more precious than everything they own. And all praise is due to Allah, Lord of the worlds.

The video continues with a series of messages for other martyrs and families of martyrs, and it concludes with a prayer:

O Allah, Revealer of the Book, Runner of the clouds, Defeater of the confederates; O Allah, defeat American and Jordanian intelligence. O Allah, defeat them and shake them. O Allah, let us kill them, O Lord of the worlds, and let us cause a great slaughter in their ranks. O Allah, accept our blood. O Allah, accept our martyrdom in Paradise. O Allah, accept our blood. O Allah, take from my blood today until You are satisfied; take from my blood until You forgive me, O Lord of the worlds. And our final prayer is that all praise is due to Allah, Lord of the world.

Al-Balawi's video is close in spirit to the rhetoric of the Palestinian martyrs discussed earlier in this chapter. The events leading up to his death are described in a way that minimizes his own agency. Rather than choosing his own path, he has heeded the signs God has sent him in the form of dreams and a string of opportunities. He had only to correctly interpret each of the intended messages and act upon them. We cannot say whether al-Balawi always had the certainty and conviction demonstrated in the video. We do not know if he always planned on betraying the Jordanians. We do not know if he was always and consistently immune to the blandishments of his Jordanian handler and really sought martyrdom from the beginning. It might be that the man we see and hear in the video has been himself entrapped by circumstances and has reconciled himself to his fate.

In the end, motivation is a black box whose contents we can never fully know, whether it is another's or our own. Al-Balawi appears in the video as a man at peace with his fate. We also see a man possessed of a divided self, a man with a gift for rhetoric who exercised that gift before the glowing late-night altar of the Internet. In those moments, it appears, he became someone else from someplace else. Humam Khalil Abu-Mulal al-Balawi from Amman, Jordan, became Abu Dujaanah from the windswept plains of Khorasan, and it was God's great gift to him—a gift not given to many—that he could become in reality the person he had invented. It was not just the self that was an invention but Afghanistan as well, refashioned as the ancient land of Khorasan, where the black banners of revolt were first raised against Umayyad tyranny centuries earlier. As it had been for Bin Laden before him, for al-Balawi Afghanistan was a mythic place and a suitable location for reinvention, and martyrdom was the ultimate demonstration and validation of this process of becoming.

The ideal of martyrdom is constructed in counter-distinction to some real or imagined set of values, in opposition to which martyrdom appears not only desirable but necessary. In al-Balawi's testimony, this is personified in Bin Zeid, his Jordanian handler, who is portrayed as both stupid and corrupt. Al-Balawi recounts a trip to the Safeway supermarket in Amman where Bin Zeid would buy food for his dog and then dispatch the receipts to his chief "as if it was purchased for [Abu Dujaanah]."

> In other words, in front of my eyes he would steal from his chief and steal from his institution! So it's all very natural: he believes that you actually believe in his religion! And he thinks that his religion is the truth. His religion is lust, his religion is money; but the fact is that for anyone who believes in Allah and in the Garden and the Fire, and believes in eternity and that there is a "Day when mankind will stand up before the Lord of the worlds" (83:6), how can a mere fistful of dollars possibly make him sell out his religion and sell out his brothers?

Opposed to the figure of Bin Zeid is the apparitional figure of al-Zarqawi, who embodies (even in disembodied form) the ideals of devotion and duty. Al-Zarqawi provides an ethical model of right thinking and action in the narrative, but he is also a figure of longing, his face "a full moon," who inspires in al-Balawi the desire to "take him to a secure place, and take him out in my car, and I also wished that we could be bombed so we could be killed together." The video constructs a narrative of repulsion and attraction, with al-Balawi moving ceaselessly away from the negative, corrupt pole of Bin Zeid toward the incorruptible example of al-Zarqawi.

On an ethical and intellectual level, martyrdom is an answer to materialism, but it has an emotional draw as well, as seen in the early poetry of jihad as well as in al-Balawi's evocation of the dead al-Zarqawi. The desires of the material world are inherently finite; those in the world beyond are infinite, as also are the torments that await those so bound to the world that they ignore the signs of what lies beyond it. The choice is clear for al-Balawi—the Garden or the Fire—and the only assurance that the former is one's destination rather than the latter is the manner of one's death.

In the West, we enlist technology to extend life, delay death, and create the illusion of perpetual youth. In Afghanistan, the machinery of sacrifice directs the believer to look in the opposite direction. Violence that cannot be avoided should be embraced. If the world offers deprivation and suffering, then martyrdom provides an alternative, and one that satisfies many of the same desires we have in the West. If living in the shadow of unending war ages you before your time, martyrdom promises eternal youth in a realm where death and the worries and anxieties of the everyday never come to mind.

From another perspective, of course, al-Balawi's sacrifice is one skirmish in what has come in the West to be called the global war on terror. Al-Balawi's martyrdom video posthumously refers to him as "the Hero of the Raid of the Shaheed Amir Baytullah Mehsud," the same Baitullah Mehsud who, as head of the Pakistani Taliban, had his greatest success recruiting suicide bombers after the United States began using drone strikes and who himself was the victim of such a strike in 2009. Al-Balawi's "raid" brings the relationship of suicide bombing and drone strikes into stark relief. Drone strikes—and the constant surveillance that precedes them—dehumanizes the people who are directly and indirectly subject to their violence, reduced to the "bare life" of the brutalized and expendable, deprived of the most basic human rights and amenities of society.

Many—perhaps most—of those who die in this way have been involved in what the United States terms terrorist activities, but they might also be killed simply because their actions have placed them within the parameters of a system whose taxonomic logic permits their murder. In this sense, they have become, in Agamben's terms, *homo sacer*—the sacred man—but the terms have changed. He who can be killed but not sacrificed (or he who can be killed *so that* he cannot sacrifice) reclaims his humanity by voiding this status, negating its negation, and offering himself as the sacrifice that the state would forbid. In the context of the global war on terror, it can be argued that the *homo sacer* has two meanings. The first, "the one who can be killed so that he cannot sacrifice," recognizes that the action undertaken by the suicide bomber is, by his lights, an act of sacrificial violence. Killing him before he can kill is intended to preempt that act of sacrifice. The second meaning is as the one who is killed to prevent him from being made subject to the juridical procedures—the sacrificial rites—of the state. The recent history of Abu Ghraib, Bagram, Guantanamo, dark sites and renditions, waterboarding and torture is sordid testament to the manner in which the global war on terror has created one long, bleak "state of exception" in which the rule of law has been sacrificed to fear and expediency.

As the preeminent recent example of the *homo sacer*, Bin Laden could not be captured. The United States had to summarily kill him and unceremoniously dispose of his body, because to bring him into custody and accord him the rites and privileges of judicial process would have exposed the vulnerability of the state to its own contradictions. In captivity and on trial, not only would Bin Laden have had an opportunity to proclaim his beliefs before a rapt worldwide audience—or be denied that opportunity, thus exposing the state's fear of its captive—but he would also have been afforded the opportunity to be martyred by the state for his beliefs. That spectacle could never have been allowed. But some of Bin Laden's subordinates, including Khalid Sheikh Muhammad, remain in suspended animation, between life and death, pleading (through prayer and judicial motions) for a martyrdom the state does not wish and cannot afford to give them.

Al-Balawi steered a passage between, on the one hand, an untimely and unplanned-for death by drone strike as suffered by al-Zarqawi and Mehsud, and, on the other, the suffering of the would-be martyr enduring the passivity of prolonged imprisonment, the fate that awaited him had he not agreed to work with the Jordanian security establishment. He avoided both these fates by arranging the place and time and manner of his own passing. Instead of passively suffering his enemy's violence, he became the agent of his own act of violence against his enemies, and he initiated that violence in the ritual manner that assured—so he believed—his own eternal salvation while also advancing the strategic cause of the ummah he was leaving behind. In so doing, *homo sacer* became shahid: the state of exception was transmuted into sacrifice.

It is impossible to know how many times al-Balawi's martyrdom video has been viewed, how influential it has been, or how important a figure he has become in death. In regard to 'Azzam and Bin Laden, we can discuss with some authority the nature and extent of their influence. With al-Balawi, such speculation is more difficult, which reflects the elusive and boundless nature of the Internet itself and why it constitutes such difficult terrain to navigate and control. However influential al-Balawi might or might not have been and however enduring or transient his legacy might be, al-Balawi represents a phenomenon that is larger than himself and that matters in part because it was not tied to any one leader or country. The Internet provides a space within which anyone can raise their voice and be listened to, no matter how strange or extreme their views. It is a place where people can reinvent themselves as something different than what they were born to be or how others assume and imagine them to be. Al-Balawi brought this prime axiom of our age to life, and, as will be discussed in the following chapter, many others are following his example.

SEVEN

Selfies

THE BOY IN THE VIDEO appears to be sixteen or seventeen years old. He is dressed in a pressed white *shalwar-kameez* and a red embroidered cap with shiny silver mirrors sewn in. He looks like he is dressed for a wedding—and, in a sense, he is (figure 22). He walks toward the camera, in a line with older, bearded men who look like ordinary Afghans from the mountains. These other men are not going to the wedding, but one of them is going to drive the boy to his big event, or at least partway there. When they have passed through the gorge and along the rutted track to the paved road, the boy will take over and drive the old SUV loaded with explosives until it crosses paths with the lead Humvee in a convoy coming the other way. Then he will detonate the explosives. We see the blast from a distance, the video editor having included arrows pointing to the two vehicles that are about to explode and take their occupants to whatever afterlife awaits them.

The video is six minutes and thirty-eight seconds long—long enough to tell a story, but short enough to download to your phone. I watched this particular video on YouTube for free, but new suicide-bomber videos and the Taliban *tarana* songs that the Taliban have been mass producing for the past several years are also being offered for sale in Afghanistan, and apparently they are selling well.[1] In 2014, an Afghan friend (who has asked to remain unnamed) was told by a Jalalabad shopkeeper that he uploads a hundred new jihadi tunes each day to keep up with the demand. Since his customers are passing the songs and videos among themselves, he has to keep buying new ones himself to refresh his stock. Most of his customers are teenage boys like the one in the video, and the songs they prefer, he says, are the ones that praise suicide bombers. Another shopkeeper told my friend that it was not just young boys who were buying these products; even government workers,

FIGURE 22. Hayatullah Mehsud. From martyrdom video, 2009.

policemen, and soldiers were uploading the songs. The market was broad and deep, and it was not showing any signs of weakening.

When my friend asked him where these songs and videos were coming from, he responded that the singers were students in the Taliban madrasas, and the products the shopkeeper sold were coming from Peshawar. Right after the Taliban government fell in 2001, the restrictions on music were lifted, and he started selling Indian and Pakistani movies and CDs. He was earning good money until around 2010, when the resurgent Taliban started attacking music centers and video shops. Ironically, the Taliban saved his business by going into the music and video business themselves. Now the shopkeeper was earning more money from the Taliban songs and videos than he did from the Bollywood CDs and the DVDs he used to sell.

When my friend asked different people why these products have become so popular, he got different answers. One is that they serve as a form of insurance (sometimes known as a "Taliban visa"). Older people, especially those who travel outside the city for their business or who work for the government, keep two separate SIM cards for their phones. The first is the one they normally use, which stores personal and work contacts along with their preferred music. The second is loaded with Taliban songs and videos. Taliban patrols routinely check mobile phones and, at the very least, will smash those that contain nonreligious music and videos. But phones containing Taliban songs are left alone, and the Taliban who stop the travelers will even upload songs they like from a traveler's phone. This is a good sign that the traveler will be allowed to go on his way. Students at Ningrahar University told my friend that they bought Taliban music for their phones because they felt "sandwiched" between the police and the Taliban: "It is difficult for us to have a cell phone. If your cell phone rings in a police station, they are asking us, 'Why do you have a Taliban ringtone?' When we are on the way home . . . Taliban are destroying our cell phones because they don't have Taliban ringtones."

Other people noted that these songs and videos represent a news source and that government officials keep them on their phones because they help them know what is going on, but my friend suspects that people simply enjoy listening to the songs, even the government officials who have the most to lose if the Taliban regain control of the country. And maybe the same is true of the videos. The video of the boy preparing to end his life is mesmerizing, and apparently I am not the only one to think so: it had 565,586 views on YouTube as of January 12, 2017.

In *Camera Lucida,* Roland Barthes writes at length about a nineteenth-century daguerreotype of Lewis Payne, one of the plotters responsible for the assassination of President Abraham Lincoln; Payne sat for the photograph in his prison cell while awaiting his execution.[2] Barthes searches Payne's face for some sign of recognition, some acknowledgment of the fate that awaits him. He must sit especially still because of the long exposures needed for photography in that era, even longer in this case because the picture is taken in the dark interior of the prison. The image is clear. There is no blurring that might suggest a nervous flinch or blink. Payne shows no fear of his impending doom; he even looks a bit bored.

Hayatullah Mehsud, the boy in the video, is surrounded by the people who are planning his death (figure 23). They are all a lot older than he is. Some have had their faces blocked out, but others are clearly recognizable, and you can only wonder about the reasons for the difference. Maybe it is because some of them are moving back and forth between the government and the Taliban side and need to conceal their involvement with the Taliban, while those who smile into the camera are already well-known in the world of martyrdom media. Whatever the case, the smiling commander seems not to have a care in the world as he chats up his young friend. The boy is another matter. We see how hard he is working at appearing casual, how he seems to

FIGURE 23. Hayatullah Mehsud (on right) and other mujahidin. From martyrdom video, 2009.

be asking polite questions about which wires attach to which terminals. He would have a hard time growing a beard even if he wanted to look like the men he is with. But it is in their interest that he looks just the way he does. Who would suspect this sweet-looking, well-dressed kid of anything?

TARANA

It is the end of black nights; the clear morning has come to us.
Deep darkness is fading away, the bright sun is rising now . . .
The beginning of our revolt is swift and triumphant.
In people's life this revival is a beautiful day of celebration . . .
Along the silky road we lead our caravan of justice.[3]

When the Taliban government was in power, they famously banned most kinds of music but made an exception for tarana: a cappella songs with religious and jihadi themes that they sang to raise their spirits when they were campaigning. Clerics had found some precedent for this kind of music in the hadith literature and deemed it acceptable so long as there was no orchestration beyond a simple kind of drum. But their leaders had not yet realized the role these songs could play in advancing their cause. They knew that singing and hearing these chants bolstered the morale of their soldiers, but they did not understand that these songs could help sell the movement to a broader audience. They also did not have the technology that is available today—the MP3 players and mobile phones, the apps for transferring songs between devices, the Internet cafes. In fact, they did everything they could to eliminate the technology they did have, like the cassette tapes whose guts still hung from electric wires when I returned to Kabul in 2003.

The Taliban fell from power about the same time that digital technology took off. The one decision they made that favored technology was to allow the newly formed Afghan Wireless telecom company to set up cell towers and relay stations to bring mobile-phone communications to Afghanistan. It is partly on the back of this network that the new Taliban are making their bid to retake power from the current U.S.-backed regime.

In the late 1960s, when the Muslim Youth Organization was first struggling to get its message out to students in the high schools and universities, it gave its members the task of making handwritten copies of the important Islamist texts, like the writings of Sayyid Qutb, as well as the pamphlets by the organization's own leaders. These handwritten texts were bound with string and quietly slipped to people the party thought might be sympathetic to its cause. If the recipients liked what they saw and wanted to get involved, they would be tasked with making five or six more copies of these writings to hand out to others, and, in this way, the movement slowly grew.[4]

When the jihad against the Marxist government began in the summer of 1978, Rafiq Jan got the idea that his poems might have an audience among the border tribes, and he hired musicians and singers to record them. He made cassettes of these recordings, which people from the mountains took with them when they went home. Listening to the tapes on their battery-operated radio-cassette players, tribesmen realized that the songs were presenting them with a challenge, both to live up to an ideal from the past, enshrined in traditional poems and stories, and to ensure their own enduring reputations as men of honor. Never before had they had the opportunity to live the ideals the way Pakhtun heroes of old had lived them. Rafiq Jan made the opportunity and the challenge clear and present to them. Through the cassettes, Rafiq Jan and other poets were able to convey their message to hundreds, if not thousands, of tribesmen in scattered villages.

Current technology has expanded this audience exponentially, and it has added images to the music. Digital media thus combine a vastly sped-up version of the "copy and distribute" structure of *dawat* proselytizing and recruitment, on which the Muslim Youth Organization built its early Islamist movement, with the early jihad approach of building morale through recorded poems and songs. Behind the music and the videos being released today is a production apparatus that has been built up in Pakistan. The target audience for this public-relations campaign is the enormous demographic bulge of young men under the age of twenty-five in Afghanistan and Pakistan.

Many of these young men have few prospects: just as the powers that supported the mujahidin in the 1980s neglected the problem and potential of refugee children, so the Afghan government and its supporters have failed to provide adequate educational and vocational alternatives to the madrasas. In fact, the government has done its best to expand the network of madrasas and Qur'an memorization centers out of fear of alienating the old jihadi leaders who sit in Parliament, accepting this as a short-term expedient while ignoring what they know to be its long-term consequences.

For their part, the young people who are so eager to upload the latest Taliban songs and suicide videos seem driven by the same sort of consumer dynamic that leads Western teenagers to want to stay current and fashionable in their musical tastes. In Afghanistan, there are two directions that taste can take you: toward the popular media that have developed in Kabul, with its burgeoning consumer and celebrity culture, or the Taliban variant that is exported from Pakistan, with its culture of sacrifice and death. Roughly analogous in the Western context might be the contrast between mainstream pop music that is deemed decent and undemanding and what is often referred to as gangsta rap: black urban music that, at least initially, existed on the margins and romanticized sex and guns.

Like Taliban tarana, gangsta rap, with its harsh beats and rhythms, is music that many adults do not like, and, partly for that reason, it found a loyal audience among suburban white teenagers who are thrilled by its edginess and danger. And just as gangsta rap brings with it a whole cultural apparatus of fashion and style as well as celebrity rappers whose exploits are followed by teenage admirers on social media, so the Taliban, with their long hair flowing from beneath their black turbans, have developed their own style and image, along with a host of celebrities, both living and dead. The appeal of gangsta rap was bolstered by stories of gang violence—Bloods and Crips, West Coast versus East Coast—and an exotic, freewheeling lifestyle centered on nightclubs, luxury rides, and sex on demand. The Taliban narrative is different, of course, centered on a brotherhood of men fighting the great American superpower, but, for young Afghans, it is likewise exotic and appealing, not only to disadvantaged young men with no jobs and few prospects but also to those idealistic enough to be discouraged by the rampant corruption and consumerism they see around them and the political paralysis that has frozen hopes for social and economic reform. Just as the rappers could claim a certain moral high ground by being black and disadvantaged, the Taliban holds the literal and metaphoric high ground by leading an ascetic life in the mountains.

The reason Hayatullah Mehsud is dressed for his wedding in the next world may be that he was unlikely to have been married any time soon in this world. Many young men cannot foresee even the possibility of marriage because their parents cannot afford the cost, which has skyrocketed since 2001. There might not be any proof of the existence either of Paradise or houris outside the realm of scripture, but the off-chance that the Taliban might be right about these matters represents the best opportunity that many young people have of realizing their dreams and releasing the pent-up frustration of teenage desire. That frustration is part of the reason why young people listen to this music and perhaps why some of them take the next step. Killing themselves offers the prospect of meeting the promised bride, whose voice is even featured in some tarana, telling the listener that she is waiting and urging him to join her in Paradise.

In this day and age of global interconnectivity, teenage boys like Hayatullah Mehsud may have seen those American rapper videos, too. Maybe part of what makes the Taliban attractive to young Afghan and Pakistani men is precisely the fact that they have seen what the West has to offer, the good and the bad, including all the varieties of do-it-yourself pornography now available on computer screens anywhere in the world. It may be that what the Taliban offers seems better and cleaner. Maybe they cannot separate the Internet images of young, voluptuous women in every variety of sexual position from the way they imagine the houris of Paradise, but they can reject the feelings of impurity that the Western porn sites elicit after the initial pleasure.

In the West, one dimension of the teenage consumer dynamic is wanting to see and hear what your parents do not want you to see and hear, and the same dynamic seems to be at work in Afghanistan. The difference, of course, is that Afghan parents are not simply worried that music will make their children dye their hair green or get a tattoo, but that it will literally drive them to their deaths. The Taliban recognize this obstacle to recruitment. Some of the songs promise their listeners not only that they will have their share of female companions in the next world but also that their act of sacrifice will ensure that their parents—whatever their sins—will be given a free pass to Paradise themselves.[5] So even if a young man cannot support his family in this world, he can support them in an even more valuable and enduring way in the next.

Taliban tarana also sometimes directly address parents, perhaps on the assumption that teenage listeners will play the music for their parents in order to obtain their blessing to pursue the path of martyrdom. These messages remind mothers of the infidelity of the regime and the abuses of the Americans—violating homes, killing children, destroying mosques, and desecrating copies of the Qur'an—and also threaten that, if their sons should make the mistake of joining the security forces or otherwise supporting the "puppet" regime, they will be killed and will suffer the perpetual torment of hell.[6] To reinforce their message, the Taliban also remind young people and parents that, though parental permission is required for most things, including participating in jihad, an exception is made when the Islamic ummah comes under the rule of an infidel regime. The implication is that parents must recognize that their children can martyr themselves with or without parental permission, so they might as well agree. By doing so, they preserve the possibility that their relationship will endure when they follow a martyred child to heaven.[7]

LOVE SONGS

I am a butterfly of the ramparts, to the ramparts I rush.
In glowing coals I suffer, but I laugh at them . . .
I am not like Majnun without any flesh.
I became red colored because of the blood from my chest.
I have gone and become the glory of whole Kabul.[8]

Many analyses of suicide bombers' motivation focus on Islamic doctrine as the primary inspiration. This might be true of suicide bombers who come out of the madrasas and have been indoctrinated over many years in the scriptural bases for jihad and martyrdom, but it is probably less true of other young people, who are unlikely to have any substantial knowledge of Islamic scripture beyond snippets from their elementary schooling at the local mosque or from the sermons that are regularly broadcast on radio and television. Although scripture is the ultimate authority for all Taliban directives and injunctions, and there is something thrilling in the resonant sound of Qur'anic recitation, it still establishes only a partial connection to the emotional circuitry of a teenage boy. Music amplifies the power of recited scripture, whose words and meanings are lost on most young Afghans, with lyrics in local dialect that are calibrated to the circumstances and needs of the moment.

Westerners who encounter the lyrics might find them awfully repetitious. The themes have been around since the beginning of the jihad, back in the 1980s. Then as now, the glory of the martyr and the infidelity of the government are the two dominant foci. New topics crop up, such as criticisms of young people playing cricket or volleyball rather than waging jihad, but the underlying message remains the same. When the Soviets arrived, the names of tribes largely disappeared from verse, and the locus of honor shifted from the tribal warrior to the mujahid, with the ultimate expression of that honor shifting from the act of killing to that of being killed. Today's poems appear very similar to those of 1984. If anything, the earlier sung poems seem marginally livelier, since they were often accompanied by drums and stringed instruments.

One way to explain the continuing popularity of this form of musical expression is by comparing Taliban songs to those heard on Western radio stations. Most pop songs refer one way or another to love. Most of the lyrics are drearily monotonous and add little to what we know of love. If anything, they trivialize our pursuit of romantic love, but still people listen, choose their favorites, and play those favorites over and over again. American radio songs, which are the only ones I can speak about from experience, have two dominant themes: eternal love, which is the type aspired to, and faithless love, the love that disappears or was false from the start—"I gave myself to you, and that love was not returned, or it was returned for a time until you saw someone else and turned away, leaving me with my heart exposed and no one to give it to." That is at the heart of a typical love song. Whatever emotive force the song manages is finally the reason we listen and maybe get a little damp-eyed when we hear it again after not hearing it for a long time.

The tarana that are most popular, according to the shopkeepers in Jalalabad, are the ones about suicide bombing, and it is not absurd to think of them as love songs. As with Western love songs, their central dynamic is the relationship between faith and faithlessness—personified, on the one hand, by the martyr who sacrifices his life for God and, on the other, by the opportunists who support the regime or wallow in material possessions and desires instead of heeding the call to jihad. In some cultures, including Afghan culture, romantic love is forbidden, except in the imagination. The expression of sexual desire threatens not only the structures of authority but also the foundations of social order. The idea of choosing one's own partner is, for most, a vivid but unattainable fantasy. Elders hold onto their right of determining familial alliances, in part because of the high cost of marriage.

Yet romantic yearning and sexual desire still exist, maybe all the more intensely for being contained. In Western societies, music is omnipresent, and the advent of iPods and earbuds have served to make it even more universal but also more inconsequential, music becoming nowadays more a way to shut out the world than to experience it. The same is not the case in Afghanistan, and though romantic love as we know it might be off-limits for most, the emotions that feed love still exist, and music may serve to direct those emotions toward other, socially acceptable objects or to disguise the nature of the desire felt under a discreet veil that masks the basic feeling that seeks expression. The martyr represents above all an object of romantic desire—not in a sexual sense, but as someone who does what lovers do, namely sacrifice themselves for love.[9]

In Afghan culture, that dimension of sacrifice is best epitomized in the classic tale of Layla and Majnun. Layla is usually depicted as the daughter of a nomad chieftain and Majnun as her faithful lover. The story has myriad variations, but, in all of them, Layla remains the unattainable object of desire, and Majnun is left to wander the mountains, heartsick, bereft, and driven mad by unrealized desire.[10] In reading the poems composed in honor of martyrs, I am often reminded of this story. The martyr poems share the story's abiding sense of lost love, with the poet cast in the role of Majnun and the martyr as Layla (or the Beloved of Sufi poetry, the God one wants to approach but can never join). Martrydom poetry, however, upends this dynamic by offering something that Majnun could never achieve, namely the fulfillment of his passion, albeit in another world. The martyr alone gains what young Afghans futilely wish for themselves, both honor and realized desire, and, in so doing, he transcends centuries of Layla and Majnun stories and generation upon generation of thwarted love.

I go on about love songs and desire to suggest that the figure of the martyr may provide for listeners a focus for emotions that crystallize the ideal that is central to both corporeal and devotional love, namely that the highest and most esteemed forms of love always entail an acceptance of loss and incompleteness. Human beings are not destined to have all they desire, but this only makes it more important for them to continue the search, sacrificing what is present and available for the absent and unobtainable ideal. The Western notion that "you can have it all" contrasts with the Afghan notion that the human condition is inevitably one of partition and separation. In Afghanistan, everyone has lost someone, and even if by some remote chance loss has not directly affected one's own family and friends, grief is all around. The figure of the martyr provides one outlet for such emotions and gives people with few opportunities to express their sadness—and much to be sad about—a way to feel good while feeling bad.

Love songs for Americans are a distraction from reality, not an alternative to it. In the end, a teenager in the United States can maintain the reasonable expectation of finding the love he desires, or at the very least sexual partners with whom to gain some experience of the postures, if not the possibilities of love. Afghans have few possibilities and fewer expectations, and so the martyr love songs of the Taliban play a different, more profound role. They offer not just a diversion but a path to fulfillment, and, in the absence of alternatives, and given the other trappings of heroic action and mastery with which the path toward martyrdom is bedecked, the lure of death for many becomes irresistible.

TALIFANS

Sharing songs and videos is one way that the Taliban and what might be called "Talifans" have of demonstrating their commitment to the cause of Islam and their willingness to consider martyrdom. Another way, and one that is potentially far more consequential, is Facebook. In the summer of 2014, a contact in Kabul gave me the Facebook name of a relative who had been trained as a suicide bomber and who had agreed to be interviewed by me, or rather who agreed to respond to the questions I submitted to him through my contact. The name he used on his account was not his own but that of someone he admired who had died on a suicide mission. While I waited for the exchange to be set up, I started following his Facebook posts, which in turn led me to the pages of his Facebook friends.

Access to the Facebook pages I viewed was not restricted, but I discovered that most of these users were keeping at least two accounts and that the accounts I had access to were not the ones they used for personal communications. Rather, these were the places where they posted material for public consumption as well as for their friends: images, memes, poems, news flashes, pious sayings, and sometimes pointed comments on the Taliban, martyrdom, Osama Bin Laden, and other topics related to Islam. The posts were numerous, and most received a positive response from friends, who expressed their approval by "liking" particular posts and making short affirmative comments such as "God is Great" and "Allah be praised" or—in response to the many posts that included a photograph or story about a compatriot's death—"May Allah accept his martyrdom."

Following from one Facebook page to the next, I discovered a seemingly limitless world of people who were using Facebook as a medium for cultivating and demonstrating their support for the Taliban and their martyrdom operations. The image one gets from this plethora of posts is very different from what one gets when reading about or seeing videos of interviews with captured or surrendered suicide bombers. This is not the world of brainwashed adolescents, kidnapped children, and cynical trainers. It is, in fact, much closer in spirit and sensibility to the world martyrdom cult that the journalist Nasra Hassan portrayed in her *New Yorker* article on the Palestinian suicide bombers in the 1990s.[11]

I have referred to the magazines put out by the Peshawar parties as having the objective of developing a cult of martyrs, but evidence of such a cult is far stronger on Facebook than it was in that milieu. It is impossible to gauge the reception of the magazines among their intended audience. They represented a top-down effort at instrumentalizing martyrdom in the service of political organizations. The exchanges I observed on Facebook, by contrast, are decentralized and appear to have no organizational connection to any particular group. Although the images and memes that circulate may nor may not be produced directly by the Taliban, they are circulated independently by Facebook users, and this appears to generate an online culture that assumes the medium belongs to no one and everyone simultaneously.

Just as it was difficult to get a sense of how and by whom the magazines were being read and their images viewed, Facebook presents its own problems of interpretation. With the exception of the original Taliban supporter and Facebook user who agreed to answer my interview questions, I have no information about the true identities of the people who are circulating these materials among themselves. I have the names attached to their accounts, but I have no evidence that they are real names and, in fact, assume that, with the exception of the accounts of well-known Taliban leaders, these publicly accessible accounts all use pseudonyms. To try to make sense of these posts and to organize the mass of materials I happened upon, I decided to focus on collecting as many posts as possible over a two-week span during the summer of 2014, using a screen-grab application to preserve images of the posts as they appeared. My collection includes roughly 260 Facebook posts by half a dozen individuals.[12]

In the summer of 2015, as I was completing the first draft of this book, I discovered that all the pages I had visited a year earlier had either been deleted or had had their privacy settings reset so that I could no longer access them. I do not know why. Perhaps word had seeped out that an American researcher was sniffing about, or perhaps the posters had become cautious in the wake of Edward Snowden's revelations about U.S. government surveillance of the Internet. In any case, I can now only provide some sense of what I originally found. I do so first through an overview of the tastes and preferences revealed by two users—one identified male and one identified female—in their choices as to what to post and repost on their Facebook pages. I then consider the effect of Facebook on the Taliban cause, showing how it serves their immediate purposes but also introduces potentially dramatic changes in the traditional Afghan culture that Taliban hold to and respect as emblematic of their own pure form of Islam.[13]

On the Internet, images and memes circulate in a limitless stream. Facebook users are exposed to only some small quantity of this material— what they see being largely determined by their past viewing choices—and they react to and comment on this material according to their own interests, beliefs, sensibility, sense of humor, and sense of the world. Although some of the users I studied might be producing their own material, I assume that most are selecting a small percentage of what they find on the Internet as of sufficient interest to take the time and trouble to repost, in the process identifying themselves with and by it.

Most of the material takes the form of photographs, poems, news stories, and screen grabs from websites and television broadcasts, but there are also a large number of memes that use computer graphic software to design assemblages of photos, texts, cartoons, fonts, and special effects that express a declaration of principle, satirize opinions they disapprove of, or present aphorisms or advice on how to live a decent Muslim life. Noticeably absent are the normal flotsam and jetsam of Westerners' Internet surfing. No cute babies or funny pets. No vacation photos shot in front of famous monuments. No images of movie or sports stars. No celebrities in general, although—as I argue later in the chapter—the martyrs whose photos are ubiquitous on Talifan posts constitute celebrities of a sort.

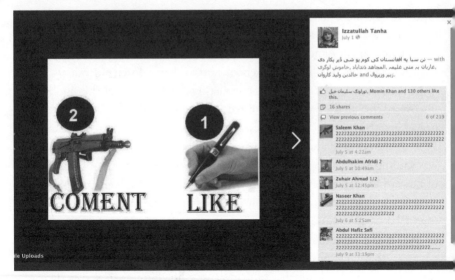

FIGURE 24. Facebook meme contrasting a machine gun and a pen.

One user I followed posted memes that juxtaposed two contrasting symbols: in one case, the Taliban (Islamic Emirate) flag and the Afghan national flag; in another, a machine gun and a pen (figure 24). He would ask people to vote for the one they preferred, and many responded to his prompting. (For the two flags, there were 679 votes in all, and—not surprisingly—the white flag of the Islamic Emirate was the hands-down choice for all but a handful of anti-Taliban Facebook users who trolled these pages.)

Many users also posted poems, though it was usually unclear whether these were their own compositions or had been taken from someone else. Here is a typical example, followed by comments from readers, the final one of which implies that the poem was lifted, with mistakes, from another source. The verse consciously or unconsciously echoes the storyline of Layla and Majnun, the poet assuming the role of the lovelorn Majnun while the unnamed Martyr is cast as the absent Beloved:

Martyr, I am crying and looking for you.
    With long hair, I am begging to find you.
I am looking for you in these mountains.
    I am looking for you on the battlefield.
Martyr, I seek you from God.
    Martyrdom, I seek you from God.

K: Mashallah, Mashallah, Mashallah.

F: Very pretty.

Da Afghanistan Islamic Emirate: Good

B: Mashallah, very pretty. Live long, Maftoon.

I: Habib, the second verse in the poem is wrong.

The subject matter of nonpoetic posts can be divided into the following categories: international affairs, internal Afghan affairs, warfare, civilian casualties, and martyrdom. By "international affairs," I mean events outside Afghanistan, but these posts are exclusively concerned with other places in the Muslim world, most often Iraq and Israel/Palestine. I was monitoring these posts as the Islamic State movement was becoming increasingly active and visible in Iraq, and a number of the posters comment on this development, but no one shows any interest in other parts of the world or other issues, such as climate change or Russian aggression in Ukraine. Posts on Afghan affairs mostly concern Afghan politics, and since my research overlapped with controversies related to the Afghan presidential race between Ashraf Ghani and Abdullah Abdullah, this topic gets considerable notice and criticism, in the forms of both satire and outright attacks on the candidates, election officials, and voters.

Warfare usually involves grisly images—mostly screen grabs—of American military vehicles that have been destroyed by roadside bombs and of U.S. soldiers, some lying near their destroyed vehicles, others photographed in rehabilitation centers getting fitted for prosthetic limbs. Civilian casualties usually involve images of children wounded or killed. The responsible parties are never identified, the unspoken assumption being that the casualties are victims of American aggression. Martyrdom material, which is by far the largest category, includes portraits of martyrs: some individual photographs taken before their deaths, some shots of their corpses, and some in pairs, often gazing at one another or clasped in what strongly suggests a romantic embrace (figure 25). Before discussing this material, I first profile Ghazi and Abida, the two Facebook users whose posts I followed.

Ghazi

Ghazi is the user with whom I was put in touch by my contact in Kabul. He is the only Facebook user about whom I have personal information from a

FIGURE 25. Facebook photograph, presumably showing a martyr being embraced by a friend.

source other than his own Facebook posts. I was able to contact him indirectly and submit questions that my contact asked on my behalf, though Ghazi refused to answer some of them and complained that others were "stupid" or "insulting." I know that he is a Pakhtun from Logar Province, that he "belongs to" the Nasiri tribe, and that his father is a doctor, though he himself only attended madrasa. This might have been because of the war—he was born in Pakistan—but it also might have been because, as he indirectly suggested, he was not a serious student and from a young age had a reputation for getting into trouble and fighting with other kids. He admitted that he was often beaten by older boys in the madrasa but also noted that he was treated even worse in his village.

Ghazi is not married, though he says that his family has sufficient funds to allow him to get engaged if he wanted to. He is single by choice because his first priority is "the freedom and peace of the country." Although he was vague in answering questions about his relationship with the Taliban, Ghazi admitted to receiving training as a suicide bomber in the town of Miranshah in North Waziristan. He did not say which organization trained him, but, because some of his Facebook posts include the logo of Jund ul Haqqani (what Western commentators refer to as the Haqqani Network) and he has posted photos of the founder of the organization, Maulavi Jalaluddin Haqqani, and his son Badruddin, both of whom had long been based in Miranshah, I assume that he is associated with this allied branch of the Taliban movement. Ghazi was evasive as to what sort of training he received in Miranshah; however, when asked if people who go on suicide missions follow particular rituals, he answered simply that "we pray and say goodbye to each other."

When asked why people volunteer for suicide missions, he replied that suicide attacks were the only response to the aerial bombardments inflicted by the Americans. In response to a question about civilian casualties that result from suicide attacks, Ghazi replied that "fewer people are killed from our attacks than from the bombardments." When asked how he pictured Paradise, he avoided a direct reply: "I don't need to picture it. It has all been explained in the Qur'an, and you can refer to the Qur'an yourself." When pressed if he thought that houris were waiting for him, he bluntly answered that the question was "stupid" and that I should read the Qur'an and hadith.

Because I knew his Facebook name was a pseudonym, I asked him why he had chosen it. He replied that he did not want his own name to appear in the media (or in my book) and that his father had already gotten angry with him for using his real name on his first Facebook account and posting pro-Taliban messages and images "because his job could be at risk and I could get arrested." Ghazi was the name of a Talib in his area who was "very sincere, brave and honest, and he served Islam and sacrificed his life fighting the enemy." Ghazi also admitted keeping two accounts, the public account I accessed and a second, private account that he uses to communicate with friends.[14] When I asked him why he posted on Facebook, he said that some Taliban use Facebook because it provides a vehicle for "doing *dawat* [summoning people to Islam] and at the same time doing jihad." In addition to Facebook, he told me, they use a variety of other social media platforms, including Twitter and Google+.

Of the dozen posters I followed, Ghazi's page had the most varied and wide-ranging content, which was fairly evenly distributed across my subject categories. However, he displayed a greater interest than other users in what was going on in other parts of the world, especially Iraq, whose Shia prime minister, Nouri al-Maliki, came in for particular abuse in his posts. Ghazi was also clearly paying attention to the early activities of the Islamic State, as he included a number of screen shots from Arab television channels (identifiable by their logos at the bottom right corner), but he didn't say whether he supported them. There were also a large number (twenty-four) of photographs of military operations—mostly explosions and destroyed American vehicles, and thirteen images of American soldiers dealing with lost limbs and other traumatic injuries—including several in which former president George W. Bush is shown visiting soldiers at a rehabilitation center. There was an equally large number of photographs of dead and injured children, the horror of the latter category implicitly justifying the suffering of the former.

The protracted crisis precipitated by the 2014 Afghan election was still going on, and Ghazi reposted many photographs and memes that criticized the two principal candidates, Ghani and Abdullah. One shot of President Ghani, who ended up winning the election, showed him dressed in a Hawaiian shirt and white slacks, cutting a long baguette in half while making a sandwich. Ghazi included no caption, but the principle at work here seemed to be a general one—that people with no power take pleasure in showing people with power in situations in which their dignity has been compromised. Real leaders, the message suggests, do not putter round the kitchen, and Ghani's indiscretion is compounded by his wearing clothing that illustrates his close ties to the Americans, in whose country he spent a large part of his adult life.

All of the users put thought into the photographs they used in their profiles. All were carefully posed, and some changed their profile photo frequently. The most distinctive profile photo, however, belonged to Ghazi, who had used graphics software to create a highly stylized and menacing image—his face obscured by a headscarf, his hands iridescent blue: one in front of his face, the other holding an AK-47 (figure 26). The impression is of a character from a video game or a movie poster. His pride in the result was indicated by his asking a friend how he liked the image. Glory, even if achieved only through the digital manipulation of images, seemed very much on his mind.

Bin Laden appeared in several of Ghazi's memes and photographs. Although Ghazi himself commented in Pashto, one of the memes he reposted took the form of photographs of "Sheikh Osama Bin Laden" and quotes him, in English, as saying, "The world has been split into 2 camps, the camp of Islam (Belief), and the camp of Kufr (Disbelief)." The person most often pictured in Ghazi's posts is Badruddin Haqqani. One of the photos shows him with his arm around an emaciated and nervously smiling Bowe Bergdahl, the U.S. soldier captured by the Taliban in June 2009 and released amid much controversy in May 2014 (shortly before I started monitoring Ghazi's Facebook posts).[15] Other photos of Badruddin have the phrase "Lover of the

FIGURE 26. "Ghazi" Facebook profile photograph.

Maidens of Paradise" (*ashuq ul hoor*) superimposed on them. Although I suspect that Ghazi was trained by the Haqqani Network, he did not tell me if he ever met the Haqqani leader himself, but it seems evident that he was the Taliban leader whom Ghazi most admired.[16]

Abida

Even though the majority of Facebook users worldwide are women, Abida is the one and only woman I encountered during my search for Talifans on Facebook. Her presence in this community, readily commenting on other people's posts and receiving comments in turn, surprised me. I have more to say about the interactions of men and women on Facebook in the next section. Here I describe without comment some features of Abida's Facebook presence. Her profile photograph shows the top half of her body, her head wrapped in a bright white, Saudi-style scarf and kerchief that obscure all but her eyes (figure 27). She wears black clothing and black gloves that contrast with her white headgear, and she poses with her right hand reaching up, as though to adjust her veil, as Western women in photographs

بی بی شیرینه
July 9

Share

301 people like this.

View 42 more comments

Abuzar Afridi masha allah,,,,bi bi sheerena
July 10 at 10:14am · 2

Md Sagor masallah a rokom akta bou amar dorkar.
July 10 at 12:31pm · 1

Md Sagor masallah a rokom akta bou amar dorkar.
July 10 at 12:31pm · 1

Kamran Butt masallah
July 10 at 1:58pm

FIGURE 27. "Abida" Facebook profile photograph.

often pose with a hand raised to brush hair out of their eyes. One of her previous profile photos, which she had kept in her Facebook photo folder, was even more striking: it was shot up close to show only her head, with her eyes, ornamented with eyeliner and eye shadow, looking away from the camera. Her face is otherwise covered by a black chador, with the Islamic creed printed in white letters on a band around her forehead. Unlike the male posters, Abida listed a number of her favorite books, music, and movies in her profile. The choices were all Islamic in orientation, but the fact that they were there at all set Abida apart.

Abida provided no information as to her schooling, though it was clear from her written Pashto that she was educated.[17] She gave Kabul as her place of residence and, like many of her male counterparts, gave her place of employment as the sangar (trench). In the summer of 2014, she had 4,925 Facebook friends. Most of these friends appeared to be male, a fact that reflects how dramatically platforms like Facebook expand the range of social contacts available to Afghan women. The photos Abida posted display the usual combination of religious propaganda, enemy treachery, child victims, and martyrs. She also included a widely circulated photograph of Abu Bakr al-Baghdadi giving his first sermon after announcing himself as the leader of the Islamic State, reflecting her early awareness of and interest in political events outside Afghanistan.

I was most interested in observing in what ways, if any, Abida was distinguishable from her male counterparts, or, to put it in more sociological terms, whether she presented a different sort of "mask" from the male posters. Certain features of Abida's self-presentation did appear different from those of male users. One was that Abida, unlike the other users, posted news reports from various battlefronts in Afghanistan. I got the impression that she was doing so, in effect, to make herself useful and thereby justify her presence in this overwhelmingly male social environment. She was also unusual in assuming the role of moral advisor on personal matters—never on major doctrinal or political issues, but on more intimate matters of decorum and appropriate action in familial settings. For example, the period of my Facebook research coincided with Ramadan, the Muslim holy month of fasting. Abida offered advice on when to serve the daily fast-breaking *iftar* meal and proverbs and advice on appropriate conduct during Ramadan. Another post contained the adage "A woman's original adornment is her modesty," a sentiment to which a number of males added their strong endorsement.

The most telling way in which Abida identified as female was in her posting of landais, a verse form associated with women. Other users posted poems, but none posted landais, which typically employ the female voice and variously encourage males to bravery or threaten them with dishonor if they fail to live up to society's expectations. In the landais Abida uploaded, the ethos of honor overlapped with and reinforced the ethos of jihad:

> What pleasure to offer your head [as a sacrifice],
>> What pleasure to walk the black mountains.
> Burn your red sheets and pillows,
>> What pleasure to lay your head on rough stone.

> I will carry the rocket on my shoulder, lover, you carry the ammunition.
>> There is a war in Helmand, there is grief for the *arbaki*.[18]
> Go, go, go, lover, there is a war in Helmand, the people are celebrating,
>> Go, go, go, lover, there is a war in Helmand.

Landai are famously provocative—not only in the sense of urging men to acts of honor but also in giving women a voice, both as arbiters of honor (no male disgrace being worse than being accused of cowardice by a woman) and as sexual beings (the implication being that it is men of honor alone who excite the admiration and desire of women).

FIGURE 28. Facebook photograph of a woman aiming an AK-47.

Unlike the male users, Abida also posted a number of photographs of women, her choices reflecting normative expectations of female modesty. All of the women portrayed wore Saudi-style clothing rather than Afghan dress. Women who adopt this style signal that they are inspired in their choice of dress by religious teachings rather than social custom. No woman in any of Abida's photos is seen in the burqa typically worn by conservative Afghan women, nor does any wear the long black chador often favored by educated women. Interestingly, several of the posted photographs showed women holding weapons, suggesting their readiness not simply to support fighters but also to assume a direct combat role. One of the posted photos portrayed a woman preparing ammunition for firing, but others showed women carrying and aiming weapons, including one photo of women whose faces were covered but who wore camouflage uniforms and carried rocket-propelled grenade launchers, and a second photo that presented a fully covered woman aiming an AK-47 over a wall in an urban setting that looks more like Iraq than Afghanistan (figure 28).

Although Facebook allows the coexistence of a virtual infinity of groups, interests, and intentions, the platform itself imposes a "structure of conjuncture" on its users. Given that it was designed in the United States by Americans and originally for Americans—in fact, for a subset of American students attending elite colleges and universities—the cultural expectations that were designed into it were those that Americans bring to social encounters, expectations that appear to them as universal but are not. Thus Facebook assumes that its users will have lots of friends and that they will want very much to have more. It also assumes that people have friends of both genders and that they inherently want to share information about themselves (if not with the whole world, then with two or three thousand of their closest friends) and that other people are so interested in learning this information that they do not mind receiving updates on their friends each and every day. Given these two assumptions, Facebook facilitates sharing personal information among those friends as a way of ensuring its own indispensability.

Facebook also is very much about faces and the visibility of faces. It was, after all, originated by male college students as a way to rate the attractiveness of their female classmates and only later became something more expansive and less sexist. But the interest in faces is still very much embedded in the platform. If you were somehow able to remove from all the Facebook pages in the world all the photographs that focus on people's faces, only a small percentage, I imagine, would remain, and many of those would be the faces of people's pets.

Here I consider the structure of the conjuncture between Facebook as a social space, with all its embedded American cultural assumptions, and the Afghans whose Facebook posts I have been considering, who seemingly would like nothing better than to see the demise of the American society that gave rise to Facebook. Further, I consider how Facebook itself changes the concepts of sacrifice and martyrdom that bring this group of users together. In doing so, I focus on two key features associated with and essential to Facebook: the underlying concept of *face* on which Facebook is based, and the functions associated with the concept of *friend* (friending, sending a friend request, liking, sharing, etc.)

Face

In Afghanistan, as in many other societies in which notions of honor are paramount, the word *face* (*makh*) is synonymous with *reputation* (*makh na lari* means "to lose face"). In America, to lose face means to suffer embarrassment and maybe even a loss of respect, but it does not imply that the damage is life altering. When an Afghan loses face, it is a far more serious matter. Enmities that bring about acts of violence begin because someone loses face. Such people may feel that it is better to abandon their homes than to stay in the community and endure the shame.

Afghans are not only much more concerned than Americans with a metaphorical loss of face but also much more careful about exposing their physical faces, and this difference is reflected in the way the two cultures deal with photographs. In America, photographs index status. The people with the highest status are photographed the most, and they have their photographs circulated in the greatest numbers to the widest circle of other people. These people—whom we can call celebrities, even if they also have some other occupation, like movie star or politician—use platforms and apps like Twitter and Instagram in order to exert some control over how and when they are photographed and to attempt to ensure that photographs show them the way they want to be shown.

Not to be photographed (or to be photographed only by those you know) is, conversely, the index of lack of status—effectively, of not existing. To be anyone in American society, you must be visible, and your visibility must be demonstrated through photographs. Seclusion as embraced by Greta Garbo or J. D. Salinger might serve in some cases to increase mystery and public interest (whether desired or not), but, for the rest of us, visibility is essential to recognition, and recognition is key to being alive in our self- and selfie-obsessed culture.

Although that culture has exerted a strong influence on other cultures around the globe, it has not necessarily made the face as central a cultural signifier as it is in the United States. In many cultures, the face is indeed a central concern, but that concern is managed not by making the face attractive and widely available for viewing but by restricting access to it. For such cultures, the advent of the camera, as well as the expansion of photography into the domain of the everyday through the mobile phone, has created as much ambiguity and uncertainty as excitement.

When I first arrived in Kabul, wooden box cameras (in which the photograph was developed inside the camera while the subject waited to receive the little black-and-white, blurry image that magically emerged) were still common. It was mostly the elite who could afford to purchase their own cameras and film, take snapshots, and get their film processed (which originally required sending the film abroad). Most people had their photos taken only to obtain a head shot for government documents or maybe to commemorate getting married, in which case the man (but rarely the woman) would go to a photo studio and have a portrait taken, perhaps holding a gun or otherwise looking fierce and manly.[19] Women were rarely photographed: the very idea of making such an image that could be viewed by outsiders was inherently dangerous and anxiety provoking. Consequently, the requirement of the government for visual documentation inevitably clashed with the personal desire for cover and protection.

When the Taliban came to power, Mullah Omar famously showed an aversion to being photographed. This was not unusual or necessarily a sign of secretiveness. Rather, he was displaying the belief common to Afghan villagers that being photographed made you more exposed and vulnerable. This belief is not the fear of witchcraft or of having your soul taken away that has sometimes been attributed to "primitive people" resistant to photography. It is, rather, the attitude of people who are wary of the intentions of outsiders, especially those associated with the state, which was the entity most responsible for disseminating photography in Afghanistan.

Afghan concerns over visibility have not diminished. The general insecurity that haunts the country leads most people to keep as invisible as possible to stay out of harm's way. However, some attitudes toward visibility have changed, especially among younger Afghans, and the fact that the Taliban now welcome and disseminate at least certain kinds of photographs is one marker of that change. More generally, the advent of the cell phone, with its built-in camera, has made taking photos easier and eliminated the fatal time lapse and expense of film cameras and the requirement that images taken by the user be handled by a third party. It has also put the process of distributing images directly into hands of those who take them and enabled much wider dissemination. By and large, the few printed photographs people might have had were kept safely tucked away and rarely shown. Images of women were not displayed except to immediate family members.

Facebook has been central to redefining the cultural significance of the human face and of visibility more generally. Abida's Facebook presence captures this change as well as the contradictions it introduces. On the one hand, by presenting herself in Saudi dress in her profile photo, she seems to be seeking greater invisibility. Unlike the burqa, traditional Saudi women's dress covers even the hands and the ankles. On the other hand, Saudi dress is in one respect actually more revealing than the burqa because it exposes the wearer's eyes, which the burqa conceals behind a mesh barrier. For Afghan men as for many others, there is nothing more sexually alluring in a woman than just the sort of almond-shaped and kohl-shadowed eyes Abida's profile photo displays.

More important, though, is the fact that Abida has chosen to make herself visible on Facebook. She has posed for these photos and uploaded them herself—the key term here being *herself*. She is the agent of her own visibility. Beyond that, Abida has chosen to upload images of other women, also dressed in Saudi-style clothing. These images show us that women are exercising the agency to choose their mode of presentation. And some of the women are shown with weapons, a symbol of agency par excellence. They are not only posing: they seem ready, willing, and able to use those weapons. The same message of female agency is contained in the landai poems Abida has posted, especially the verse representing the female poet carrying a rocket on her shoulder. Thus, although the female faces of pro-Taliban Facebook users are not made visible, Facebook has nevertheless enabled them to express their desire for and intention to assume ever-greater forms of agency in their personal and political lives.

Our immediate assumption when we hear of women taking on the role of suicide bomber is probably to assume coercion or brainwashing as the cause, but Abida's example might in fact indicate that how we view agency has to be defined more broadly than we tend to understand it. It might very well be that a woman who secretes a bomb beneath her burqa and blows herself up at the gate of a police station has been forced into this position by male relatives, but that is not necessarily the case. We can, for example, imagine Abida putting on a burqa, a mode of dress she otherwise would seem to disdain, in order to fulfill a role that her posts indicate she might be destined for. In doing so, she would be demonstrating in her actions that agency is tied neither to the visibility of the face nor the identity of the subject. The true believer knows that the only judgment that matters in the end is not the judgments that men and women daily make about the appearance of people's faces and physiques. It is, rather, the judgment God will make on the last day, when the dead rise from their graves and face their Maker, or, in the case of martyrs, immediately after their deaths.

In the Western media, and probably on Facebook as well, the most commonly seen faces are those of beautiful women and celebrities. On the Talifan Facebook pages I observed, the most commonly displayed faces were those of the dead. Some of the martyr photos were taken before the martyrs' deaths,

FIGURE 29. Facebook photograph of a dead martyr.

but many are after-death shots. Some of the dead martyrs' faces seem to have had makeup applied; in all cases, the aim appears to have been to make the face appear peaceful and undamaged (figure 29). In contrast, for example, to Catholic martyr iconography, which usually emphasizes the agony suffered by the saint—the instruments of torture often being included in the image as the primary means of distinguishing one martyr from another—the images of jihadi martyrs' faces on Facebook suggest the satisfaction they have discovered on the other side of death. Earlier in this book, I discussed Abdullah 'Azzam's book of martyr miracles, many of which center on the incorruptibility of the martyr's body and the sense of satisfaction and tranquility that is said to radiate from it. These photos make those stories come alive. Maybe more to the point, they separate the martyr from the violence of the act he committed, leaving behind only images that represent the act as clean and purifying.[20]

The fact is, however, that suicide bombings (like drone strikes) dismember the attacker's body, leaving behind only scattered body parts and shredded flesh that are difficult to distinguish from those of the attacker's victims, much less bury. Those realities are not what believers want to see on the Web.

Better the image of young Hayatullah Mehsud, the boy in the video dressed in his finest clothing, or most any of the other close-up photos of the undamaged, peaceful faces of martyrs who are all but nameless and story-less as they leave this world. In the tribal world discussed at the beginning of this book, a hero's immortality is vested in the stories of his exploits that survive him. Facebook creates a parallel universe of its own, one in which images matter more than stories, and images never die but continue circulating, image on top of image, pixilated perhaps but otherwise incorruptible so long as the electric power holds out.

In looking at the faces of martyrs in the photos posted on Facebook, I am reminded of Bernini's famous sculpture of the ecstasy of Saint Teresa that shows her in a state of divine bliss, the model for which one can only assume to have been sexual orgasm. Like Bernini, martyr photographers seek to represent the moment of human apprehension of the divine, but they have far more limited resources available for creating a work of art than Bernini had. In the first place, the photographs require the simultaneous availability of camera and a reasonably intact body, or at least a face. The photographer can put a cap on the martyr's head. He can tie a cloth around the chin to keep the mouth closed. He can put rouge on the cheeks and encircle the face with flowers. But, ultimately, the photographer has the same problem as the mortician in preparing a body for viewing, and fewer tools.

The results consequently tend to fall short of conveying ecstatic transport but do convey a sense of peace. For conveying intense emotional effects, video offers more scope. In Hayatullah Mehsud's video, the moment of the blast is shown through a telephoto lens as a flash of red light, after which the video immediately cuts to a photo of the martyr superimposed on a radiant blue sky, illuminated by shafts of sunlight (figure 30). In the background, the text of a Qur'anic *surah* scrolls up toward heaven as a muezzin intones the words. This is not the single moment of ecstasy that Bernini captured in his sculpture, but it combines the same elements: the shafts of light, the face of the saint, and the symbols signaling that the moment is to be understood in religious terms.

Bernini's *Ecstasy of Saint Teresa* is a singularity, placed within a completely realized theatrical environment intended for cultic veneration. The worshippers do not imagine themselves experiencing what Saint Teresa experienced or aspire to her level of divine grace. Instead, they seek to worship her and thereby to gain her intervention on their behalf. The martyr photos and videos are different. Even though they are individually identified, their value is

FIGURE 30. Hayatullah Mehsud ascending to Paradise after his sacrifice. From martyrdom video, 2009.

in their multiplicity and not their uniqueness. Their subjects are not to be worshipped or asked for intercession, either of which would be a sin in Islam (or at least in the Salafi and Wahhabi variants).[21] The martyrs are also not saints: traditionally, Muslim saints are people who, through years of devoted study, spiritual exercise, and isolation from society have become "friends" of God. The martyrs, by contrast, achieved their status through a single act of devotion, irrespective of what they did or did not do before. Unlike Catholic or Sufi saints, martyrs are primarily objects of emulation, not veneration. What matters is not their transhistorical singularity but the fact that they have taken their places in a line of martyrs, a caravan if you will, extending back to the time of the Companions and followers of the Prophet and forward into the future, when all bodies will rise to account for the consequences of the actions they performed in life.

More than saints (or heroes), martyrs resemble celebrities—the transient, "known for being known" sort of celebrities that have proliferated in recent years. Our best guide for translating the lessons of celebrity to the world of martyrs is Andy Warhol, who predicted that "in the future everyone will be world-famous for fifteen minutes." Though he is perhaps best known for his representations of Campbell's soup cans, Warhol was as fascinated by martyrdom as he was by consumer culture, perhaps because he spent hours as a boy staring at the iconostasis of martyred saints in his local Orthodox church in Pittsburgh. One aspect of Warhol's genius was in recognizing in subjects like Marilyn Monroe and Jackie Kennedy iconic representations of the ways in which private grief and public exposure are produced for mass consumption.[22] Consumer culture had changed art and artists, as it had every other aspect of contemporary life. Rather than bemoan that fact, Warhol embodied and embraced it, focusing on the dynamics of celebrity as a significant and visually potent realm of consumer culture. Above all, Warhol understood that the artist was part of the larger culture of mass production and consumption and that celebrity had to be understood in the aggregate rather than the individual instance, in repetition rather than uniqueness, in seriality rather than singularity. All of these lessons apply as well to martyrdom as a form of celebrity culture today.

In the early days of the jihad in Afghanistan, the martyr was represented as a romantic figure, unique and semi-divine. Thirty-plus years later, martyrs have become commonplace, and their mystique derives not from their uniqueness but from their multiplicity. In this context, they have less in common with Bernini's representation of Saint Teresa than with Warhol's many Marilyns, whose enigmatic half smile, beneath the wash of garish color Warhol has applied like mortician's rouge, evokes not only the false promise of glamour and fame but also a premonition of her early death. It is the photograph's ability to capture the interplay of life and death that fascinated Warhol, to look back in time for the foreshadowing of what we later come to experience and know. Something similar is going on with the "smiling martyr" photographs on Facebook and similarly inspired videos on YouTube, both of which offer evidence to those who want to see and believe for what happens after life ends.[23]

Friends

Friendship is the social linchpin of Facebook. The understanding that underlies the Facebook phenomenon is not only that people value their friends but also that they want as many of them as possible, and they want to share with their friends as many details of their lives as they can manage through frequent posts and status updates. The friends who view the photos and keep up with their friends' activities are expected in turn to communicate their care and commitment to their friends by liking, sharing, and commenting on the images and personal information their friends provide. All of these are new responsibilities now associated with friendship that did not exist in the past, and, in creating these new expectations, Facebook has transformed the dynamics of friendship in ways we probably do not fully realize. This being the case, we must consider how much more dramatic and far-reaching might be the implications of Facebook when transplanted to other cultures, which have their own established friendship ideals and sometimes conflicting expectations related to other social matrices, most importantly kinship and religion.

The early poetry of martyrdom reflects the importance of friendship both in war and in Afghan society more generally. Although the poems are formulaic in many way, they nevertheless reveal the importance of emotional ties and personal loyalty between friends. This dimension of the Afghan conflict was always missing from the analyses I was reading and my own early attempts to analyze what I was seeing. As I thought more about the founding of the Muslim Youth Organization, however, and looked back over my interviews with early members, I began to appreciate the importance of friendship in forging the ties on which the party depended for both its expansion and its security. The Muslim Youth Organization—the precursor to the Islamist parties that rose to prominence in Peshawar in the 1980s—depended on personal contact for recruiting potential members and for the labor of copying the pamphlets that new members would distribute to others they thought might be sympathetic to the party message. These individuals then formed five-person cells, which were kept intentionally small and intimate to reduce the possibility of infiltration.

By sharing not only pamphlets but also secrets and risks, the early party members forged the sort of enduring friendships that can only be formed in youth and only in the heat of shared danger and adventure. Ideology and submission to the party regimen and structure thus presupposed friendship among party members. The martyrs who were pictured on the covers and in the lead pages of the Peshawar martyr magazines were likewise not just party members but friends as well. Although I have emphasized the instrumental reasons why the party foregrounded these student martyrs over the mujahidin, for some of the more experienced members of Hizb-i Islami and Jamiat-i Islami in Peshawar—those who began their careers in Afghanistan before their immigration to Pakistan—these fallen heroes of jihad were also the friends of their youth, with whom they shared the responsibility and the exhilaration of building an organization and making history.

FIGURE 31. Facebook meme comparing popularity of Facebook with the Qur'an.

With Facebook, the growth and expansion of the movement—particularly into the uncharted waters of middle-class and elite society—is now based on individual, interpersonal relationships, much as it was in its earliest days. With their rhizomic, decentered mode of communication, Facebook and other social media platforms generally allow individual users to select the people with whom they have contact and to choose what material to share and how to respond to what is shared with them. Militants and sympathizers no longer need to pass pamphlets from hand to hand as they did in the 1970s. Nor do they depend on a central party command to tell them what to share or with whom. Rather, they pick and choose from myriad options that they come across on the websites that interest them and that support the causes and beliefs they espouse.

The old way of communicating reinforced the central doctrine of submission. In the domain of the new "digital dawat," submission is ensured not through the dictates of any central command but through online peer pressure. The central Taliban authority sends out its own messages, photos, videos, and songs and controls its own social media presence, but it cannot dictate who will repost or create links to the materials it provides. This creates more freedom and autonomy for individual Facebook users, but they know that their online friends will not hesitate to criticize them should they post material that is thought to be un-Islamic or detrimental to the cause the Taliban espouse (figure 31).

Social media platforms have also changed the gendered nature of traditional friendships. When I first came across Abida's Facebook page, I found a notice that Abida was now "friends with" Ibrahim Achekzai (another pseudonym, one presumes). Ibrahim's photograph showed him to be a glowering, middle-aged man with a long beard, turban, and dark glasses. Yet if one Afghan were to tell another in public that Abida was "friends" with Ibrahim, the implication would be that they were engaged in an illicit affair, and both of them would be liable to summary execution, whether or not they had ever had sex. On Facebook, however, friendship is expanded but also neutered and devalued. Facebook users can become friends with any other users with whom they share an interest.

I doubt very much that, in real life, Abida has anywhere close to the 4,925 friends she lists on Facebook. She may have only a handful of female friends outside her own family, friends she rarely sees because of the constraints on movement for young women. Assuming that she is unmarried, Abida's male friends are likely confined to her brothers and those cousins who are not potential marriage partners because they are too young, too old, or already married to one of her close kin. In other words, though Abida composes (or reposts) verse in which she imagines herself in the mountains pursuing jihad with her lover, in all likelihood she is either stealing time on an office computer to visit her Facebook page or she is from an elite family that has its own computer and Internet access. Assuming Abida to be the virtuous young Muslim woman she presents herself to be, she would have precisely zero real-life male friends outside her family.

So what does it mean that Abida is now Facebook friends with Ibrahim Achekzai? Facebook provides only one possible mode of friendship. There are no separate, more nuanced categories for "acquaintance," "platonic friend," "correspondent," or "fellow Muslim with whom I agree on most issues." There is just the one category of friend, so you are either that or nothing, or a lurker like me, observing someone's digital life from the margins (in the process mashing together traditional participant-observation, celebrity voyeurism, and panoptic surveillance).

Like everyone else who tries to make sense of social media while being immersed in it, all I can really do is to point to the very interesting domain of Afghan male-female relationships and to wonder aloud how they are being reshaped by a technology that allows this strange melding of public and private realms, at once detached and intimate.[24] And there are other questions, some more directly pertinent to the subject of this book, including whether

Abida's contact with a world of virtual men makes her imagine her own capabilities and real-world choices differently, especially with regard to martyrdom and sacrifice.

Beyond gender relations, there are other issues related to how friendship on Facebook affects jihad and, specifically, the machinery of sacrifice—particularly, how Facebook friendship reinforces social and ideological conformity. Like anyone who has spent time living and working in Afghanistan or among Afghans, I have spent long hours in conversation over tea. As much as anyone, Afghans enjoy banter. Conversations are long and lively, involving harangues and jokes. Contrary opinions are expressed. But always, or almost always, the dialogue is kept within bounds of civility. It usually takes place in the guestroom in someone's house. The guests demonstrate their respect for their host by keeping their words in check. But what happens on the Internet when there is no physical space of conversation, no eye contact, no body language, no tea?

In my experience, communication changes in dramatic ways. The civility at the heart of all Afghan rituals of hospitality tends to split into two kinds of discourse on the Internet. One is the hostile, obscenity-strewn, back-and-forth rants that can break out between people of opposite opinions who share an email list or a comment space; the other kind is the too-strict conformity and unanimity of the type I found among the Talifans, who seem eager to best each other in the degree of their piety and devotion to the cause. The conversation, in other words, divides into the two camps of extreme incivility toward those with whom one disagrees and extreme conformity among those with whom one agrees, with civility itself—defined here as the open expression of different views, wherein exists the possibility of compromise and convergence—an abandoned space in the middle.

This development seems not altogether coincidental or accidental. To the contrary, it seems built into Facebook and other social media platforms by the tools they provide and the algorithms they employ. Central to this dynamic are Facebook's Like and Share buttons, introduced in 2010. In 2013, their developer commented that these buttons are pushed over 22 billion times daily on more than 7.5 million websites. Clicking buttons, as we have all come to realize, has implications. If, at some point, you search Google for children's furniture, you will later find that the sidebar ads on every website you visit feature merchandise targeted at parents of young children. In the case of Facebook, the Like algorithm, as one commentator observes, has "two goals: to increase the broader visibility of promising items in the Newsfeed and to appeal to specific individuals more apt to like particular content."[25]

Facebook's algorithm selects the content of each user's newsfeed based on the preferences indicated through the materials typically posted and the user's apparent satisfaction with those and similar materials, as indicated by use of the Like button. This process also tends to reinforce the ties between friends who like the same things and to increasingly isolate them within their own group of the "like-minded":

> Once an item is noticed and Liked initially, the button targets others who might Like it as well. To do this, the Like mechanism highlights mutual Friends (particularly those with whom it knows a user has an affinity) who have also Liked the item and separates their names out of the aggregate. Seeing trusted ties have Liked something makes it a more appealing action to engage in. . . . On Facebook, socially approved content *is* the most relevant content. Social influence is not extra noise in the system that distorts our preferences but the very barometer for those preferences. In this way, positive endorsements from close individuals can facilitate mass affirmation and even facilitate the viral spread of a particular item.[26]

The Facebook algorithm thus helps ensure that a Talifan reads the same news, sees the same photos, and watches the same videos as other Talifans and that they know that others with the same beliefs are reading, seeing, and watching the same things. Other social media platforms employ similar algorithms to guide users toward congenial material. Of course, no one is limited to these platforms: everyone is free to surf the Web, even venturing into zones that contradict the values of their affinity groups. Most people, however, are unlikely to stray too far from safe, familiar online territory.

One of the Facebook users I followed was a young man I will call Habib. He was an avid poster with a passion for photographs of martyrs, collecting and trading martyr portraits the way I collected and traded baseball cards as a kid. But Facebook adds an additional dimension to this obsession, because with most of the portraits he posted, Habib posted a note encouraging his friends to show their approval with the Like feature. He always received an enthusiastic response:

> I want to see how many people will like and share this picture of this lion! (283 Likes, 14 Shares)

> Is there anyone who would not like this picture? Like it as soon as possible. (976 Likes, 77 Shares)

> Mashallah, he is a real fighter. If you like this man, like this picture. (643 Likes, 113 Shares)

Martyr A.K. Do not forget to like and share. (491 Likes, 36 Shares)

Martyr A.R. is forever asleep. Honor him with at least 100 Likes. (543 Likes, 17 Shares)

Martyr N.A. I want to see how many likes you guys give him. (733 Likes, 33 Shares)

Habib's requests for likes and shares raise the question of whether the repeated liking and sharing of images associated with martyrdom itself becomes an inducement to martyrdom. If you vociferously praise the martyrs' path, are you not honor-bound to follow it yourself? Whatever their ideological position, and no matter how fervently they affirm Muslim features of their identity, these Facebook users are still Afghan, and, in Afghan culture, talk needs to be followed up by action. Failure to live up to your words brands you as *be ghairati* (cowardly) and *be namusi* (dishonorable). These ideals of honor are not just external social pressures; they are internalized. Thus, one wonders to what extent the casual act of pressing the Like button to praise the bravery of others eventually requires a person to step out of the virtual world into the world of real-life martyrs to become the one who is praised.

DAESH AND THE FUTURE OF SACRIFICE

At the same time as radical madrasas continue to recruit and prepare martyrs for eventual deployment to the markets, streets, and assemblies that have become the loci of sacrificial violence, social media has moved martyrdom into a broader virtual world outside the control of traditional institutions. As national boundaries and divisions of culture and language erode, social media is recruiting a greater range of would-be martyrs from many countries who volunteer for missions of their own accord. This new generation is influenced less by religious authorities and more by the emotional pull of well-edited videos that combine the powers of song, image, and testimony. It seems quite probable that would-be martyrs will increasingly come not from the ranks of madrasa students but out of the global society of consumers who are tuning into jihadi websites even when they know little about Islam.

The most striking example of this new stage in the evolution of sacrifice is centered not in Afghanistan but in the transnational propaganda campaign undertaken by the Islamic State, or Daesh, as it is more commonly known in the Islamic world. Daesh began as an al-Qaeda affiliate in Iraq led by

Abu Musab al-Zarqawi, whose own first experience of jihad was in the waning days of the Soviet occupation in Afghanistan. Al-Zarqawi is reported to have had a strained relationship with Bin Laden. There has been much speculation as to the causes of this rift, but one factor was al-Zarqawi's brutality, particularly in his attacks against Shia Muslims in Iraq.[27] It might seem strange that, of the two, the architect of the September 11 attacks was more restrained in his approach to violence, but in a 2005 letter to al-Zarqawi, Bin Laden's deputy, Ayman al-Zawahiri, expressed his distaste for the videos al-Zarqawi had produced that showed him beheading a hostage. In al-Zawahiri's view, presumably shared by Bin Laden, such scenes of violence would inevitably alienate the moderate Muslims whose support they were seeking.[28]

Al-Zawahiri's letter did not dissuade al-Zarqawi or those who took over the leadership of the organization after he was killed in a U.S. air strike in 2006. To the contrary, they refined al-Qaeda's improvised and unrehearsed representation of violence and put it at the center of their organizational identity and elaborate media operation. Thus, where al-Zarqawi's original decapitation video was grainy and poorly produced, Daesh's productions use high-definition cameras and advanced video editing and graphics software. Rather than distribute speeches by its leaders, which has been al-Qaeda's standard operating procedure, Daesh puts its martyrs and fighters at the center of its productions. Al-Zawahiri was concerned that al-Zarqawi's beheading videos would alienate ordinary Muslims who would never find palatable scenes of slaughter, but Daesh's strategy has been to focus not on "the Muslim populace" referred to in al-Zawahiri's letter but on an entirely different audience, many of whom were from Muslim families living in Europe and North America who knew little about Islam and had not previously thought of themselves in religious terms.[29]

Unlike al-Qaeda, which was looking for "a few good men" to train as paramilitaries, Daesh is trying to create a state from scratch. Its goal is to bring into the fold not only young men for combat roles but also young women to service the young men as brides and provide a domestic infrastructure for their new society. To attract this cohort, doctrinal appeals are less important than emotional ones that induce a sense both of familiarity and of adventure. Although Daesh videos show buildings being constructed and crops harvested with modern combines, violence is the core of the group's propaganda strategy, and the media wing of the organization ensures that the violence it depicts meets the technical standards that young people are familiar with and have come to expect from Hollywood action movies and first-person shooter games.

Daesh's media staff uses drones to hover above and film suicide attacks, and it produces footage shot with GoPro cameras mounted on AK-47s to create the immediacy of a video game. Analysis of the beheading videos distributed by Daesh reveals that scenes have been "rehearsed and shot in multiple takes over many hours" and that the film crews demonstrate "professional-caliber attention to lighting, sound and camera positioning."[30] According to one former Daesh cameraman, it is the film crew who supervises executions rather than any legal authority:

> They brought a white board scrawled with Arabic script to serve as an off-camera cue card for the public official charged with reciting the condemned man's alleged crimes. The hooded executioner raised and lowered his sword repeatedly so that crews could catch the blade from multiple angles. . . . The beheading took place only when the camera crew's director said it was time to proceed.[31]

Writing before the rise of Daesh, Faisal Devji noted that al-Qaeda resembled a multinational corporation that did not wish to control territory but rather engaged in "a series of indirect and speculative investments."[32] It was an apt analogy for al-Qaeda's style of jihad. But where Bin Laden's organization could be seen as a franchise operation with little oversight over the actions of its franchisees, Daesh seeks control both of the action of its scattered affiliates and of the territorial base that legitimates its claim to caliphal status. And if it resembles a corporation, it is in the mold of media conglomerates like the Walt Disney Company, which develops its own signature content, distributes that content on a wide variety of social media platforms, invests rigorously to protect its distinctive brand, and pursues its target audience through focused marketing.[33]

At the center of all Daesh media content, as predictable as a spunky hero or heroine and a moral message in a Disney film, is the spectacle of sacrificial violence, represented in both the actions of its own martyrs and the ritual execution of its prisoners. Daesh suicide bombers who speak to the camera before setting off on their missions are earnest and confident. Daesh corpses recovered from the battlefield are arranged in poses that exalt their sacrifice, with blood washed away, the corners of their mouths lifted to create the appearance of a satisfied smile, and their index fingers raised skyward.[34] Executions are presented as ritual affairs, usually with the condemned wear-

FIGURE 32. Execution of an Afghan police officer. Daesh video.

ing Abu Ghraib and Guantanamo–inspired orange jumpsuits and forced to kneel with heads bowed before they are shot or their heads are cut off from behind by masked and uniformed Daesh soldiers who stand at attention until directed to begin their killing.

One video produced by the Afghan branch of Daesh shows masked Daesh fighters standing behind a group of older men who are on their knees with hands bound behind their backs. On cue, the Daesh fighters bend over and begin sawing off the heads of their captives, some of which are then displayed for the camera. The same video shows a captured Afghan police officer, first wearing a bright red woman's dress and a few shots later dressed in an orange jumpsuit. The man is shot in the back of the head while bent over the metal railing of a bridge. His body is then thrown in the river and is shown floating downstream in bloodstained water (figure 32).

These are difficult images to watch, all the more so because the old men have committed no crime. They are elders of their community. Not so long ago, these men might have ritually sacrificed a sheep to make peace among themselves, but today Daesh slaughters men like these as spectacles it can film and distribute online. The policeman in the video is no more guilty of wrongdoing than the elders. Like many others who have joined the government, he probably did so in order to support his family. The humiliation of making him wear a dress, turning his death into a display of degradation, and not affording him the dignity of proper burial seems intended simply to accentuate the horror of what the viewer has witnessed and is likely never to forget.

Never forgetting, it seems, is central to Daesh's media strategy, and in this respect Daesh can be seen as the bastard offspring of the Baathist regime in Iraq, a regime for which many Daesh leaders once worked. Like Daesh, the Baathists specialized in creating horrifying spectacles of violence—in public events and on television—intended to instill what Samir al-Khalil referred to as "a new kind of fear" that would be "etched on the memory" of a populace and render them "unable to 'think' or accumulate experience in dealing with itself" and consequently become "more prey than ever to believing the most fantastic lies."[35]

Saddam Hussein did not inaugurate the Baathist reign of terror in Iraq. It started well before his own rise to power, but he understood better than his predecessors that the violence inflicted by the state needed the illusion of purpose, and he supplied that purpose in the form of a cult of personality around himself. Daesh has not tried to resurrect that cult. To the contrary, Abu Bakr al-Baghdadi, Daesh's leader, has so far stayed in the shadows, putting his martyrs and executioners in the spotlight. This makes sense, because what separates and defines Daesh's spectacles and gives them meaning and purpose is the sacred imprimatur supplied by sacrifice.

The conceit underlying Daesh's violence is that all the scattered acts of sacrifice are preparation for and necessary precondition of the ultimate conflagration that will end history as we know it. Today's small sacrifices serve to divide the world into the two forces of faith and infidelity that will ultimately face one another in the final apocalyptic battle that has been prophesied to occur on the plain of Dabiq in present-day Syria. From the perspective of eschatology, the failure of Saddam's vision was that it was tied to a single individual. The failure of al-Qaeda was to invest its resources in a few spectacular acts of terrorist violence with no follow-up plan of action and no way to respond when the United States marshaled its resources to hunt down the group's leaders.

For its part, Daesh is keeping its eyes on the future. Everything in the present is tied to and in preparation for what will happen next. Theirs is a vision that cannot be refuted, only postponed. In one sense, it is a timeless vision, older than the Qur'an or the Bible, but Daesh has refashioned ancient End-Time prophecy using the technological resources of the contemporary world. Never before has it been possible to project a doctrine of global war instantaneously to a global audience. Never before has there been a global audience so alienated and disconnected from where it actually resides and so willing and eager to reside someplace else. Armageddon is an idea that especially appeals to people insecure in the present and anxious about the future, regardless of their knowledge of the past. Those attracted to Daesh's vision do not seem to care that Daesh's images are staged. Nor do they care whether or not the people who are the victims of Daesh violence are guilty or if they have received fair trials before their sentences were handed down. Like Humam Khalil Abu-Mulal al-Balawi, those who live outside of Daesh's zone of control create for themselves an "echo-chamber" in which they hear and see what reinforces what they already believe, and, when they are physically present in Daesh-controlled areas, they are subject to the enforced acceptance complicity that Daesh's spectacles of violence sustain.[36]

Daesh's retooling of the machinery of sacrifice is both deeply rooted in mythic narratives of sin and redemption and responsive to the contemporary world of social media and global interconnectivity. Daesh stages, films, and distributes myriad small acts of sacrificial violence to transform abstract, ill-formed, and passive faith into practical action and irrevocable commitment on the part of those responsive to its message and vision. Each small sacrifice is an instantiation of Daesh's ultimate vision of a final glorious battle that will lead either to God reigning supreme and unchallenged over a global ummah or to a world in flames with the faithful dying as martyrs and reborn in paradise.

Yet Daesh has also turned sacrifice into a form of voyeuristic entertainment in which sadism is recast as sacrality, and it is reasonable to question how long a movement based on ever more grotesque depictions of human death can maintain its appeal. Daesh has established its political brand on what are, essentially, snuff films, and, like all purveyors of violent pornography, it faces the challenge of coming up with ever more novel ways to portray the act of harming human beings. We must hope, ironically, that al-Zawahiri will eventually be proved right in his judgment that Daesh will discredit itself through its viciousness and that the voices of moderation within the Muslim ummah will speak louder and stronger and ultimately win out over those of brutality and violence. There is, of course, no guarantee that this will happen or that, after being retooled so many times before, the sacrifice machine will somehow seize up and cease to function in the future as it has in the past. That is an eventuality we should not expect, even if it is one we desire.

EIGHT

The Widening Gyre

PRAGUE, 2016

I completed this book where I started writing it two years earlier, in the city of Prague. I do not think it is coincidental that the book finally came to fruition in this particular place. Geographically, the Czech Republic is roughly halfway between the United States and Afghanistan, and, though it is a modern country, far closer in its material aspect to America than to Afghanistan, in certain respects it bears a nearer resemblance to Afghanistan. Both, after all, are landlocked nations whose histories have been defined by the machinations of their more powerful neighbors. Both have a history of invasion and occupation. And, to an even greater degree than in Afghanistan, martyrdom runs in the Czech bloodstream. The mythic founder of the Czech nation, the tenth-century Václav (King Wenceslas), was murdered and later canonized as Saint Václav; the patriarch of the Hussite movement (and one of the founders of the Protestant Reformation), Jan Hus, was burned at the stake for criticizing priestly abuse of the sacraments; the patron saint of Czech Catholics, Jan of Nepomuk, was thrown off a bridge and canonized for upholding the Catholic sacraments; the patron saint of communists, Julius Fučík, was executed by the Gestapo and turned into a folk hero whose record of his imprisonment was required reading for generations of Czechs under communist rule; and the student saint of anticommunists, Jan Palach, immolated himself in 1969, following the Soviet occupation of his country, at the base of Saint Václav's memorial in the center of Prague.

The list of Czech martyrs goes on and on, but in a sense the whole country can be said to have been offered up for sacrifice—first following the Battle of White Mountain in 1620, with the execution of twenty-seven Protestant noblemen in Old Town Square and the subsequent return of the Czech Lands to Catholic control, and in more recent times at the altar of Nazi appeasement at the Munich Conference in 1938 and then again at the Yalta Conference in 1945 to satisfy Moscow's desire for satellites and compensation for its wartime sacrifices. But for all their importance in Czech history, martyrdom and sacrifice still sit uneasily on the Czech conscience, as it has not always been obvious just what the Czech martyrs died for. Saint Václav, for example, is held up as the founding figure of the Czech nation, but his death can be attributed to fratricidal jealousy as readily as to providential sacrifice. The significance of Hus's death is muddled by the fact that his countrymen ultimately resubmitted themselves to the papal control he gave his life to oppose. Jan of Nepomuk's story was pretty clearly a fabrication intended to transform a low-level bureaucrat into a pious divine to provide the Czechs with a native-born saint and thereby counter any lingering nostalgia for Hus.[1] Fučík was a hardcore Stalinist whose cult of personality, enduring long after the revilement of Stalin himself, represents a lingering embarrassment to middle-aged Czechs who were brought up revering him. And Jan Palach embodies for many Czechs the shame of their acquiescence to Soviet subjugation for two more decades after his act of self-sacrifice.[2]

For me, the most telling symbol of Czech unease over the meaning of sacrifice can be seen in the village of Ostřešany, a kilometer or so from my mother-in-law's house in Pardubice, an hour east of Prague: a memorial commemorating soldiers from the community who fell in World War I. It is located in what was once a town square but is now more of a sideways glance for occupants of cars that skirt its edge on the way to someplace else.

The memorial is a bronze statue of a man falling to the ground (figure 33). His face is obscured by his helmet and the high collar of his greatcoat. His fists are clenched, and one leg extends over the base of the statue. It is the figure of an unarmed man who is about to die. The inscription on the base includes the years 1914–18 and, on the sides, the names of the fallen and the dates of their deaths.[3] No other words are included—no words of inspiration, no telling epigraph. It is as though saying more would be saying too much, and anyway, what could have been said? There was no Czech Republic or Czechoslovakia during those years. There was just the tattered flag of the Austro-Hungarian Empire, and there were as many soldiers from this part of Bohemia fighting against that banner as there were soldiers fighting under it. The statue references martyrdom, but what is commemorated is the moment of death itself and, indirectly, the private grief of those who lost their loved

FIGURE 33. World War I memorial, Ostřešany, Czech Republic. Author's photograph, 2016.

ones—whatever the cause they thought they were fighting for or the army into which they were conscripted. The sacrifice machine is operating here, but it is locked in neutral. Sacrifice is acknowledged, but it is not directed to any particular ends.

My understanding of the centrality of sacrifice has been sharpened and clarified by spending time in the Czech Republic and learning more about what the historian Richard Burton refers to as "the Czech self-definition through martyrs."[4] But the Czech example also shows that important though the act of sacrifice may be, its meaning is in no way certain. One way to view sacrifice is as a machine for forging symbols; but symbols, by their nature, are capable of speaking multiple truths and of relating to social and political contexts in unpredictable ways that are transformed as those contexts change. Without these examples and patterns in mind, I do not know that it would have occurred to me that the diverse forms of death and dying, consecration, condemnation, and commemoration analyzed in this book all belonged together, or that it might make sense to group them under the umbrella of sacrifice. After years of looking perhaps too closely at one place on the map, it required the triangulation of vision provided by close observation of a second foreign culture to see the first more clearly. Maybe it also helped that I was looking at Czech history with the eyes of a newcomer and from a middle distance, unencumbered by close familiarity with people and place beyond my affinal family. Sometimes knowing too much can lead to concluding too little, just as having too schematic and panoramic a view can lead one to too-quick conclusions. Laying one history on top of another sometimes allows an outline to appear.

SACRIFICE AND SUICIDE BOMBING

In my two earlier books on Afghanistan, I focused on the interactions of cultural and political forces, arguing that one should not view politics in Afghanistan solely through the lens of the state. Over many generations, Afghans had developed a political system centered on the interplay of tribes, state, and Islam. I examined this system in terms of the moral codes that animated these larger social and political forces. Viewing the components of that system in a broader historical context, we can see that its very indeterminacy—the characteristic that made it so difficult for Westerners to understand and respond to—was also what had allowed generations of people in the region to withstand multiple invasions and protracted periods of conquest and foreign rule. It involved a continual jockeying for advantage among representatives of the three moral orders, with the general result that, whenever one order gained an advantage, representatives of the other two aligned themselves in such a way that the advantage would be undercut and the triangle of tribe, state, and Islam would regain its balance.

In the positioning and skirmishing that constituted Afghan history before the coming of Marxism and the Soviet occupation, ideas and practices related to sacrifice, and specifically martyrdom, were never of central importance. Afghans have never seen themselves as victims, and they have always been far more likely to revere living heroes than dead martyrs. What I observed in Peshawar, therefore, was the beginning of a fundamental transformation that—if present trends hold—will have permanently destroyed the triangle of forces that have been at the heart of Afghan political culture for centuries. At the center of this change has been the transformation of sacrifice into something very different from what it was and what it represented at the beginning of the war.

It was in the context of the refugee crisis spawned by the war, a crisis that led three and a half million Afghans to flee to Pakistan, that the Islamic political parties in Peshawar began to publish magazines memorializing martyrs and extolling the virtues of self-sacrifice in the service of jihad. By themselves, these magazines did not alter the equation; however, they reflect a broader shift toward Islamic piety over tribal honor and a changing culture in which death would be more valued than life and the political potential of that change could be realized. From an unfortunate occurrence to be grieved and lamented, death became something laudable and then, over time, something desirable.

It is difficult to say whether the original motivation behind this initiative was more commemorative or instrumental, but pushing martyrs to the forefront of popular attention changed the nature of political discourse, as martyrdom became one of the key pivots around which events and disputes revolved and the standard by which they were judged. As in the Czech Lands, martyrs and martyrdom were neither new nor unique, but never—at least in recent times—had they taken on the political form and saliency that they did during the Soviet occupation of Afghanistan. Whether or not their symbolic potency was recognized at the outset and consciously manipulated, they quickly became a lever by which the more extreme parties, which had no traditional base of influence and authority in Afghan society, were able to position themselves in the political competition unleashed by the Soviet occupation and the erosion of traditional forms of political authority.

Ten years of occupation and five of civil war wore down the machinery of sacrifice. The followers of formerly respected mujahidin commanders became guerrilla groups that established local fiefdoms and preyed on local populations—a source of unease and suspicion, if not outright loathing, for the people these groups oppressed. Martyrdom in this context lost much of its meaning and political force. However, the Taliban recycled the parts and repurposed the machinery of sacrifice so that the focus of ritual death shifted from the martyr to the criminal, whose public execution became a force binding authorities and spectators together in catharsis and culpability. Public punishments were a means by which the state demonstrated its right to exercise judicial control, but they had a second, symbolic dimension as well. Those executed were not just criminals whose deaths or dismemberments righted a commensurate wrong; they were also scapegoats whose punishment implicated the populace and solidified—if only by intimidation—the authority of the rulers.

All the while that the Taliban were trying to firm up the foundations of their rule, their nominal guest, Osama Bin Laden, was busy refashioning sacrifice according to his own design. This process had begun ten years before the Taliban came to power, with the efforts of Abdullah 'Azzam to redirect the spiritual and mystical powers formerly associated with Sufism into the institution of martyrdom. This shift made the martyr, rather than the saint, the focus of admiration and longing, if not of cultic veneration. 'Azzam's primary audience was not Afghans but Arabs. His efforts to interest this larger audience in events in Afghanistan and turn it into a stage on which they could reinvigorate their own spiritual identity were crucial for internationalizing the conflict and globalizing jihad. The Soviet Union, the United States, Pakistan, Iran, and other states had been engaged in the conflict well before 'Azzam arrived in Peshawar, but 'Azzam created a means for individual Muslims, irrespective of national origin or citizenship, to engage as combatants.

It was left to his successor, Bin Laden, to more fully exploit the political potential of sacrifice. Bin Laden was never interested in Afghanistan except—as the name of his organization, al-Qaeda (the Base), implied—to serve as a center for training his men and launching operations. More than anyone before him, Bin Laden recognized the symbolic and political potency of sacrifice and created a small army of *fedayeen* who willfully and purposefully used their bodies as instruments of jihad. The manual of instructions for the September 11 hijackers had not a word to say about the operational details of the mission. The more immediate concern of these men as they faced their deaths was the ritual nature of their deed, framed as an impending wedding rather than the wanton carnage it became—a ceremony of innocence that masked the blood-dimmed tide being loosed upon the world.

The Arab connection does not end with Bin Laden. Palestinian militants indirectly supplied the Taliban with the techniques they needed to downscale the airborne technology of destruction devised by al-Qaeda to the level of the street, replacing the singular conflagration with a multitude of mini-9/11s, each of which affected a smaller cohort of people but in equally tragic and profound ways. Embracing this path, the Jordanian doctor Humam Khalil Abu-Mulal al-Balawi found in Afghanistan a place to put into practice a vision he had created for himself in the solitude of late-night Internet postings. As with 'Azzam and Bin Laden, Afghanistan was the place of al-Balawi's self-invention, the stage-set for the realization of his own narcissistic dream of becoming.

In recent years, Syrian-based Daesh has broadened the use of the Internet to break down national borders altogether in the creation of a new generation of mujahidin—who, for the most part, are ignorant of Islam but fully conversant with social media and desperate to make a connection to something real in the midst of their estranged and alienated everyday reality. The means of that connection has been through the transformation of their captives into human sacrifices in carefully choreographed spectacles of violence and the repurposing of their own bodies as walking bombs.

Discussions of suicide bombing have been dominated, on the one hand, by analysis of psychological factors that propel individuals to join the ranks of suicide bombers and, on the other hand, by organizational and strategic perspectives. In this book, I have tried to make a case for why it is important to consider other dimensions of this phenomenon as well. In doing so, I have staked out several claims, the first of which is that we cannot understand suicide bombing by seeing it solely through the lens of terrorism. The rhetoric of terror obscures the motivations and the mechanics that are expressed through the act of self-destruction, in the process confusing effects with causes. A second claim is that it is a mistake to see Islam as the sole or even primary source of suicide bombing. Some subset of those who become suicide bombers may be inspired primarily by Islamic ideas, but we cannot assume that to be the case with all or to conclude from the fact that the Taliban dispatched a suicide bomber that the matter of individual motivation is thereby explained.

The approach I have followed in this book is to assume, first of all, that suicide bombing has a history. It did not arrive on the scene fully wrought or thought out. In fact, it is a phenomenon that Afghans could not have imagined when the war that has devastated their country first began and, indeed, that they have difficulty even to this day reconciling with their sense of themselves and their culture. One way to view this history is through the circuitry of transference of the practice from one location to another, but this sort of history of passage is inadequate in itself. We must also understand how and why suicide bombing took root in different places and how it connected to the social and political histories and formations that exist in different countries and cultures.

Here again, Islam as often as not impedes understanding as aiding it, for we have the tendency to assume that suicide bombing is a religious practice, that it is an expression of Muslim identity, and that fundamentally all Muslims are alike and are motivated in similar ways toward similar ends. But Palestinian Muslims (or Muslim Palestinians), for example, are different from Afghan Muslims (which is to say, Muslim Afghans), and both of these (and other) aspects of identity have to be accounted for in explaining why people from these different religio-cultural worlds would choose to blow themselves up.

Suicide bombing not only has a history in the traditional sense in which we think of history (namely, as a narrated sequence of events orchestrated and undertaken by determinative agents over a duration of time); it also has what can be called a "deep structure," and I have tried to locate one dimension of that deep structure in the ritual of sacrifice. In using the term "ritual," I am not referring to any particular ritual but rather to the general notion of a patterned set of actions that some group of people recognize as something that they have done in the past, that is good for them to do now, and that they should keep doing in the future.

This patterned set of actions revolves around the act of killing a living being, a killing that is understood as a "giving back" and that is further understood as part of a sequence of exchanges that will involve a "getting back" for those who undertake the sacrificial act. This something that they will "get back" can be moral benefit, as Henri Hubert and Marcel Mauss propose.[5] It can be a sense of security for having followed a religious command. It can be an increase in social status that one will gain from one's peers. It can be the promise of a future reward, whether in this world or the next.

On one level, the entity on the other end of the exchange is probably most often conceived of in supernatural terms, and the giving up something of value now (a sheep or oneself) likewise carries with it the expectation of getting something back (for example, an eternal afterlife). This way of focusing on the thing that is promised in return (for example, the seventy-two virgins) causes us to overlook what is more important in the grand scheme of things, namely the deep structure of exchange itself—the fact that the act undertaken is expressive of something larger and continuing and that ramifies outward from the act itself to implicate other actors and future situations.

Although it is important to recognize that one aspect of exchange centers on the supernatural exchange with God, we also need to be cognizant of another form that is ultimately, in the Afghan context, equally or more consequential: the exchange of honor. In the analysis of the Dog Feud, I argued that the act of sacrifice served as a switch by which warring factions changed communicative registers, from the register of reciprocal violence to the register of talking about peace. But my analysis of suicide bombing has demonstrated how sacrifice in the form of suicide bombing and in the context of occupation has come to function as an extension of rather than an answer to the logic of reciprocal violence.

Over the course of the American intervention in Afghanistan, as the American military has removed itself from the battlefield, all the while inflicting lethal damage from a safe distance and in a way that cannot be specifically traced to particular agents, it has become increasingly difficult for those who have suffered violence (or who feel themselves to have been aggrieved by that violence, even if they have not suffered its direct consequences) to find a means of reciprocation. The debt of honor cannot be repaid in any ordinary way with the enemy removed from the field of battle, so the body itself must be used as the vehicle for overcoming the nullity that results from being unable to repay the debt of honor.

The imbalance of power between the United States and Afghanistan, and the ability of the Americans to apply overwhelming force in the pursuit of their ambitions, results in feelings of shame at one's inability to respond, humiliation at one's loss of status and identity, and resentment at those responsible for creating this situation. These terms are universal ones that can be applied in many contexts, but it is important to recognize that the way these feelings are expressed, how individuals respond to them, and even how they are felt in the first place are cultural matters as much as psychological ones, though the cultural dimension of this articulation has generally been ignored, perhaps because it requires considerable time, attention, and empathy in situations that do not lend themselves to attaining any of these states of mind and connection.

One response to this toxic mix of shame, humiliation, and resentment is the traditional response associated with the logic of the feud, which itself embodies the Maussian logic of exchange, though in a negative sense—the exchange of gifts being replaced by the exchange of violence. The radical disconnection of the enemy, however, precludes the traditional embodiment of the feud response (the deft application of violent riposte against a member of the offending party). Suicide bombing provides at least a partial solution—partial in the sense that the responsible enemy might not be effectively targeted—but complete in that, for the individual, it eliminates negative feelings altogether, while bequeathing to posterity (or so the suicide bomber might imagine) the residual memory of a hero/martyr who had the courage to end his life to reclaim his lost honor. The cost of that reclamation, however, is extremely high, for though suicide bombing relieves the individual once and for all of the debt of honor, it does so at the expense of those left behind, who must live with the certainty that each suicide detonation will entail successive acts of retaliatory violence, each of which will, in all likelihood, be more devastating than the one before.

In highlighting this dynamic, I find myself cycling back again to the story of Sultan Muhammad Khan that I referred to earlier in this book, the story that I told in the first chapter of my first book on Afghanistan.[6] In my analysis of that story, I remarked on how the extreme actions undertaken by Sultan Muhammad to reclaim his honor after the murder of his father (actions that included disobeying his father, blinding his mother, and killing his best friend) could be taken both as an example of the difficulties that a true man must endure to salvage his name and as a warning to those hearing the story of what happens when the desire for personal honor is taken so far that it undermines the negotiation and compromise on which social life is based. The same can be said of suicide bombing and the destruction it brings about, even as it allows the individual recompense for wrongs done to him.

To this point, the recapitulation of the theoretical argument of *Caravan of Martyrs* presented here has focused on the aspects of the book that serve to extend the analytical framework provided by Hubert and Mauss in their essay on sacrifice and by Mauss alone in his essay on the gift. Yet, as brilliant and enduring as their insights are, I have encountered certain difficulties in applying them to contemporary cases, in large part because these works, in particular the early essay on sacrifice, are focused on Vedic and biblical rituals (and, in the later work, on exchange rituals in small-scale, bounded societies) and so are far removed from the complicated, globally intertwined world in which suicide bombing has emerged as a potent modern form of sacrificial ritual.

I have tried to address this disconnect by proposing the analogy of sacrifice to a simple machine. I have found this analogy useful for a number of reasons, the first of which is that, when we strip sacrifice of the particular ritual coating that adheres to it in different contexts, we can see that it does what all simple machines do: convert energy of one sort into another sort, in the process amplifying that energy by giving it both emotional force and cultural meaning. The analogy has seemed useful as well because sacrifice, like the simple machines we are familiar with (levers, pulleys, wedges, etc.), can be modified and elaborated in various ways to suit particular situations and tasks. At its core is the simple act of killing, but that simple act releases tremendous energy that can be harnessed in many different ways to serve many ends, even if the ultimate purposes to which any machine might be put cannot be presupposed or predicted.

Hubert and Mauss were convinced that sacrifice "nourished social forces," that it renewed "that character, good, strong, grave, and terrible, which is one of the essential traits of any social entity." And they believed that "individuals find their own advantage in this same act. They confer upon each other, upon themselves, and upon those things they hold dear, the whole strength of society."[7] They never could have imagined that sacrificial rites could have such enduring power in the modern world, that these rites could be modified and extended as they have been, or that, while attempting to rekindle the sputtering flame of collective caring, sacrifice could simultaneously loose such violent and destructive energies upon the world. That transformation in the ritual of sacrifice is what the forever war in Afghanistan has forged, and it is a legacy that we must also shoulder and share.

LESSONS FROM THE COLD WAR

First our funds, then our indifference, and now our drones have helped create the space occupied by the Taliban, al-Qaeda, and, lately, Daesh. September 11 provided reason enough for retaliation, but again our often tone-deaf and sometimes indiscriminate response helped establish the conditions for ever more virulent forms of predation and violence. When al-Qaeda operatives blew up the American embassies in Kenya and Tanzania in 1998, it was less the terrorist act that provided al-Qaeda with its advantage than the U.S. response: the cruise-missile strikes against al-Qaeda bases in Paktia Province rallied the local population to reverse or at least neutralize their sympathies and support their formerly unwelcome Arab guests. The same dynamic has been playing out ever since with ever more deadly results, and we have yet to figure out a way to break the chain of retributive violence that has created a deepening divide between us and those we have sought to influence and assist.

The willingness of some to sacrifice their bodies should not be assumed to demonstrate a general societal fatalism or indifference to the value of human life. Nor can it be explained solely in ideological or cultural terms. Rather, it reflects a realistic assessment of the nature of the conflict and an understanding of where strategic and tactical advantage resides. When the enemy you are facing uses unmanned drones to kill, the most effective response might be to go to the opposite extreme, matching the disembodied nonpresence of the drone with the embodied presence of the suicide bomber. If your enemy wants the conflict to be as bloodless for them as possible, then the best expedient might be to make it as bloody as humanly possible for everyone close at hand, even those who have had no part in the conflict themselves.

In making these assessments, I do not mean to excuse or justify the actions of the Taliban, much less al-Qaeda or Daesh. In offering their lives to the Afghan jihad, the Arab volunteers gave to Afghanistan a poisoned gift that has brought only suffering and devastation to the country. But the process did not begin there, and it was not only outsiders who were at fault. We are now on the third or fourth generation of fighters in Afghanistan, and each generation has been more intolerant than the one before and more ready to give up the meager hopes of the present for the prospect of a better life in the next world. Parallel to these developments, outsiders have arrived to fill the political vacuum with their own credos. Again each generation has been more venomous than the last, Bin Laden's Afghan Arabs now giving way to followers of Daesh who revel in the opportunity to create their videos of torture and suffering.

To seek out the roots of this catastrophe is not to apply to it the kind of weak-kneed moral relativism of which anthropologists are sometimes accused. Representing the native point of view in order to understand it does not mean embracing or justifying it. Making sense of the behavior of people in other social worlds is what anthropologists do. It is critical that we hold to that duty now, when the voices of intolerance are stronger and shriller than they have been at any time in memory. Suicide bombing is a plague, and it is a plague that affects Muslims more than anyone else. Combating that plague requires careful understanding of the causes and conditions that have brought it into being, and it requires recognition of the oldest lessons of all— that violence begets violence, and that, to end that cycle, each side must make sacrifices and demonstrations of good faith. We must also show respect and compassion across lines of difference and in the face of blind incomprehension. We should remember as well that the machinery of sacrifice can exhaust itself of its own accord, but that intemperate actions to extinguish it can keep the engine running.

In considering our response to the violence emanating from the Middle East, we might do well to look backward to an earlier decisive moment when the West was confronted with the threat of annihilation from without and intolerance and suppression from within, another moment when shrill voices echoed in the corridors of power and in the media to strike first and fast against enemies foreign and domestic, never mind the consequences. That moment came in the wake of World War II, as the West was beginning to reckon with the challenge of an adversary potentially more powerful than Nazi Germany and one quickly developing the capacity to match American nuclear might with similar weapons of its own. At a critical juncture, George F. Kennan, then a mid-level diplomat, dispatched his now-famous "long telegram" to his State Department superiors that enunciated a strategy of containment as an alternative to confrontation and preemptive nuclear strikes.[8]

The essence of Kennan's analysis was that the contradictions within Soviet society ensured the "seeds of its own destruction" and that an overly aggressive approach to the Soviets would only delay that inevitable process of internal collapse. At the same time, Kennan argued, the belief animating Soviet policy was that "it was desirable and necessary that the internal harmony of our society be disrupted, our traditional way of life be destroyed, the international authority of our state be broken, if Soviet power is to be secure." The only strategy for allowing the Soviet's internal process of disintegration to play itself out and to forestall their efforts to bring about the internal destruction of the Western democracies was patient containment of the Soviet threat, careful attention to the "health and vigor of our own society," and the projection to other nations of "a much more positive and constructive picture of [the] sort of world we would like to see than we have put forward in [the] past." Kennan concluded his telegram by noting, "We must have courage and self-confidence to cling to our own methods and conceptions of human society.... After all, the greatest danger that can befall us in coping with this problem ... is that we shall allow ourselves to become like those with whom we are coping."[9] The moral balance that once existed in Afghanistan may not survive this prolonged and brutal war, but we should make sure that the principles that have preserved and sustained the United States over the centuries do not suffer the same fate.

AFGHAN CHRONOLOGY (1964–2015)

1964–65   Constitutional monarchy and parliamentary democracy introduced.
Political parties and newspapers established.

Late 1960s   Widespread demonstrations on campuses. Increasing political
agitation and covert organizing by Marxist and Islamist
parties.

1973   Muhammad Daud seizes power in a coup d'état from his cousin,
King Zahir Shah, and expands alliance with the Soviet Union.

1975   Islamists attempt to ignite a popular revolt against regime. Efforts
fail and leaders flee to Pakistan, where they establish political parties
to coordinate antigovernment resistance.

1978   President Daud overthrown and killed by military officers aligned
with the Khalq faction of the Marxist People's Democratic Party
of Afghanistan (PDPA). New regime introduces widespread socialist reforms. Local insurrections against the regime begin within
months. Islamic parties headquartered in Pakistan gradually gain
control of scattered local fronts.

1979   Soviet Union sends 100,000 troops to prop up failing Marxist
regime, beginning decade-long occupation. Soviets install Babrak
Karmal, the leader of the Parcham faction of the PDPA, as
president.

1980   Antigovernment opposition intensifies. United States steps up covert
assistance to mujahidin fronts. Pakistani intelligence agency (ISI) bans
all secular political parties and funnels arms and aid to Islamic parties.
An estimated 4 million Afghans become refugees in Pakistan, Iran,
and other countries.

1984   Abdullah 'Azzam and Osama Bin Laden establish Maktab al-
Khedamat to assist mujahidin. Beginning of a large influx of Arabs
in support of the jihad.

1986	Karmal replaced by Mohammad Najibullah as head of Soviet-backed regime. Bin Laden sets up base for "Afghan Arabs" in the area of the Jaji tribe in Paktia Province.
1987	Government troops attack Bin Laden base in Jaji but fail to capture it.
1988	Afghanistan, the USSR, the United States, and Pakistan sign peace accords, and Soviet Union begins pulling out troops.
1989	Last Soviet troops withdraw from Afghanistan. Assassination of 'Azzam in Peshawar. Siege of Jalalabad by mujahidin parties fails to dislodge regime and leads to splintering of the jihad movement and the outbreak of civil war. Many "Afghan Arabs" leave to pursue jihad in their home countries.
1990	United States initiates Gulf War to bring down regime of Saddam Hussein. Bin Laden fails to convince Saudi rulers to allow him to mobilize an army of Afghan Arabs to attack Saddam.
1991	Bin Laden moves to Sudan.
1992	Najibullah's government finally toppled. Coalition government comprising mujahidin political parties formed in Kabul, but fighting continues as local commanders attempt to maintain control in local areas.
1993	Ramzi Youssef, nephew of Khalid Sheikh Muhammad, later mastermind of the September 11 attacks, explodes a truck bomb in the underground parking lot of the World Trade Center.
1995	Taliban emerge as powerful political force in southern Afghanistan and quickly expand to other regions, gaining popular support for their opposition to predatory mujahidin commanders. Group seizes control of Kabul and introduces shari'a-based social reforms. Public punishments initiated.
1996	Publication of Bin Laden's *A Declaration of War against the Americans Occupying the Land of the Two Holy Places*.
1998	Al-Qaeda operatives bomb U.S. embassies in Kenya and Tanzania, resulting in 253 people killed, including 12 Americans. United States steps up campaign to capture Bin Laden and launches missile strikes at suspected al-Qaeda base at Zhawar in eastern Afghanistan.
1999	United Nations imposes embargo and financial sanctions to force Afghanistan to hand over Bin Laden for trial.
2000	The USS *Cole* is bombed off coast of Yemen.
2001	Ahmad Shah Massoud, leader of the Northern Alliance opposition to the Taliban, is assassinated in first suicide attack in Afghanistan. Two days later, on September 11, al-Qaeda launches attacks against New York City and Washington, D.C. United States responds by

initiating attacks on Afghanistan designed to dislodge Taliban and capture Bin Laden. Afghan expatriate groups meet in Bonn and agree to establish a power-sharing interim-government led by Hamid Karzai. United States fails to capture Bin Laden at Tora Bora.

2002 Deployment of NATO-led International Security Assistance Force (ISAF) to serve as peacekeepers in Kabul. U.S. and allied Coalition forces begin protracted campaign to dislodge Taliban from remaining strongholds in southern Afghanistan and along the Pakistani border. *Number of suicide attacks: 1 (total deaths: 2; wounded: 0).*[1]

2002 Loya Jirga, or grand council, elects Hamid Karzai as interim head of state. *Number of suicide attacks: 1 (total deaths: 1; wounded: 3).*

2003 Bin Laden distributes video encouraging suicide attacks. NATO takes control of security in Kabul. *Number of suicide attacks: 2 (total deaths: 9; wounded: 31).*

2004 Hamid Karzai wins presidency in democratic election. *Number of suicide attacks: 3 (total deaths: 6; wounded: 15).*

2005 Afghans vote in first parliamentary elections in more than 30 years. Former jihad commanders gain many of the seats. *Number of suicide attacks: 20 (total deaths: 50; wounded: 144).*

2006 NATO assumes responsibility for security across the whole of Afghanistan. *Number of suicide attacks: 105 (total deaths: 279; wounded: 771).*

2007 U.S. Marines kill 19 civilians in Ningrahar Province. NATO forces kill as many as 150 Taliban in Operation Mountain Fury in Paktia Province. *Number of suicide attacks: 140 (total deaths: 604; wounded: 1,154).*

2008 Suicide-bomb attack on Indian embassy in Kabul kills more than 50. President George W. Bush sends an extra 4,500 U.S. troops to Afghanistan, in a move he describes as a "quiet surge." *Number of suicide attacks: 126 (total deaths: 587; wounded: 1,306).*

2009 Karzai reelected as president. President Barack Obama boosts U.S. troop levels in Afghanistan to 100,000. Baitullah Mehsud, leader of the Pakistani Taliban, killed in drone strike. Jordanian suicide bomber Humam al-Balawi kills 8 CIA officers and contract employees and a Jordanian intelligence official in a retaliatory suicide attack at Camp Chapman in Khost. *Number of suicide attacks: 99 (total deaths: 512; wounded: 1,267).*

2010 United States raises troop levels and more than doubles the number of drone strikes to 115 from 50 the previous year. General Stanley McChrystal resigns as commander of U.S. forces in Afghanistan and is replaced by General David Petraeus. Afghan parliamentary elections held. *Number of suicide attacks: 110 (total deaths: 449; wounded: 1,187).*

2011   Taliban launch assault on Kandahar. Bin Laden assassinated by U.S. Seal Team 6. President Karzai's half-brother and Kandahar governor, Ahmad Wali Karzai, and ex-president Burhanuddin Rabbani killed in separate suicide attacks. At least 58 people are killed in twin attacks at a Shia shrine in Kabul and a Shia mosque in Mazar-i Sharif. President Obama announces drawdown of troops. *Number of suicide attacks: 111 (total deaths: 647; wounded: 1,645).*

2012   A series of high-profile abuses by American troops, including release of a video showing troops urinating on dead Taliban soldiers and the murder of 16 civilians in Kandahar, create widespread anger among Afghans. Nationwide protests erupt over burning of copies of the Qur'an by U.S. soldiers at the Bagram airbase. *Number of suicide attacks: 92 (total deaths: 514; wounded: 1,258).*

2013   National Directorate of Security headquarters attacked by team of suicide bombers. United States hands over main prison facility in Bagram to Afghan government. *Number of suicide attacks: 87 (total deaths: 377; wounded: 1,071).*

2014   Taliban attack popular restaurant in Kabul, killing 21. An attack on the luxury Serena Hotel kills 9. Ashraf Ghani succeeds Karzai as president of Afghanistan. Islamic State (Daesh) establishes branch in Afghanistan and begins recruiting efforts. *Number of suicide attacks: 116 (total deaths: 503; wounded: 1,276).*

2015   Taliban mount attack on Afghan parliament. Taliban capture parts of Kunduz city. An American AC-130 gunship attacks Médecins Sans Frontiéres (Doctors Without Borders) hospital in Kunduz, killing 30. Death of Mullah Omar in 2013 announced by Taliban. *Number of suicide attacks: 77 (total deaths: 394; wounded: 1,230).*

2016   Daesh suicide bombers attack demonstration by Shia Hazaras. Ninety-seven people reported killed, with 260 wounded. Afghan forces backed by U.S. air support attack Daesh bases in Ningrahar Province. Suicide bombers attack Afghan police convoy, killing 40 recently graduated cadets. Taliban attack American University in Afghanistan, killing 13. *Number of suicide attacks: 27 (total deaths: 258; wounded: 781).*

NOTES

1. *Jihad Watch,* Sept. 11, 2007.
2. See, e.g., Said 1994.

ONE. SACRIFICE

1. "Army Staff Sgt. Eric J. Lindstrom," Honor the Fallen, *Military Times,* accessed July 27, 2016, http://thefallen.militarytimes.com/army-staff-sgt-eric-j-lindstrom/4190548.
2. See my books *Heroes of the Age: Moral Fault Lines on the Afghan Frontier* (1996) and *Before Taliban: Genealogies of the Afghan Jihad* (2002).
3. Illouz 2007, 3.
4. My translation. Throughout this book, translations are my own unless otherwise indicated.
5. The film that resulted from this trip is *Kabul Transit* (2006), available for streaming at http://kabultransit.org.
6. Williams 2007.
7. For statistics on suicide attacks, see the Chicago Project on Security and Terrorism, Suicide Attack Database, accessed June 14, 2016, http://cpostdata.uchicago.edu/search_new.php. See also UNAMA 2007.
8. See Crews 2015 and Marsden 2016.
9. The Arabic terms (intehar and intehari) are used in both Dari and Pakhtu. Other terms are also used, including *zanwazhana* (Pakhtu) and *khudkushi* (Dari Persian) for the act of suicide bombing, and *zanmargai* (Pakhtu) and *khudkush* (Dari) for suicide bomber. These terms, or variants of them, are also used for the act of committing suicide (as opposed to engaging in an act of suicide bombing). Context and changes of verb indicate whether the act being referred involves killing

oneself alone or killing oneself in order to kill others. See Finn 2012 for a critique of the terms *suicide bombing* and *suicide bomber.*

10. Nasser Abufarha (2009) takes a somewhat similar approach to my own in his excellent study of suicide bombing in the West Bank. An anthropologist by training, Abufarha is also concerned about grounding his analysis in the way suicide bombing is conceptualized by its practitioners and the members of the community with which those practitioners are associated. This orientation leads him to focus on suicide bombing as a manifestation of local ideas and ideals associated with sacrifice, and he, too, draws inspiration from Hubert and Mauss 1964. See also Strenski 2003 on the importance of sacrifice in analyzing contemporary Muslim "human bombers."

11. Hubert and Mauss 1964.

12. In a foreword to an edition of *The Gift*, Mary Douglas noted a connection between *Sacrifice*, written at the beginning of Mauss's career, and *The Gift*, written at the end. In Douglas's view, it is "likely that Mauss did get the idea of a morally sanctioned gift cycle upholding the social cycle from the Vedic literature that he studied in that first major research" (Douglas 1990).

13. Hubert and Mauss 1964, 50.

14. Ibid., 58.

15. Ibid., 60.

TWO. HONOR

1. See Anderson 1979.

2. *Qurban* is the usual noun form, *qurbani* usually used as an adjective; however, there are contexts in which *qurbani* can used as a term for a sacrifice being offered for a particular purpose.

3. *Sadaqa* (pl. *sadaqat*) comes in three varieties: *farz,* or obligatory donations, such as those mandated by the Islamic principle of *zakat; wajib,* which is also obligatory and includes charitable gifts given during religious holidays; and *mustahab,* or voluntary donations. *Kherat* ("good deed") is a voluntary contribution given to a needy person, sometimes in response to something positive happening in a person's life (e.g., the birth of a male child). A third form of donation, *nazar,* refers to gifts pledged in hopes of something positive happening or of something bad not happening. For detailed information on sacrificial rites in Islam, see Ådna 2014.

4. The petitioning group fully expects that the honor of their women will be respected by their enemies. Dispatching the women is, in this sense, a confirmation of the understanding that, whatever their disagreements and the immediate cause of their enmity, both sides are committed to "doing Pakhtu."

5. If the opposing side refuses to agree to the requested truce, they can return the sacrificial animal, sometimes also giving veils (*chadar*) to the women as a sign that their honor has not been compromised.

6. The religious personnel who attend these rituals are usually not themselves members of the tribe. In some cases, they might be descendants of a Sufi saint. In

others, they might be respected clerics who are not personally connected to either side of the dispute in question and whose neutrality can therefore be ensured.

7. Ahmed 1980, 107.

8. Edwards 1996, 35.

9. Muhammad Daud Khan was the cousin of King Zahir Shah and, at the time of the Safi War, was serving as minister of defense. He became prime minister in 1953 and continued in that capacity until 1963. Ten years later, he staged a coup against his cousin and installed himself as president. He was overthrown and killed along with his family in the Marxist coup in April 1978.

10. *Niyat* here refers to the Islamic precept that a course of action should be undertaken with full intentionality, because God judges the rightness of an action by the sincerity of its purpose.

11. Ignaz Goldziher (1967 [1889–90]) and Alois Musil (1928) drew attention to the importance of poetry in Middle Eastern Muslim societies. In recent decades, anthropologists in particular have added a rich body of scholarship on poems as an expression of cultural values and on poetic composition and recitation as central spaces for the performances of cultural meaning. Of particular significance for my understanding of the role of poetry in Afghan society have been the work of Michael Meeker (1979), Lila Abu-Lughod (1986), and Stephen Caton (1990) on poetry in Middle Eastern contexts, of Inger Boesen (1983) and Benedicte Grima (1992) on Pakhtun women's poetry, and of Alex Strick Van Linschoten and Felix Kuehn (2012) on Taliban poetry.

12. Biddulph 1890, vii.

13. My interview with Rafiq Jan, Sept. 4, 1983.

14. On causes of the failure of the Marxist regime, see, among many other works, Shahrani and Canfield 1984; Roy 1986; Rubin 1995; and Edwards 2002.

15. See Edwards 1987, 1996, 2002 for longer discussions of the lashkar and its limitations.

16. Poems by Rafiq Jan have all been transcribed from tape cassettes I purchased in Peshawar in 1983–84. Original translations and background information on tribes, people, events, and objects referred to in the poems was provided by Shah-mahmood Miakhel.

17. Boesen 1983, 121.

18. Last two couplets from Shahmahmood Miakhel, personal communication.

19. In the first stage of the fighting against the Marxist regime, Afghans used the term *ghaza* to describe their military actions against the government more often than the term *jihad*, while referring to themselves as *ghazi* (plural, *ghaziyan*) rather than as *mujahidin*. The terms originally derive from pre-Islamic Arabic words related to the raids that Bedouin tribes conducted against each other. With the coming of Islam, the terms were adopted to describe the raids that the Muslims under the Prophet Muhammad undertook against their enemies. The implication is that these military actions reflected both the tribal principles and ambitions of many of the Prophet's early followers and allies as well as the religious principles and ambitions he was promoting and that would ultimately supersede all others. As the

Afghan war progressed and the Islamic parties in Peshawar took control of the various fighting fronts, the terminology of ghaza/ghazi was gradually replaced by jihad/mujahid.

20. On the various terms used to describe martyrs, the theological distinctions and controversies related to what constitutes a legitimate act of martyrdom, and what rewards accrue to martyrs, see Cook 2007 and Hatina 2014.

21. Hubert and Mauss 1964, 102.

22. Ibid., 102–3.

THREE. MARTYRDOM

1. The poem appears on a cassette tape I purchased in the Peshawar market in 1984. Like the tapes of Rafiq Jan's poetry, this cassette and others discussed in this chapter were labeled only with the name of the poet. Because I was able to contact and interview Rafiq Jan, I could determine when his poems were written, recorded, and circulated. However, I was unable to locate Gul Sha'er or any of the other poets discussed in this chapter, so I cannot provide contextual background on the poet or the production. Consequently, my dating of these poems to the second stage of the war is speculative. It is also possible that these poems were composed as early as Rafiq Jan's and that they represent not a later development but simply a more religiously centered discourse that coexisted with Rafiq Jan's all along (as the religiously oriented poetry of the seventeenth-century Pakhtu poet Rahman Baba coexisted with the heroic tribal poetry of Khushal Khan Khattak). In either case, it is clear that the kind of honor-centered poetry that Rafiq Jan composed at the beginning of the war was quickly eclipsed by the martyr-centered poetry.

2. Rahman Baba 1977, 95, 55. Quoted in Lindholm 1982, 240–41.

3. Lindholm 1982, 240–41.

4. Many landais romanticize an ideal of forbidden love from a female perspective, in the figure of the man willing to defy society and risk censure, even death, to secretly meet with his lover. The poems thus embody for women the same fundamental contradiction that animates Pakhtun society from the male perspective: between the desire for individual autonomy and the demands of social conformity and control.

5. For a detailed discussion of the Peshawar parties, see Edwards 2002. For a discussion of the prior publications of the Muslim Youth Organization, see Edwards 1993a, 1993b.

6. From video footage and photos in the collection of the Afghan Media Resource Center, it is clear that some mujahidin groups, at least, carried these magazines (along with other pamphlets and basic reading and writing primers) when they traveled from their bases in Pakistan to the fronts in Afghanistan.

7. Prisons also feature in Sufi narratives, though their meaning differs from that of latter Islamist discourse. In one such story that I discuss in *Heroes of the Age*, Amir Abdur Rahman Khan repeatedly imprisons a dissident Sufi leader but finds that

every time he manages to slip through the bars until finally the amir must admit that the pir has miraculous powers that exceed his own (Edwards 1996, 158–67).

8. See Edwards 1993b.

9. Hubert and Mauss 1964, 97.

10. *Hedayat ul-mujahidin* (*mufti sangar*) was written by Maulawi Gul Rahman Deobandi from Ningrahar Province, approved by a council of eighteen clerics whose names are listed at the beginning of the pamphlet, and published by the Seven-Party Alliance of Afghan mujahidin. My copy of the pamphlet is the third edition, printed in 1982.

11. *Mufti sangar* stipulates three conditions under which jihad is compulsory: for adults present when an enemy attacks; for adults whose home is attacked; and when the *imam* (prayer leader) or *mufti* (Islamic legal authority) announces that participation is obligatory (17–18).

FOUR. VIRTUE AND VICE

1. The woman in the video was named Zarmina and had been convicted of murdering her husband. The story of her purported crime and the domestic abuse leading up to it can be found on the RAWA website (www.rawa.org/zarmeena2 .htm).

2. Margaret Mills has speculated that the enormous popularity of *Titanic* in Afghanistan might have something to do with the fact that DiCaprio's character was a "martyr for love," a fate that resonates well with characters in Afghan folklore whose romantic aspirations are thwarted by family opposition and class and ethnic differences (Mills, personal communication, Jan. 2016).

3. Bearak 1998.

4. Jamiat-i Islami was led by Burhanuddin Rabbani, but Massoud, who commanded Jamiat's front in the Panjshir Valley, was its most prominent figure.

5. Matinuddin 1999, 25.

6. An alternative view holds that Najibullah's execution was ordered by Mullah Muhammad Rabbani, an important Taliban official, to avenge the killing of his brother by Najibullah. Kamal Matinuddin (1999, 87–88) repeats the allegation that Rabbani's subsequent sacking was due to Mullah Omar's unhappiness at this usurpation of authority. Rabbani was later brought back into the ruling circle of the party.

7. Verdery 1999, 5. The attack against the Buddhas was carried out arguably less to prove the superiority of Islam over Buddhism than to demonstrate the authority of the Taliban as stronger than that of previous Afghan regimes, which had not only tolerated the statues' continued existence but also used them to promote tourism to the country by non-Muslims. The Buddhas needed to fall precisely because the international community said they should stay. Thus, just as Taliban rule required ridding the country of the stain of corruption by former mujahidin commanders, so it required symbolic affirmation of the sovereignty of Islamic law over all alternative writs.

8. Anderson 1979.

9. Douglas 1966, 13.

10. Ibid., 67.

11. Agamben 1998, 30. See also Caton 2006.

12. Verdery 1999, 33.

13. Ibid., 38.

14. Hubert and Mauss 1964, 60.

15. Verdery 1999, 32–33.

16. Girard 1977, 39–67.

17. For an insightful discussion of such rites, see Wyatt-Brown 1986.

18. Hubert and Mauss 1964, 60.

19. Ibid., 60.

FIVE. FEDAYEEN

1. "Afghan Arabs" are also often referred to with the words reversed, as "Arab Afghans." I choose the former term, first, because there is an existing non-Arabic speaking ethnic group in Afghanistan known as Arab Afghans and, second, because there was very little that was "Afghan" about the foreign fighters who traveled to Afghanistan and who became defined by their association with the country.

2. For additional biographical information on 'Azzam, see Hatina 2014, 137–43.

3. Although 'Azzam created the context in which such attacks could be imagined, it is quite possible that he would have opposed them. He advocated developing a robust Islamic state in Afghanistan before extending jihad to other regions and countries. This became an important bone of contention between 'Azzam and Bin Laden, with Bin Laden's view prevailing after 'Azzam's death.

4. Abdullah 'Azzam, *Join the Caravan,* https://archive.org/stream/JoinThe-Caravan/JoinTheCaravan_djvu.txt.

5. Abdullah 'Azzam, *Signs of Allah the Most Merciful in the Afghan Jihad (Ayat al-Rahman fi Jihad al-Afghan),* accessed Feb. 22, 2016, https://archive.org/stream/MiraclesOfJihadInAfghanistan-AbdullahAzzam/Signs_of_ar-Rahman_djvu.txt.

6. On the importance of miracles in 'Azzam's writings, see Hatina 2014, 141.

7. For an insightful discussion of this treatise, see Daryl Li (2012) who notes that, for all of 'Azzam's concern for empirical proof, the miracles associated with martyrs were not universally recognized. Indeed, one of Li's informants commented that he had never encountered any of the sort of miracles that 'Azzam claimed were so numerous (cited on p. 15).

8. For a detailed examination of miracles in the Afghan Sufi context, see Edwards 2002.

9. Abdullah 'Azzam, *The Lovers of the Maidens of Paradise,* accessed Feb. 22, 2016, https://archive.org/stream/BlackFlagsE-bookSeries/_1-Ushaq-al-Hoor—Lovers-of-the-Maidens-of-Paradise—Abdullah-Azzam-AfghanJihad1979–89#page/n3/mode/2up.

10. Li 2012, 21. Many observers have noted 'Azzam's ideological contribution to the founding of al Qaeda, but few have given adequate attention to the importance of his writings on shahadat, especially the hagiographies and miracle stories, which arguably had a larger impact in terms of drawing recruits to Afghanistan than 'Azzam's theological or ideological writings. Many, if not most, of the recruits 'Azzam drew to Afghanistan reportedly were not well-informed on Islamic matters, and what seems to have appealed to them were 'Azzam's more romantic and sensationalist accounts of miracles and martyrs. See Hegghammer 2008 for an example of the relative emphasis on ideology over martyr and miracle narratives in Western discussions of 'Azzam's influence. The sample of 'Azzam's writings included with Hegghammer's otherwise excellent essay on 'Azzam excludes contemporary stories of martyrs and the miracles associated with them, though the selection does include writings related to the definition and qualifications for martyrdom (Kepel and Milelli 2008, 102–43).

11. Hamid and Farrall 2015, 82. Mustafa Hamid and Leah Farrall's book is invaluable for understanding the role Bin Laden played in Afghanistan and the development of al-Qaeda. In reading it, one has to keep in mind that Hamid was an interested party to these events and that the approach he recommended was different from Bin Laden's. Nevertheless, his unique and insightful perspective not only fills in many of the gaps in our understanding of the Arab role in Afghanistan but also helps correct for distortions in Western interpretations of this history, especially the tendency to overestimate al-Qaeda's coherence and integration.

12. Ibid., 82.

13. Ibid., 82.

14. Ibid., 36–37.

15. Ibid., 299.

16. Ibid., 77. According to Hamid and Farrall (2015), Bin Laden had made earlier trips to Paktia but always as part of well-organized tours that sought to show the jihad in the best possible light. It was only when Bin Laden journeyed to Paktia on his own that he saw the real conditions in which the mujahidin were operating.

17. Ibid., 84.

18. Ibid., 148.

19. Ibid., 122.

20. Li (2012, 17) has taken me to task for asserting that Afghans as a rule disliked Arabs. The basis for his criticism was a report that Afghans prayed at the graves of Arab martyrs, which in his view demonstrated their respect for these fallen heroes. That might be the case, but Li never comments on the fact that the Afghans were visiting these graves in apparent defiance of the widely known fact that most of the Arabs who came to fight in the jihad—like their mentor, Bin Laden—subscribed to the Wahhabi doctrine that forbade venerating and seeking divine intervention from the dead. Shrines aside, whenever the topic of Arabs has come up during my fieldwork, Afghans have been quick to characterize them as arrogant, unmannered, and bossy. There were undoubtedly exceptions to this rule, on both sides, but I have

heard the opinion expressed often enough that I give it some validity, if only as a widely accepted stereotype.

21. Hamid and Farrall 2015, 74.

22. Ibid., 151.

23. Ibid., 165.

24. See Miller 2015.

25. On the background and contents of the tape, its message, and its publication, see Miller 2015.

26. Miller 2015, 237. The speech was transcribed and translated by Flagg Miller from one of the cassettes contained in the collection sent to me in 2002.

27. Ibid., 237.

28. Ibid., 236.

29. As Ignaz Goldziher noted (1967 [1889–90]), early Islamic authorities viewed tribal poetry with considerable disdain and apprehension. Like the Afghan tribal poetry discussed in chapter 2, pre-Islamic tribal poetry exalted ancestors, urged listeners to be as brave as their forebears, and mocked those who failed to live up to the expectations of bravery in battle, hospitality to guests, and the other tenets of the tribal code of honor. For many Muslims, this old code represented a challenge to the code of conduct introduced by Muhammad, particularly the expectation that believers would submit to the authority of their leaders. Bin Laden, for his part, recognized the value in salvaging the pre-Islamic honor code and using it to energize his doctrine of jihad.

30. Miller 2015, 239.

31. The literature on September 11 is too vast to summarize, but some of the works that stand out include Wright 2006; Fouda and Fielding 2003; and Atwan 2006.

32. Kippenberg 2005. A number of scholars have written insightfully on the text, including Kanan Makiya and Hassan Mneimneh (2002), Bruce Lincoln (2003), Juan Cole (2003), David Cook (2002), David Cook and Olivia Allison (2007), and Margo Kitts (2010). Of particular importance are works by Hans Kippenberg (2005) and by Hans Kippenberg and Tilman Seidensticker (2006), which provide invaluable background and analysis of the text.

33. Fouda and Fielding 2003, 115. On the provenance of the document, see Kippenberg and Seidensticker 2006; Cook 2005; and Kitts 2010.

34. Hubert and Mauss 1964, 19–20.

35. Ibid., 25.

36. Ibid., 9–10.

37. Ibid., 97–98.

38. Kippenberg and Seidensticker 2006, 16.

39. Makiya and Mneimneh 2002, 20.

40. Ibid., 20.

41. Feldman 1991, 78.

42. Devji 2005, xvi.

1. Hassan 2001. Although there were earlier suicide operations, including the 1983 attack on the U.S. Marine barracks in Beirut, the Palestinian model is most pertinent to understanding subsequent developments in Afghanistan.

2. Ibid.

3. Ibid.

4. Ibid.

5. See Khalili 2007 and Abufarha 2009 for insightful, in-depth analyses of suicide-bombing operations in Palestine.

6. Ahmad 2011a.

7. Ibid.

8. Ahmad 2011b.

9. Pajhwok Reporter 2014.

10. Baidar 2011.

11. Khpalwak 2011.

12. Pajhwok Reporter 2011.

13. There is another "why" question, of course: Why do the Taliban use suicide bombing as a tactic of war? In this study, I have intentionally avoided the organizational and strategic dimensions of this question on the assumptions, first, that it has received ample attention to date, and, second, that I can make a greater contribution by offering an anthropological perspective on the cultural and moral logic that informs an individual's decision to engage in a suicide mission, rather than asking why the Taliban found this strategy to be to their political benefit.

14. UNAMA 2007, 85. The Taliban have sometimes been accused of kidnapping children, but, as BBC reporter Syed Shoaib Hasan has noted, the Taliban "don't really kidnap children. . . . The Taliban convince them it is their duty to carry out jihad. . . . [But] how much convincing does a child need? . . . Especially when promised adventure?" (ibid., 107).

15. Ibid., 106.

16. Ibid., 89.

17. Ibid., 77.

18. According to these informal estimates, 15 percent of attacks are thought to be in revenge for the loss of family members in the course of operations by the Afghan government and American-led international coalition; 10 percent are said to be the result of the influence of Taliban recruitment and propaganda on illiterate Afghans and Pakistanis; and around 5 percent are the result of personal enmities. Danish Karokhel, editor of the Pajhwok News Agency, personal communication, July 12, 2014.

19. There are significant differences in the orientations of Pakistani and Afghan madrasas, with different institutions subscribing to a variety of theological and ideological doctrines associated with Deobandi, Salafi, Wahhabi, and other Islamic schools of thought. Despite these differences, or maybe because of them, there has

been a more general movement toward more literal interpretations of Qur'an and hadith and the obligation of Muslims to adhere strictly to the fundaments of the faith as discerned through the example of the Prophet. Along with this has come increasing intolerance toward those who espouse more moderate interpretations.

20. There is considerable disagreement as to the number of madrasas in Pakistan and their relative influence in comparison to nonreligious schools. According to one report, the number of madrasas has risen from fewer than 300 when the country was founded to more than 35,000 today, with an estimated 3.5 million students. Estimates of the number of madrasas in Khyber Pakhtunkhwa range from 1,354 to 3,136 (Khalil 2015). C. Christine Fair (2007), among other scholars, has argued that the madrasa/militancy connection is overblown (see also Andrabi et al. 2005). Fewer students attend madrasas in Afghanistan, where for many years their expansion was suppressed by a combination of a communist government and an ongoing war. Since the end of the war, however, their growth has been substantial. An article published by the Pajhwok News Agency indicates that the number of seminaries and Qur'an memorization centers in Afghanistan had risen from 222 in 2001 to 581 in 2010, while the total number of students had expanded from 76,000 to 143,000 (Ayubi 2010).

21. Goldberg 2000.

22. Muhaq 2010.

23. Ibid.

24. Danish Karokhel, personal communication, July 12, 2015.

25. Lansford 2012, 141.

26. Undated affidavit of an interview with a captured suicide bomber provided to me by the Pajhwok News Agency.

27. One exception is anthropologist Scott Atran, who has written perceptively on the subject of suicide bombing (see, e.g., Atran 2006). However, Atran's work differs from mine in being oriented toward the global phenomenon of suicide bombing—what characteristics link people in different societies who have resorted to suicide bombing—rather than toward an in-depth analysis of suicide bombing in one particular place and culture.

28. An example of this sort of analysis is Mia Bloom's *Dying to Kill: The Allure of Suicide Terror* (2005), which focuses on the rational calculation, at both the organizational and individual level, underlying suicide attacks. Individual motivations here are framed in terms of incentives. Organizations that sponsor suicide attacks do so, in part, as "a tactic of coercive bargaining which includes the risks of outbidding because of the competition among rival organizations utilizing the tactic. Under conditions of group competition, there are incentives for further groups to jump on the 'suicide bandwagon' and ramp up the violence in order to distinguish themselves from the other organizations" (94).

29. Post 2007, 185.

30. Pedahzur 2006, 35, summarizing Lackhar 2002. See also DeMause 2002.

31. Stern 2003, 38. See also Stern 2004.

32. The UNAMA report notes that, in early 2006, General Rahmatullah Raufi, the corps commander of the Afghan National Army in Kandahar, explained that "the explosives come from Pakistan, and the drivers come from Pakistan and foreign countries. It is very difficult for an Afghan to persuade himself to commit suicide" (UNAMA 2007, 65).

33. One major difference between the moral bases of suicide attacks in Palestine and those in Afghanistan lies in the significance ascribed to land. Nasser Abufarha depicts the pivotal importance of the land for Palestinians: "Sacrifice is the medium of exchange between the fida'i body and the land of Palestine. This exchange is achieved by situating the sacrificed body and the land of Palestine in a 'homologic relation' in which the blood of the sacrificed Palestinian body corresponds to the water feeding the streams and rivers of Palestine" (2009, 45). The idea of homeland is important in Afghan sacrificial ideology as well, but, perhaps because of Afghanistan's larger size, more diverse geography, and more complicated ethnic composition (as well as the fact that its land has never been successfully occupied or colonized), land per se is less idealized than it is among Palestinians; I would argue its significance is largely subsumed under the concept of namus.

34. See Edwards 1996, 56.

35. See ibid., chap. 2, for a more complete discussion of the dynamics of honor.

36. It should be noted that there can be gaps between what should happen and what does happen. Specifically, in cases of sexual misconduct, both the male and the female parties to the affair should be punished by death, but it sometimes happens that the female dies and the male does not. This can be rationalized in relation to the belief that, since women are more prone to carnal desire (*nafs*), they are more likely to be at fault and responsible for leading the man astray. It is equally likely that those enforcing the collective decision of the group will have compromised on the principle of equal justice for the man and woman to avoid the greater enmity of the man's family. Nevertheless, as in the Dog Feud, it would not be surprising in such situations for the male responsible for the infraction to be exiled from his home, effectively ceasing to exist and no longer reminding the other family of the different punishments handed out to their family member.

37. To Soviet soldiers, the Afghans they were fighting against were ghosts (*dukhi*), a term that reflects both the unreality of the situation they found themselves in and the way that covert mujahidin attacks haunted both their waking lives and their dreams. See Coll 2004, 17.

38. UNAMA 2007, 81.

39. Edwards 1996, 35.

40. It is important to note that it is not only acts of violation and violence—such as house searches and drone strikes—that engender the sense of lost honor. Benevolent distribution of aid, however well intentioned, can accomplish the same end, insofar as it too demonstrates that the power is entirely with one part to the exchange and not with the other. During his tenure as president, Hamid Karzai was often chastised by Americans for his ingratitude when he would publicly criticize U.S.

officials when giving speeches to Afghan audiences. However, another way to see these public acts of lashing out at the officials who were supplying his regime with so much aid was as an attempt to reclaim his own and his country's honor in a situation in which he and they had little power, autonomy, or opportunity for reciprocation.

41. Reuters 2016. It should be noted that U.S. Air Force drone strikes constitute only a portion of the total, because the CIA controls its own, classified drone program.

42. Serle and Sargand 2015.

43. Bergen and Tiedemann 2010 reports that between 1,584 and 2,716 "militants" were killed in Pakistan between 2004 and early 2010, and between 152 and 191 civilians (130–268 casualties were classified as "unknown"). The Bureau of Investigative Journalism, which does not use the "militant" label in its datasets, reports that drones killed between 474 and 881 Pakistani civilians between 2004 and 2011, out of 2,562–3,325 total deaths (International Human Rights and Conflict Resolution Clinic 2012). Given the reliance on circumstantial evidence to identify insurgents, it is doubtless the case that some number of victims identified as legitimate targets and therefore excluded from the category of "civilian casualty" were not members of the Taliban.

44. Rohde 2012.

45. Quoted in International Human Rights and Conflict Resolution Clinic 2012, 98. This report contains numerous testimonies as to the psychological, social, and economic harm done to communities under threat of drone strikes.

46. Ibid., 81–82.

47. Ibid., 84.

48. Ibid., 45.

49. Ibid., 60, 93–94. See also Grima 1992 on the importance of funeral rites in Pakhtun culture.

50. Rodriguez 2011.

51. Ibid., 37.

52. Ibid., 43.

53. Devji 2005, 9.

54. See Ackerman 2014.

55. UNAMA 2007, 70.

56. In its ongoing monitoring of drone-strike casualties, the Bureau of Investigative Journalism estimates the number of civilian deaths in the June 23, 2009 attack at between 18 and 45 (www.thebureauinvestigates.com/category/projects/drones/drones-pakistan/). It is also estimated that more than 11,000 houses belonging to the Mehsud tribe in South Waziristan were destroyed by the Pakistan government during Operation Rah-i Nijat beginning in June 2009 (Mehsud 2016). See also Mayer 2009.

57. Agamben 1998. See also chapter 4 of this book for a fuller discussion.

58. Balawi 2010. All subsequent quotes from al-Balawi come from this source.

SEVEN. SELFIES

1. The video can be seen at https://www.youtube.com/watch?v = NQUv9UuA_jM.

2. Barthes 1981, 96.

3. Pelevin and Weinreich 2012, 56.

4. See Edwards 1993a, 1995.

5. According to one hadith, God will pardon seventy relatives of a martyr in heaven. Another hadith, attributed to Abu Daud, affords the martyr six privileges: (1) forgiveness of previous sins; (2) seeing his place in heaven at the moment of his death; (3) protection from the torments of the grave; (4) bestowal of a crown of rubies on Judgment Day that will be greater than all the goods of this world; (5) marriage to seventy-two virgins; and (6) forgiveness for seventy relatives (www .dorar.net/enc/aqadia/2535).

6. A high school teacher in Ningrahar told an Afghan friend that parents are "very careful and treat [their] sons with caution," because they know that the boys might make good on their threats to join the Taliban. The teacher said that there were "hundreds of examples" of young boys leaving their homes after playing Taliban ringtones and video clips.

7. Another target audience for Taliban ringtones and video clips is members of the army and the police, whom they hope to inspire to so-called "green on blue" attacks, in which an Afghan policeman or soldier will turn his government-issued weapon against his superiors or the government's Coalition allies. There have been many such attacks, including some against top Coalition officers. Although it is rarely clear what specific factors influenced the attacker to open fire on the people who gave him a job and were paying his salary, it appears likely that propaganda instruments like ringtones and videos play a role, particularly since such people rarely encounter the Taliban in person.

8. Pelevin and Weinreich 2012, 56.

9. On the theme of "martyrs of love," see Cook 2007, chap. 6.

10. Margaret Mills (personal communication, Sept. 2015) has noted that *majnun* in Arabic means "jinn-struck," or possessed, and thus the character's name is an epithet that derives from his having been driven insane by love. Mills has also pointed out that, in both Sufi devotional poetry and secular verse, the purest love is the love that persists even though—or because—it is unconsummated. The Beloved, whether imagined as God or as a flesh-and-blood person, remains at a distance, beckoning but out of reach, and the poet's devotion is signaled by his acceptance of his state of incompleteness.

11. Hassan 2001.

12. Although I assume that most of the Facebook users I was following were Afghans, given that they presented themselves as such, it was not always clear whether or not they lived in Afghanistan. In some cases, I could tell that a user was probably living outside of Afghanistan, for example by the fact that posts were typed

on an Urdu keyboard. But such signs are not conclusive evidence. I also cannot say much of anything about the backgrounds of those who use Facebook to advance the cause of jihad and promote martyrdom. I do not know how many there are, how representative they are, or how their numbers compare, for example, to those who follow particular Bollywood stars or football teams. I do not know where the posters come from. I do not know their class background. I can speculate to some degree about their level of education and age by their use of language, but language can be modified to obscure identity, and profile photographs can be faked. So, for better or worse, I have to admit to the limits of my research. In contrast to my fieldwork experience in Afghanistan, in this instance I operated as an unseen, presumably unnoticed observer in a foreign land, a lurker in Internet parlance, who—with one exception—did not make contact with the people whose posts I was reading. In retrospect, I wish that I had interjected my own comments to people's posts, though I am not sure that such contacts would have provided much more in the way of information and insight. In any case, my comments in this chapter must be read for the impressions they are.

13. I acknowledge that anonymous Internet research, even among people who want to see the death and destruction of my country and my culture, is ethically ambiguous terrain. I therefore use pseudonyms to disguise the online identities of the individuals I profile and quote. I do this knowing that in all likelihood they were already doing the same thing, so that what I present here are probably pseudonyms of pseudonyms—which pretty well captures the strange social space of the Internet.

14. In July 2015, I accessed an account that uses the same name, Ghazi, and provides the same home area, Logar. However, if this is the person I interviewed and whose posts I collected in the summer of 2014, the account has been scrubbed of all content related to martyrdom and the Taliban.

15. The photo was picked up by international news services, but it was circulated on social media before it made its way to the mainstream media. It must have been taken at least two years before I first saw it on July 8, 2014 (it appeared in press reports two days later, on July 10), because Badruddin was killed in a drone strike in North Waziristan in July 2012.

16. In 1984, I interviewed Badruddin's father, Maulavi Jalaluddin Haqqani, in Peshawar and received permission from him to visit mujahidin bases in Paktia controlled by his faction of Hizb-i Islami. On the way to and from Paktia, I stayed in Haqqani's home in Miranshah and met several of Haqqani's sons, including Badruddin, who was then a young boy.

17. This judgment is based on the opinion of educated Afghans with whom I have discussed these posts.

18. *Arbaki* are locally recruited police and militias paid by the government to maintain law and order.

19. Afghans often do not smile for photographs. Smiling is considered undignified, and since having a photograph taken is still a rare and solemn occurrence among those who do not yet have mobile phones, they believe photographs should exhibit sufficient gravitas to preserve the dignity of the subject.

20. The search term "smiling martyrs" brings up dozens of videos on YouTube. The facial expressions of the martyrs are seen as evidence of their having espied what awaits them as a reward for their sacrifice.

21. See Li 2012.

22. Warhol also fabricated images of newspaper headlines detailing deaths caused by tainted food tins and photos of car wrecks. These were part of what was known as his Disasters series.

23. In *Heroes of the Age* (1996), I wrote about the importance to earlier generations of Sufi mystics of the phrase *lifting the veil* and the concept behind it. In lifting the veil of ordinary perception through the performance of miracles, Sufi saints allowed their devotees to view the power of God and his continuing involvement in and oversight of human affairs. Miracles of the sort I described in that book are no longer commonplace, but martyr photographs also serve the function of "lifting the veil" and thereby providing evidence to the living of the supernatural domain that exists beyond the range of normal perception.

24. In the West, Facebook has become a vehicle for finding lost loves, for connecting and reconnecting. It is a place ripe with desire and longing, a place that lends itself to late-night temptation. Does it play a similar role for these Facebook users? Do Abida's male Facebook friends stare into her dark eyes and wonder, what if? I will certainly never know. What I do know is that such desire would never be admitted. The pressure toward conformity is too strong for the personal to seep through the facade of propriety. Expanding on this theme, Margaret Mills (personal communication, Sept. 2015) has noted that the personal and confessional mode has always been a feature of Persian and Afghan poetry, and it may be that Facebook and other social media platforms intersect with this domain of Afghan expressivity. In both, there is a mode of speech that is at once personal and detached.

25. Fallon 2014, 18.

26. Ibid., 19–20.

27. See Byman 2015 and Zelin 2014.

28. Zawahiri 2005.

29. According to captured Daesh in-take records obtained by the Syrian opposition site Zaman al-Wasl, 70 percent of recruits crossing from Turkey into Syria to join Daesh were judged by Daesh officials who interviewed them to have only rudimentary knowledge of Islam, with only 5 percent rated as having advanced knowledge. See Batrawy, Dodds, and Hinnant 2016.

30. Miller and Mekhennet 2015.

31. Ibid. In addition to recruiting young people to the movement, Daesh is using media to appeal to its own citizenry. This population is subjected to a "constant stream of utopian messages . . . designed to convince residents, in Soviet-style fashion, of the superiority of the Islamic State" (Miller and Mekhennet 2015). In cities controlled by Daesh, screens are set up in neighborhoods for evening video nights at which local residents watch government-approved videos streamed on a laptop. According to one witness who was present at a film screening near the University of Mosul, "the Islamic State's most notorious videos—including those showing the

beheadings of Western hostages and the burning of a caged Jordanian fighter pilot—were shown over and over ... long after their audiences beyond the caliphate dissipated" (Miller and Mekhennet 2015). What struck him in particular that evening was the fascination of the children in the audience for the violence they were seeing. Especially popular was the figure of Muhammad Emwazi, the notorious "Jihadi John," whose black, quasi-Ninja outfit a number of the children imitated in their own dress. See Miller and Mekhennet 2015.

32. Devji 2005, 9.

33. See Winter 2015a, 2015b; Miller and Mekhennet 2015; Koerner 2016.

34. Miller and Mekhennet 2015.

35. Khalil (the former pseudonym of Kanan Makiya) 1989, 58–61. Many former Baathists who survived the overthrow of Saddam Hussein and were then purged from the military during the American occupation of Iraq refashioned themselves as Muslim fundamentalists under Daesh. Among them were al-Baghdadi's deputy, Abu Muslim al Turkmani, who was killed in a U.S. air strike in August 2015 (see Sly 2015; Coles and Parker 2015).

36. On the role of the Internet in creating the mindset of Daesh recruits, see Shane, Apuzzo, and Schmitt 2015; Vidino and Hughes 2015.

EIGHT. THE WIDENING GYRE

1. On the role of saint cults in the Counter-Reformation, see Louthian 2009. On sacrifice in Czech history generally, see Pynsent 1994; Sayer 1998; and Burton 2009.

2. The payment of the debt that Palach's martyrdom incurred required another "sacrifice," that of a student demonstrator, Martin Šmíd. Reports of his death at the hands of government police generated a groundswell of outrage that brought people into the streets in sufficient numbers to help topple the government in November 1989. Later, it was discovered that there was, in fact, no Martin Šmíd, nor did any protester die on November 17, but the story was enough to ignite the revolution a few hundred meters from where Palach had died two decades earlier.

Palach's legacy endures even twenty-plus years after the Velvet Revolution expelled the communist regime. In the summer of 2016, the National Museum hosted an exhibition of the work of artist Jiří Sozanský titled *1969 Rok Zlomu (Breaking Year)*. Sozanský's work is dedicated to the memory of Palach. This is the wall text that accompanied the paintings on display:

When words lost meaning
All those, who were physically confronted with the military invasion in August 1968, standing against soldiers ready to use their weapons upon an order, went through an extreme life experience, which was a mix of helplessness and humiliation.

All those, who were confronted with the helplessness of Czechoslovakia representatives against the aggressor after the invasion of the "allied" armies, felt the deadly indeterminateness of the situation. The persistent failures of the political elites, with whom they identified during the Prague Spring, represented a clear signal of the failure of an unfulfilled ideal.

The truth was replaced with lies. Reality was re-marked by the propaganda. The words lost their meaning. That was probably the reason why Jan Palach decided for a demonstration with his own body, when all the other means failed.

I was not surprised by his deed. It was an ultimate reaction to an ultimate situation. Just like me and all the male part of the generation, Palach was standing at the threshold to adult life. Our bodies were not different in any significant way, but we did not follow him.

Some of us perceived this as a hardly definable failure. Including me. That is perhaps why Jan Palach became my shadow, which I did not manage to escape. I can only cope with his constant presence through the process of work, which is why I must repeatedly return to the theme of Palach. —Jiří Sozanský

3. The names and death dates of the fallen of World War II were later added to the back of the base.

4. Burton 2009, 197.

5. Hubert and Mauss 1964.

6. Edwards 1996, chap. 2.

7. Hubert and Mauss 1964, 102.

8. Kennan 1946.

9. Ibid.

AFGHAN CHRONOLOGY (1964–2015)

1. Suicide-attack statistics are from the Chicago Project on Security and Terrorism (http://cpostdata.uchicago.edu/).

GLOSSARY

AMIR: commander, ruler, king; used also for chief of a political party or group

AMR BIL MA'RUF WA NAHI AN AL-MUNKAR: Department for the Promotion of Virtue and Prevention of Vice, administrative unit under the Taliban government responsible for ensuring popular compliance with religious rules and regulations

'AQL: intelligence, reason, sense (quality often associated with men and contrasted with **nafs**—carnal desires—the quality often associated with women)

ARBAKI: locally recruited police and militias paid by the government

'ASHUQ UL HOOR: "lover of the maiden of Paradise"

AWLIYA (SING. WALI): "friend of God," Sufi saint

BADMASH: reprobate or outlaw, troublemaker

BE GHAIRATA: coward

BE GHAIRATI: cowardly, lacking in integrity

BE NAMUSI: dishonorable; someone who cannot defend himself and whose "possessions" are subject to violation by others

BURQA: tent-like veil worn by some Afghan and Pakistani women

CHADAR: veil

CHARPAI: wood-and-rope bed

CHILLA: period of ascetic retreat (usually forty days)

CHILLA KHANA: cave, room, or building where ascetic retreats are undertaken

DALA: cuckold; someone who is insipid or of impoverished self-esteem

DAM: breath; the curative act of reciting verses of the Qur'an while blowing on a sick or injured individual

DAR AL-HARB: "realm of war" (Arabic), used for those places controlled by infidels against whom Muslims are engaged in jihad

DAR AL-ISLAM: "abode of Islam" or "realm of peace" (Arabic), used for those places controlled by Muslims and living under Islamic shari'a law

DAUS: cuckold; especially a man unable to protect the sexual honor of his female kin; a pimp or sellout

DAWAT (FROM ARABIC DAWA): proselytizing, summoning people to the faith

DEOBANDI: someone who has studied at the Dar Uloom Deoband madrasa or who subscribes to the Deobandi school of Islamic thought

DIN: religion

DOST: friend

DRUND: heavy, great, consequential

DUKHI: ghost; term used by Soviet soldiers for Afghan mujahidin

EID AL-AZHA: "Festival of Sacrifice," second of the two Muslim feast days, commemorating the willingness of Ibrahim to sacrifice his son Ismail as an act of submission to God (also referred to by Afghans as **Eid-i Qurban** [Dari], "Feast of the Sacrifice," and **Loya Akhtar** or **Ghat Akhtar** [Pakhtu], "Great Feast")

FARZ 'AIN: a compulsory duty for all Muslims

FARZ KIFAYA: a duty required for some but not all Muslims

FATWA: religious decree (usually pronounced "fitwa" in Afghanistan)

FEDAYEEN: "those willing to sacrifice themselves," a term so-called Afghan Arabs used to refer to themselves; Afghans sometimes used the term **fedayan** to refer to Afghan Arabs

FIRMAN: proclamation, command, order

FITNA: sedition, discord, anarchy

GHAIRAT: courage, zeal, bravery; self-determination

GHAZA: war or raid (term associated with the early Muslim attacks on Meccans during the lifetime of the Prophet Muhammad); used by Afghans prior to the Soviet invasion to refer to the battle against the Kabul regime. The term **ghazi** (pl. **ghaziyan**) is used for those who participated in these battles. Less commonly used after the Soviet invasion and supplanted by the terms **jihad, mujahid** (pl. **mujahidin**)

GHAZAL: a poetic form using rhyming couplets and refrains particularly associated with expressions of loss or separation, often separation from God

HADITH (PL. HADITHS): tradition or saying associated with the life of the Prophet Muhammad

HAJI: honorific title for man who has completed the pilgrimage to Mecca

HANAFI: one of four principal schools of Islamic thought within Sunni Islam

HARAM: domestic area, off-limits, forbidden

HAZARA: one of the main ethnic groups in Afghanistan, concentrated primarily in the central part of the country

HIZB-I ISLAMI: one of the main Islamic resistance parties founded during the Soviet occupation that continued to operate after the American invasion at a much reduced level as an opposition force loosely aligned with the Taliban

HOURA (PL. HOURI): a beautiful woman who resides in Paradise and is promised as a reward to those who are martyred in **jihad** (also known as **hoor**)

HUDUD: punishments according to Islamic law

HUJRA: guesthouse

IFTAR: meal that breaks the fast of Ramadan

IMAM: prayer leader

INTEHAR: suicide bombing (originally Arabic, used in both Dari Persian and Pakhtu)

INTEHARI (PL. INTEHARIYAN): suicide bomber

IZZAT: honor

JAHILI: pre-Islamic society

JAHILIYYA: Age of Ignorance, term referring to the era prior to Islam

JAMIAT-I ISLAMI: one of the main Islamic resistance parties founded during the Soviet occupation; later became a principal component of the Northern Alliance that opposed the Taliban

JANG: war or fighting, usually tribally based and without the imprimatur of Islamic authorities

JANNAT: Paradise

JIHAD: effort, struggle on behalf of Islam; holy war

JIHAD UL-AKBAR: "the greater jihad," i.e., the spiritual struggle to defeat the carnal self

JIRGA: tribal council or assembly

KAFAN: shroud

KAFIR: unbeliever, infidel

KALAMATULLAH: "There is no god but Allah, and Muhammad is His Prophet"

KARAMAT: miracle

KHALQ: "Masses," one of the two principal Soviet-backed communist parties (followers are **Khalqis**)

KHAN: title/honorific used for leader of a tribal group

KHANAQAH: Sufi center

KHAROB: spoiled, ruined, unauthorized

KHARWAR: large unit of weight

KHA TZWAN: "good youth"; a young man who adheres to Pakhtun norms

KHERAT: charity; voluntary donation given to a needy person, sometimes in response to something positive happening in a person's life (e.g., the birth of a male child)

KHUDKUSH: suicide bomber

KHUDKUSHI: suicide or suicide bombing

KUFR: infidelity, disbelief

LANDAI: short verse form generally composed by women

LASHKAR: tribal fighting force

LEWANAI: mad, insane

LUCHAK: naked, shameless

MADRASA: religious school

MAJNUN: crazy, love-struck; the name of a well-known folk hero

MAKH: face (*makh na lari*—"to lose face")

MAKTAB: school

MAKTAB AL-KHEDAMAT: name of the organization founded by Abdullah 'Azzam and Osama Bin Laden to support Afghan jihad during the Soviet occupation

MAL: property

MAMA: maternal uncle

MASADAH, AL-: "Lion's Den," base in eastern Paktia Province established by Osama Bin Laden during Soviet occupation

MASHREQI: eastern border region of Afghanistan

MAULANA: advanced religious scholar, similar to **maulavi,** albeit more often associated with those whose training has been in India or Pakistan

MAULAVI: advanced religious scholar; see also **maulana**

MELMASTIA: obligation to offer hospitality

MUFTI: Islamic legal authority

MUJAHID (PL. MUJAHIDIN): someone who pursues jihad; holy warrior

MULLAH: man who earns all or part of his income supervising a mosque, teaching religious lessons, or otherwise engaging in religious activities

MOULUD: celebration of the Prophet Muhammad

NAFS: passions, senses, carnal desires (qualities most often associated with women)

NAMAZ: prayer

NAMUS: honor; a man's assets and possessions whose violation brings about his disgrace (used principally for a man's female relatives)

NANAWATI: Pakhtun custom of requesting pardon by a person or the family of a person who has committed a crime or transgression

NANG: honor; reputation, esteem

NAZAR: gifts given in hopes of receiving good luck

NERKH: tribal law

NIYAT: intention

NUFUS: selection of army conscripts by government, based on population (from **nufus,** population)

PADSHAH: king

PAIGHUR (SING. AND PL.): taunt, reproach

PAKHTUN: one who speaks the **Pakhtu** (Pashto) language and who claims descent in one of the commonly recognized lines of Pakhtun tribal descent (also known as Pashtun, Pushtun, and Pathan)

PAKHTUNWALI: Pakhtun code of honorable behavior

PARCHAM: "Flag," one of the two principal Soviet-backed communist parties in Afghanistan

PATU: woolen shawl

PIR: mystic, leader of a Sufi order

QAUMI: selection of army conscripts by tribal elders (from **quam,** tribe)

QISAS: form of punishment in Islamic law that gives the right to a murder victim's nearest kin to exact revenge

QUR'AN: Islamic scripture revealed to the Prophet Muhammad

QURBAN/QURBANI: offering, sacrifice, martyr

RAFIQ: friend

RAMADAN: ninth month in the lunar calendar; Islamic month of fasting (commonly pronounced "Ramazan" in Afghanistan)

ROZA: fasting

SADAQA (PL. SADAQAT): donation

SALAFI: Islamic reform movement advocating a return to the original scripture and teachings of the Qur'an and emulation of the actions of the Prophet Muhammad and his Companions

SALAM: "peace" greeting

SANGAR: trench, bunker, place of battle

SAR KALAI: first hair-cutting ceremony

SHAHADAT: martyrdom

SHAHID (PL. SHAHIDAN, SHUHADA [ARABIC]): martyr

SHALWAR KAMEEZ: traditional clothing worn in Afghanistan and Pakistan ("kameez" is the long shirt worn with the "shalwar" or baggy pants)

SHARI'A: religious law

SHIRK: polytheism

SHURA: council

SUHOOR: meal taken in the morning before the start of the fast

SUNAT: term used to refer to all ritual obligations enjoined on Muslims; also used in Afghanistan to refer specifically to the ritual of male circumcision

SURAH: chapter in the Qur'an

TAKFIR: accusation of infidelity or apostasy

TAKFIRI: a Muslim who accuses another Muslim of infidelity or apostasy

TALIB UL-'ELM (PL. TALIBAN): religious student, seeker of sacred knowledge (more often referred to as **talib**)

TARANA: a form of musical composition favored by the Taliban and other conservative Muslim groups because of its reliance on the voice and lack of instrumentation

TOPAKIAN: gunmen

TORSARA (PL. TORSAREE): "black-head," a term of respect for a woman

TURA: sword

UMMAH: Muslim community

'UZR: "excuse" or "apology," usually an animal as a sacrifice, offered by an individual who seeks a negotiated truce

WAHHABI: school of religious thought associated with Arab reformer Abdul Wahhab and sponsored by the Saudi government

WATAN: homeland, home territory

ZAKAT: religious tax required of all Muslims

ZANMARGAI (PL. ZANMARGEE): suicide bomber (Pakhtu)

ZANWAZHANA: act of suicide bombing (Pakhtu)

ZIARAT: saint's shrine

ZIKR: mystical practice associated with Sufism involving the repeated recitation of sacred phrases

REFERENCES

Abufarha, Nasser. 2009. *The Making of a Human Bomb: An Ethnography of Palestinian Resistance.* Durham, N.C.: Duke University Press.

Abu-Lughod, Lila. 1986. *Veiled Sentiments.* Berkeley: University of California Press.

Ackerman, Spencer. 2014. "41 Targeted but 1,147 People Killed: US Drone Strikes—The Facts on the Ground." *The Guardian,* Nov. 24. www.theguardian.com/us-news/2014/nov/24/-sp-us-drone-strikes-kill-1147.

Ådna, Gerd Marie. 2014. *Muhammad and the Formation of Sacrifice.* Frankfurt am Main: Peter Lang.

Agamben, Giorgio. 1998. *Homo Sacer: Sovereign Power and Bare Life.* Stanford, Calif.: Stanford University Press.

Ahmad, Khwaja Basir. 2011a. "Pakistani Taliban Use Children for Suicide Attacks." *Pajhwok Afghan News,* Feb. 26. www.pajhwok.com/en/2011/02/26/pakistani-taliban-use-children-suicide-attacks-nds.

———. 2011b. "Boys Being Forced into Suicide Attacks." Pajhwok News Agency, Apr. 12. www.pajhwok.com/en/2011/04/12/boys-being-forced-suicide-attacks-nds.

Ahmed, Akbar S. 1980. *Pukhtun Economy and Society: Traditional Structure and Economic Development in a Tribal Society.* London: Routledge and Kegan Paul.

———. 2013. *The Thistle and the Drone: How America's War on Terror Became a Global War on Tribal Islam.* Washington, D.C.: Brookings Institution.

Allen, Nick. 2013. "Using Hubert and Mauss to Think about Sacrifice." In *Sacrifice and Modern Thought,* edited by Julia Meszaros and Johannes Zachhuber, 147–62. Oxford: Oxford University Press.

Andrabi, Tahir, Jishnu Das, Asim Ijaz Khwaja, and Tristan Zajonc. 2005. "Religious School Enrollment in Pakistan: A Look at the Data, Evidence for Policy Design." Kennedy School, Harvard University, Dec. http://epod.cid.harvard.edu/files/epod/files/khwaja_a_-_religious_school_enrollment_in_pakistan_madrassa_cer_deco5.pdf.

Anderson, Jon. 1979. "Doing Pakhtu: Social Organization of the Ghilzai Pakhtun." Ph.D. diss., University of North Carolina, Chapel Hill.

Asad, Talal. 2007. *On Suicide Bombing*. New York: Columbia University Press.

Atran, Scott. 2006. "The Moral Logic and Growth of Suicide Terrorism." *Washington Quarterly* 29, no. 2: 127–47.

Atwan, Abdel Bari. 2006. *The Secret History of al Qaeda*. Berkeley: University of California Press.

———. 2015. *Islamic State: The Digital Caliphate*. Berkeley: University of California Press.

Ayubi, Sultana Rahim. 2010. "Mushrooming Seminaries Fail to Tackle Admission Hassle." Pajhwok News Agency, Sept. 23. http://archive.pajhwok.com/en/2010/09/23/mushrooming-seminaries-fail-tackle-admission-hassle.

Baidar, Obaidullah. 2011. "Human Smuggler Detained; Children Rescued." Pajhwok News Agency, Oct. 23. www.pajhwok.com/en/2011/10/23/human-smuggler-detained-children-rescued.

Balawi, Humam Khalil Abu-Mulal al-. 2010. "An Interview with the Shaheed Abu Dujaanah al-Khorasani, Hero of the Raid of the Shaheed Amir Baytullah Mehsud." Interview transcript. Accessed Feb. 25, 2016. www.scribd.com/doc/27777898/CIA-Base-Bomber-s-Last-Statement-The-Raid-of-the-Shaheed-Baytullah-Mehsud.

Barfield, Thomas. 2010. *Afghanistan: A Cultural and Political History*. Princeton, N.J.: Princeton University Press.

Barthes, Roland. 1981. *Camera Lucida: Reflections on Photography*. New York: Hill and Wang.

Batrawy, Aya, Paisley Dodds, and Lori Hinnant. 2016. "'Islam for Dummies': ISIS recruits have poor grasp of faith." *AP Big Story*, Aug. 15. http://bigstory.ap.org/article/84c09c4cbfd1408a8ca08cbddcefbd97/islamic-state-gets-know-nothing-recruits-and-rejoices?utm_campaign = SocialFlow&utm_source = Twitter&utm_medium = AP.

Bearak, Barry. 1998. "Pul-i-Charki Journal; Afghan Beard Code: Like Castro, Si, Pavarotti, No." *New York Times,* Oct. 13. Accessed Aug. 3, 2016. www.nytimes.com/1998/10/13/world/pul-i-charki-journal-afghan-beard-code-like-castro-si-pavarotti-no.html.

Bell, Kevin. 2013. *Usama bin Laden's 'Father Sheikh': Yunus Khalis and the Return of al-Qaida's Leadership to Afghanistan*. West Point, N.Y.: Combating Terrorism Center.

Bergen, Peter, and Katherine Tiedemann. 2010. *The Year of the Drone: An Analysis of U.S. Drone Strikes in Pakistan, 2004–2010*. Washington, D.C.: New America Foundation. http://vcnv.org/files/NAF_YearOfTheDrone.pdf.

Biddulph, C.E. 1890. *Afghan Poetry of the Seventeenth Century: Being Selections from the Poems of Khushhal Khan Khatak*. London: Keegan Paul.

Bloom, Mia. 2005. *Dying to Kill: The Allure of Suicide Terror*. New York: Columbia University Press.

Boesen, Inger W. 1983. "Conflicts of Solidarity in Pakhtun Women's Lives." In *Women in Islamic Societies: Social Attitudes and Historical Perspectives,* edited by Bo Utas, 104–27. London: Curzon Press.

Burton, Richard. 2009. *Prague: A Cultural History*. Northhampton, Mass.: Interlink Publishing.

Byman, Daniel L. 2015. *Comparing Al Qaeda and ISIS: Different Goals, Different Targets*. Washington, D.C.: Brookings Institution, Apr. 29. www.brookings.edu /testimonies/comparing-al-qaeda-and-isis-different-goals-different-targets/.

Caton, Stephen. 1990. *"Peaks of Yemen I Summon": Poetry as Cultural Practice in a North Yemeni Tribe*. Berkeley: University of California Press.

———. 2006. "Coetzee, Agamben, and the Passion of Abu Ghraib." *American Anthropologist* 108, no. 1 (Mar.): 114–23.

Chamayou, Grégoire. 2015. *A Theory of the Drone*. New York: The New Press.

Cole, Juan. 2003. "Al-Qaeda's Doomsday Document and Psychological Manipulation." Paper presented at Genocide and Terrorism: Probing the Mind of the Perpetrator, Yale Center for Genocide Studies, New Haven, Conn. Apr. 9.

Coles, Isabel, and Ned Parker. 2015. "How Saddam's Men Help Islamic State Rule." *Reuters,* Dec. 11. www.reuters.com/investigates/special-report/mideast-crisis-iraq-islamicstate/.

Coll, Steve. 2004. *Ghost Wars: The Secret History of the CIA, Afghanistan, and Bin Laden, from the Soviet Invasion to September 10, 2001*. New York: Penguin Press.

Cook, David. 2002. "Suicide Attacks or 'Martyrdom Operations' in Contemporary Jihad Literature." *Nova Religio: The Journal of Alternative and Emergent Religions* 6, no. 1 (Oct.): 7–44.

———. 2005. *Understanding Jihad*. Berkeley: University of California Press.

———. 2007. *Martyrdom in Islam*. Cambridge, Engl.: Cambridge University Press.

Cook, David, and Olivia Allison. 2007. *Understanding and Addressing Suicide Attacks: The Faith and Politics of Martyrdom Operations*. Westport, Conn.: Praeger Security International.

Crews, Robert. 2015. *Afghan Modern: The History of a Global Nation*. Cambridge, Mass.: Harvard University Press.

Davis, Natalie. 1973. "The Rites of Violence Religious Riot in Sixteenth-Century France." *Past and Present* 59 (May): 51–91.

DeMause, Lloyd. 2002. "The Childhood Origins of Terrorism." *Journal of Psychohistory* 29, no. 4: 340–80.

Devji, Faisal. 2005. *Landscapes of Jihad: Militancy, Morality, Modernity*. Ithaca, N.Y.: Cornell University Press.

———. 2008. *The Terrorist in Search of Humanity: Militant Islam and Global Politics*. New York: Columbia University Press.

Douglas, Mary. 1966. *Purity and Danger*. New York: Praeger.

———. 1990. "Foreword—No Free Gifts." In *The Gift*, by Marcel Mauss, vii–xviii. New York: W. W. Norton.

Edwards, David. 1987. "Origins of the Anti-Soviet Jihad." In *Afghan Resistance: The Politics of Survival*, edited by Grant Farr and John Merriam, 21–50. Boulder, Colo.: Westview Press.

———. 1993a. "Summoning Muslims: Print, Politics, and Religious Ideology in Afghanistan." *Journal of Asian Studies* 52, no. 3: 609–28.

———. 1993b. "Words in the Balance: The Poetics of Political Dissent in Afghanistan." In *Russia's Muslim Frontiers: New Directions in Cross-Cultural Analysis*, edited by Dale Eickelman, 114–29. Bloomington: Indiana University Press.

———. 1994. "Afghanistan, Ethnography, and the New World Order." *Cultural Anthropology* 9, no. 3: 1–16. Reprinted in Antonius C. G. M. Robbins and Jeffrey A. Sluka, eds. *Ethnographic Fieldwork: An Anthropological Reader*, 2d ed., 387–98. Oxford: Wiley-Blackwell, 2007.

———. 1995. "Print Islam: Media and Religious Revolution in Afghanistan." *Anthropological Quarterly* 68, no. 3: 171–84. Reprinted in June Nash, ed. *Social Movements: An Anthropological Reader*, 99–116. Oxford: Blackwell, 2005.

———. 1996. *Heroes of the Age: Moral Fault Lines on the Afghan Frontier*. Berkeley: University of California Press.

———. 2002. *Before Taliban: Genealogies of the Afghan Jihad*. Berkeley: University of California Press.

———. 2010. "Counterinsurgency as a Cultural System." *Small Wars Journal* (Dec.). *http://smallwarsjournal.com/blog/2010/12/counterinsurgency-as-a-cultura/*. Reprinted in Paul A. Erickson and Liam D. Murphy, eds. *Readings for a History of Anthropological Theory*, 4th ed., 545–61. Toronto: University of Toronto Press, 2013.

Edwards, David, Gregory Whitmore, and Maliha Zulfacar, directors. 2006. *Kabul Transit*. Bullfrog Films. kabultransit.org.

Elphinstone, Mountstuart. 1815. *The Kingdom of Caubul*. London: Longman Hurst, Rees, Orme, Brown, and Murray.

Fair, C. Christine. 2007. "Militant Recruitment in Pakistan: A New Look at the Militancy-Madrasah Connection." *Asia Policy* 4 (July).

Fallon, Rebecca. 2014. "Facebook Official: Affirmation, Validation and Ambivalence among the Children of the Social Network." Bachelor's thesis, Williams College.

Feldman, Allen. 1991. *Formations of Violence: Narratives of the Body and Political Terror in Northern Ireland*. Chicago: University of Chicago Press.

Finn, Melissa. 2012. *Al-Qaeda and Sacrifice: Martyrdom, War and Politics*. New York: MacMillan.

Foucault, Michel. 1979. *Discipline and Punish: The Birth of the Prison*. New York: Vintage Books.

Fouda, Yosri, and Nick Fielding. 2003. *Masterminds of Terror: The Truth behind the Most Devastating Terrorist Attack the World Has Ever Seen*. New York: Arcade.

Fussell, Paul. 1973. *The Great War and Modern Memory*. Oxford: Oxford University Press.

Girard, René. 1977. *Violence and the Sacred*. Baltimore, Md.: Johns Hopkins University Press, 1977.

Goldberg, Jeffrey. 2000. "Inside Jihad U: The Education of a Holy Warrior." *New York Times Magazine*, June 25.

Goldziher, Ignaz. 1967 (1889–90). *Muslim Studies*. Reprint. Chicago: Aldine.

Grima, Benedicte. 1992. *The Performance of Emotion among Paxtun Women: "The Misfortunes which Have Befallen Me."* Austin: University of Texas Press.

Hamid, Mustafa, and Leah Farrall. 2015. *The Arabs at War in Afghanistan.* London: Hurst and Co.

Hassan, Nasra. 2001. "An Arsenal of Believers, Talking to the 'Human Bombs,'" *New Yorker,* Nov. 19. www.newyorker.com/magazine/2001/11/19/an-arsenal-of-believers.

Hassan, Riaz. 2014. *Suicide Bombings in Afghanistan.* ISAS Working Paper, No. 191, June 17. Singapore: Institute of South Asia Studies.

Hatina, Meir. 2014. *Martyrdom in Modern Islam: Piety, Power, and Politics.* Cambridge, Engl.: Cambridge University Press.

Hegghammer, Thomas. 2008. "Abdallah Azzam, the Imam of Jihad." In *Al Qaeda in Its Own Words,* edited by Gilles Kepel and Jean-Pierre Milelli, 81–101. Cambridge, Mass.: Harvard University Press.

———. 2010. "The Rise of Muslim Foreign Fighters: Islam and the Globalization of Jihad." *International Security* 35, no. 3: 53–94.

Holmes, Stephen. 2005. "Al-Qaeda, September 11, 2001." In *Making Sense of Suicide Missions,* edited by Diego Gambetta, 131–72. Oxford: Oxford University Press.

Hubert, Henri, and Marcel Mauss. 1964. *Sacrifice: Its Nature and Functions.* Chicago: University of Chicago Press. Originally published in French in 1898 as *Essai sur la nature et la function du sacrifice.*

Illouz, Eva. 2007. *Cold Intimacies: The Making of Emotional Capitalism.* Cambridge, Engl.: Polity Press.

International Human Rights and Conflict Resolution Clinic (Stanford Law School) and Global Justice Clinic (NYU Law School). 2012. *Living under Drones: Death, Injury, and Trauma to Civilians from US Drone Practices in Pakistan.* Stanford, Calif., and New York: IHRCRC/GJC.

Johnson, Thomas H. 2009. *Poetry: Why It Matters to Afghans?* Monterey, Calif.: Naval Postgraduate School.

Kennan, George F. 1946. "Long Telegram," George Kennan to George Marshall (Feb. 22). Photocopy. Harry S. Truman Administration File, Elsey Papers. www.trumanlibrary.org/whistlestop/study_collections/coldwar/documents/pdf/6–6.pdf.

Khalil, Samir al- (Kanan Makiya). 1989. *Republic of Fear: The Inside Story of Saddam's Iraq.* Berkeley: University of California Press.

Khalil, Umair. 2015. *The Madrasa Conundrum: The State of Religious Education in Pakistan.* Karachi: Hive.

Khalili, Laleh. 2007. *Heroes and Martyrs of Palestine: The Politics of National Commemoration.* Cambridge, Engl.: Cambridge University Press.

Khosrokhavar, Farhad. 2005. *Suicide Bombers: Allah's New Martyrs.* London: Pluto Press.

Khpalwak, Ahmad Omaid. 2011. "Bombing Suspect Says Pakistani Mullahs Brainwashed Him." Pajhwok News Agency, July 28. www.pajhwok.com/en/2011/07/28/bombing-suspect-says-pakistani-mullahs-brainwashed-him.

Kippenberg, Hans G. 2005. "'Consider That It Is a Raid on the Path of God': The Spiritual Manual of the Attackers of 9/11." *Numen* 52, no. 1: 29–58.

Kippenberg, Hans G., and Tilman Seidensticker. 2006. *The 9/11 Handbook: Annotated Translation and Interpretation of the Attackers' Spiritual Manual*. London: Equinox.

Kitts, Margo. 2010. "The Last Night: Ritualized Violence and the Last Instructions of 9/11." *Journal of Religion* 90, no. 3: 283–312.

Koerner, Brendan I. 2016. "Why ISIS Is Winning the Social Media War." *Wired*, Mar. www.wired.com/2016/03/isis-winning-social-media-war-heres-beat/.

Lackhar, John. 2002. "The Psychological Make-up of the Suicide Bomber." *Journal of Psychohistory* 20: 349–67.

Lansford, Tom. 2012. *9/11 and the Wars in Afghanistan and Iraq: A Chronology and Reference Guide*. Santa Barbara, Calif.: ABC-Clio.

Li, Daryl. 2012. "Taking the Place of Martyrs: Afghans and Arabs under the Banner of Islam." *Arab Studies Journal* 20, no. 1: 12–33.

Lincoln, Bruce. 2003. *Holy Terrors: Thinking about Religion after September 11*. Chicago: University of Chicago Press.

Lindholm, Charles. 1982. *Generosity and Jealousy: The Swat Pukhtun of Northern Pakistan*. New York: Columbia University Press.

Louthian, Howard. 2009. *Converting Bohemia: Force and Persuasion in the Catholic Reformation*. New York: Cambridge University Press..

Makiya, Kanan, and Hassan Mneimneh. 2002. "Manual for a 'Raid.'" *New York Review of Books*, Jan. 17.

Marsden, Magnus. 2016. *Trading Worlds: Afghan Merchants across Modern Frontiers*. London: Hurst and Co..

Matinuddin, Kamal. 1999. *The Taliban Phenomenon: Afghanistan 1994–1997*. Karachi: Oxford University Press.

Mauss, Marcel. 1954 (1924). *The Gift: The Form and Reason for Exchange in Archaic Societies*. Reprint. New York: Norton.

Mayer, Jane. 2009. "The Predator War." *New Yorker*, Oct. 26. www.newyorker.com/magazine/2009/10/26/the-predator-war.

McNally, Lauren, Alex Amiral, Marvin Weinbaum, and Antoun Issa. 2016. "The Islamic State in Afghanistan: Examining Its Threat to Stability." Middle East Institute Policy Focus Series, May. Washington, D.C.: Middle East Institute. www.mei.edu/sites/default/files/publications/PF12_McNallyAmiral_ISISAfghan_web.pdf.

Meeker, Michael. 1979. *Literature and Violence in North Arabia*. Cambridge, Engl.: Cambridge University Press.

Mehsud, Sailab. 2016. "Pashtun Tribe Lost 11,000 Houses in Pakistan's Waziristan Offensive." *Gandhara*, Aug. 17. http://gandhara.rferl.org/a/pakistan-waziristan-mehsud-houses/27929086.html?ltflags = mailer.

Miller, Flagg. 2015. *The Audacious Ascetic: What the Bin Laden Tapes Reveal about Al-Qaeda*. London: Hurst and Co.

Miller, Greg, and Souad Mekhennet. 2015. "Inside the Surreal World of the Islamic State's Propaganda Machine." *Washington Post*, Nov. 20. www.washingtonpost

.com/world/national-security/inside-the-islamic-states-propaganda-machine
/2015/11/20/051e997a-8ce6–11e5-acff-673ae92ddd2b_story.html.

Moghadam, Assaf. 2008. *The Globalization of Martyrdom: Al Qaeda, Salafi Jihad, and the Diffusion of Suicide Attacks*. Baltimore, Md.: Johns Hopkins University Press.

Muhaq, Mohammad. 2010. "Madares-i Taliban, az kudak azari ta entakhar" (Taliban Madares: From Child Abuse to Suicide Attack). *Radio Zamaaneh.com*. http://zamaaneh.com/humanrights/2010/07/post_643.html.

Musil, Alois. 1928. *The Manners and Customs of the Rwala Bedouin*. New York: American Geographical Society.

Naji, Abu Bakr. 2010. *The Management of Savagery: The Most Critical Stage Through Which the Umma Will Pass*. Translated by William McCants. https://azelin.files. wordpress.com/2010/08/abu-bakr-naji-the-management-of-savagery-the-most-critical-stage-through-which-the-umma-will-pass.pdf.

Norland, Rod. 2011. "For a Long-Term Afghan-American Accord, Night Raids Are a Sticking Point." *New York Times*, Dec. 4. www.nytimes.com/2011/12/04 /world/asia/for-afghan-us-accord-night-raids-are-a-sticking-point.html.

Pajhwok Reporter. 2011. "Boy Resorts to Suicide Attack after Marriage Denial." Pajhwok News Agency, Sept. 12. www.pajhwok.com/en/2011/09/12/boy-resorts-suicide-attack-after-marriage-denial.

———. 2014. "Students Abused in Pak Seminaries." Pajhwok News Agency, Jan. 29. http://archive.pajhwok.com/en/2014/01/29/students-abused-pak-seminaries-nds.

Palaver, Wolfgang. 2014. "Sacrificial Cults as 'the mysterious center of every religion': A Girardian Assessment of Aby Warburg's Theory of Religion." In *Sacrifice and Modern Thought*, edited by Julia Meszaros and Johannes Zachhuber. Oxford: Oxford University Press.

Pape, Robert A. 2005. *Dying to Win: The Strategic Logic of Suicide Terrorism*. New York: Random House.

Pedahzur, Ami, ed. 2006. *Root Causes of Suicide Terrorism: The Globalization of Martyrdom*. London: Routledge.

Pelevin, Mikhail, and Matthias Weinreich. 2012. "The Songs of the Taliban: Continuity of Form and Thought in an Ever-Changing Environment." *Iran and the Causcasus* 16 (2012): 45–70.

Post, Jerrold M. 2007. *The Mind of the Terrorist: The Psychology of Terrorism from the IRA to al-Qaeda*. New York: Palgrave MacMillan.

Pynsent, Robert. 1994. *Questions of Identity: Czech and Slovak Ideas of Nationality and Personality*. Budapest: Central European University Press.

Rahman Baba. 1977. *Selections from Rahman Baba*, translated by J. Enevoldsen. Herning, Denmark: Poul Kristensen.

Raverty, H. G. 1862. *Selections from the Poetry of the Afghans: From the Sixteenth to the Nineteenth Century*. London: Williams and Norgate.

Reuter, Christoph. 2004. *My Life Is a Weapon: A Modern History of Suicide Bombing*. Princeton, N.J.: Princeton University Press.

Reuters. 2016. "US Drone Strikes Outnumber Warplane Attacks for the First Time in Afghanistan." *The Guardian,* Apr. 21. www.theguardian.com /world/2016/apr/21/us-drone-strikes-outnumber-warplane-attacks-for-first-time-in-afghanistan.

Rodriguez, Alex. 2011. "Pakistan Death Squads Go After Informants to U.S. Drone Program." *Los Angeles Times,* Dec. 28. http://articles.latimes.com/2011/dec/28 /world/la-fg-pakistan-death-squads-20111228.

Rohde, David. 2012. "The Drone Wars." *Reuters Magazine,* Jan. 26. www.reuters .com/article/us-david-rohde-drone-wars-idUSTRE80P11I20120126.

Roy, Olivier. 1986. *Islam and Resistance in Afghanistan.* Cambridge, Engl.: Cambridge University Press.

Rubin, Barnett R. 1995. *The Fragmentation of Afghanistan: State Formation and Collapse in the International System.* New Haven, Conn.: Yale University Press.

Sahlins, Marshall. 1979. *Historical Metaphors and Mythical Realities: Structure in the Early History of the Sandwich Islands Kingdom.* Ann Arbor: University of Michigan Press.

Said, Edward W. 1994. *Orientalism.* New York, Vintage Books.

Sayer, Derek. 1998. *The Coasts of Bohemia: A Czech History.* Princeton, N.J.: Princeton University Press.

Serle, Jack, and Payenda Sargand. 2015. "Get the Data: Drone Wars." *Bureau of Investigative Journalism,* Feb. 12. www.thebureauinvestigates.com/2015/02/12 /us-drone-war-afghanistan-list-american-air-strikes-2015/.

Shah, Saira. 2001. *Beneath the Veil.* Documentary film. London: Independent Television News.

Shahrani, M. Nazif, and Robert L. Canfield. 1984. *Revolutions and Rebellions in Afghanistan: Anthropological Perspectives.* Berkeley: University of California Press.

Shane, Scott, Matt Apuzzo, and Eric Schmitt. 2015. "Americans Attracted to ISIS Find an 'Echo Chamber' Online." *New York Times,* Dec. 9. www.nytimes .com/2015/12/09/us/americans-attracted-to-isis-find-an-echo-chamber-on-social-media.html.

Sly, Liz. 2015. "The Hidden Hand behind the Islamic State Militants? Saddam Hussein's." *Washington Post,* Apr. 4. www.washingtonpost.com/world/middle_east /the-hidden-hand-behind-the-islamic-state-militants-saddam-husseins/2015/04 /04/aa97676c-cc32–11e4–8730–4f473416e759_story.html.

Stern, Jessica. 2003. *Terror in the Name of God: Why Religious Militants Kill.* New York: Harper Collins.

———. 2004. "Beneath Bombast and Bombs, a Caldron of Humiliation." *Los Angeles Times,* June 6. http://articles.latimes.com/2004/jun/06/opinion/op-stern6.

Strenski, Ivan 2003. "Sacrifice, Gift, and the Social Logic of Muslim 'Human Bombers.'" *Terrorism and Political Violence* 15, no. 3: 1–34.

Strick Van Linschoten, Alex, and Felix Kuehn. 2012. *Poetry of the Taliban.* New York: Columbia University Press.

United Nations Assistance Mission to Afghanistan. 2007. *Suicide Attacks in Afghanistan (2001–2007).* September.

Verdery, Katherine. 1999. *The Political Lives of Dead Bodies.* New York: Columbia University Press.

Vidino, Lorenzo, and Seamus Hughes. 2015. *ISIS in America: From Retweets to Raqqa.* Washington, D.C.: Program on Extremism, George Washington University, Dec. www.stratcomcoe.org/download/file/fid/2828.

Warrick, Joby. 2012. *The Triple Agent: The al-Qaeda Mole Who Infiltrated the CIA.* New York: Vintage Books.

Williams, Brian Glyn. 2007. "Suicide Bombings in Afghanistan." *Islamic Affairs Analyst,* Sept. www.brianglynwilliams.com/IAA%20suicide.pdf.

———. 2008. "Mullah Omar's Missiles: A Field Report on Suicide Bombers in Afghanistan." *Middle East Policy Council* 15, no. 4 (Winter). www.mepc.org/journal/middle-east-policy-archives/mullah-omars-missiles-field-report-suicide-bombers-afghanistan?print.

Winter, Charlie. 2015a. "Documenting the Virtual 'Caliphate.'" *Quilliam Foundation Report,* Oct. www.quilliamfoundation.org/wp/wp-content/uploads/2015/10/FINAL-documenting-the-virtual-caliphate.pdf.

———. 2015b. "Understanding Islamic State's Propaganda Strategy." *Quilliam Foundation Report,* July. www.quilliamfoundation.org/wp/wp-content/uploads/publications/free/the-virtual-caliphate-understanding-islamic-states-propaganda-strategy.pdf.

Wright, Lawrence. 2006. *The Looming Tower: Al-Qaeda and the Road to 9/11.* New York: Alfred A. Knopf.

Wyatt-Brown, Bertram. 1986. *Honor and Violence in the Old South.* London: Oxford University Press.

Zawahiri, al-. 2005. "Letter to Abu Musab al-Zarqawi, 2005" (English translation). *2005 Intelligence and Security News,* Intelligence Resource Program, Federation of American Scientists. https://fas.org/irp/news/2005/10/letter_in_english.pdf.

Zelin, Aaron Y. 2014. "The War between ISIS and al-Qaeda for Supremacy of the Global Jihadist Movement." Research Notes No. 20, June. Washington, D.C.: Washington Institute of Near East Policy. www.washingtoninstitute.org/policy-analysis/view/the-war-between-isis-and-al-qaeda-for-supremacy-of-the-global-jihadist.

INDEX

Abdullah, Abdullah, 177, 180

Abdullah, King, 156

Abdur Rahman Khan, Amir (aka "Iron Amir"), 224–225n7

Abida (female Facebook user), 181–184, *182*, 187–188, 195–196, 234n17, 235n24

Abu Daud, 233n5

Abufarha, Nasser, 222n10, 231n33

Abu Ghraib, 161, 200–201

Afghan Arabs (*fedayeen*), xii, 94–95; Afghan Arabs as term, 95, 226n1; as audience of 'Azzam, 103–105, 209; Bin Laden and practical support for, 106–107, 227n16; departures from Afghanistan, 109, 111; detachment from Afghans, 107–108, 227–228n20; ever-increasing radicalization of, 215; *fedayeen* as term, 94; frustration of, with combat training and lack of miracles, 105; and Jaji, battle of, 108, 111; Jalalabad siege and, 108–109; and martyrdom as sought-after goal, 95, 104–105; reckless disregard for personal safety of, 97, 104–105; Soviet occupation and, 95, 97, 106–107; splinter groups referred to as Jalalabad School, 109. *See also* Balawi, Humam Khalil Abu-Mulal al-; martyrdom, pursuit of; September 11, 2001

Afghan army: conscription into, Safi war over, 32–35, 223nn9–10; suicide attacks by soldiers of, on government or Coalition, 233n7; tribal armies (*lashkar*) and

resistance to, 38–39; weaponry of, 44–45

Afghan secret police (KHAD), 12

Afghan Wireless (telecom company), 167

Agamben, Giorgio, 87, 152–153, 160

agency, 16; of women, Facebook and, 188

Ahmadzai tribe, 82

Ahmed, Akbar S., 30–31

AK-47 (Kalashnikov), 43, 184, *184*, 200

Algeria, 109

'Ali (the Prophet's son-in-law), 121, 122

Ali, Muhammad (informant), 27, 32, 35

Al-Jihad magazine ('Azzam), 108

al-Qaeda: al-Balawi (suicide bomber) and, 157; Daesh distinguished from, 198–199, 200, 202; embassy attacks in East Africa (1998), 98, 214; founding of, xiv, 94, 209, 227n10; franchise-like structure of, 200; Jalalabad School as undermining, 109; overestimation of, by Westerners, 227n11; as target of U.S. invasion of Afghanistan, 73. *See also* Bin Laden, Osama; September 11, 2001

Al-Quds al-Araby (Arabic-language newspaper), 110

amulets, 68

animal sacrifice, xi, *xii*, 9–10, 29–30, 89, 122, 201, 222n5

anthropology: flexibility of discipline, 6–7; on global phenomenon of suicide bombing, 230n27; and history, stories embedded in, 7; methodological problems of Internet/Facebook research, 173, 174–175,

Eastern Shura (a council), 76–77
education: Islamic political party-run schools (*maktab*), 69–71; lack of alternatives to madrasas, 168; literacy classes for mujahidin, 69; orthodoxies in, 138–140; Pakhtu reading primer, 69–71; Taliban shuttering of, for girls, 75. *See also* illiteracy; madrasas
Eid-i Qurban, xi, 29, 119–120
Elphinstone, Mountstuart, 35–36
embassy bombings and attacks, East Africa (1998), 98, 214
emotion: Daesh and appeals to, 199–200; prescribed words and actions to avoid distractions of, in ritual sacrifice, 117, 118, 120; and psychological studies of terrorism, 141–142; and ritual, 10. *See also* romantic aspirations
employment: demographic bulge of young men and lack of prospects for, 168; madrasas and, 135; religious mindset and, 71
Emwazi, Muhammad ("Jihadi John"), 235–236n31
End-Time prophecy: Daesh and, 202–203; evoked in Bin Laden's "Declaration," 111, 123
Enzeri Mullah Sahib (Sufi saint), 78
Ettihad-i Islami (Islamic political party), and Jalalabad, siege of, 108–109
exile, as punishment, 231n36
extralegal rendition, 161

Facebook: American cultural assumptions embedded in, 185; faces, 185–192; friends, collection of and sharing with, 185, 192–193; friendship, single category of, 195; friends of both genders, 185, 195–196, 235n24; and incivility-conformity split of discourse, 196; Like and Share buttons, 196–198; and lost love, 235n24; newsfeed, 196–197; as parallel universe, 190; Taliban official presence on, 194. *See also* Facebook, "Talifans" and
Facebook, "Talifans" and: agency of women and, 188; and *caravan of martyrs*, as term, xiv, *xv*; and cult of martyrdom,

174; as decentralized form of communication, 174, 194; and faces/visibility, 185–188; friendship and, 194; and methodology, problems of, 173, 174–175, 233–234nn12–14; multiple accounts for users, 173–174, 179, 234n14; peer pressure and, 194; pseudonyms used, 173, 174–175, 179. *See also* Facebook, "Talifans" and—content of
Facebook, "Talifans" and—content of: Abida (female user profile), 181–184, *182*, 187–188, 195–196, 234n17, 235n24; Ghazi (male user profile), 177–181, *181*; martyrdom material, 177, *178*, 188–192, *189*, 197–198, 235n23; memes and images, *xv*, 174, 175–176, *176*, 180, 182–183, *194*, 234n15; nonpoetic material, 177; photographs of people/faces, 177, *178*, 180–183, *181–182*, 184, 187–192, *189*; poetry, 176–177, 183, 188, 195, 235n24
face/to lose face, 185–186
family/parents: isolation from, and suicide bomber training, 140; martyrs instructed to commemorate parents, 120, 121; permission for martyrdom, 170; and psychological studies of suicide bombing, 141; of suicide bombers, 127, 169–170, 233nn5–6; visibility and invisibility of, honor and, 145–147, 149
fantasy films, 114–115
farming, difficulty of return to, 78, 80
Farrall, Leah, 227nn11,16
fatwas, training toward and authority to make, 137
fedayeen, as term, 94. *See also* Afghan Arabs
Federally Administered Tribal Area (FATA), 149
Feldman, Alan, 17, 122–123
Feminist Majority Foundation (U.S.), 72
feud dynamic of Pakhtun tribal society: and balance, importance of, 27, 42–45; clerical supervision and observation of sacrifice, 30–31, 222–223n6; the dead and, 31, 34, 35; Dog Feud story, 26–27, 29, 32, 34, 211, 231n36; female delegation to sue for peace, 29–30, 32, 34, 222nn4–5; generation and role of, 27–28; and the jirga, 27, 30, 31, 150; martyrdom as

feud dynamic of Pakhtun tribal society
(continued)
disconnected from, 31; poetry and logic
of, 42, 45; sacrifice and, 29–30,
222nn3,5; sacrifice as cover for later acts
of violence, 122; and self-determination
vs. conformity to social norms, as
balance, 28–29, 30; tribal customs and
institutions in tension with Islam,
30–31, 222–223n6; weaponry and
changes to, 42–45, 43–44. See also
tribal society
Fielding, Nick, 116
fitna, 86
Fouda, Yosri, 116
"freedom fighters," as American government term, 6, 104. See also mujahidin
friendship: conversation, Afghan concern
for, 196; Facebook and (see under Facebook); between genders, as disallowed,
195; importance to Islamist movement,
193–194
Fučík, Julius, 204, 205
funerals. See burials/graves
Fussell, Paul, 35

gangsta rap, 168–169
Gauhar (poet), 50–51, 55, 95
Ghani, Ashraf, 177, 180
ghaza/ghazi vs. jihad/mujahid terminology,
and anti-Marxist uprising, 223–224n19
Ghazi (male Facebook user), 177–181, 181
Girard, René, 88–90, 91–92, 93, 123
global interconnectivity: consumer
dynamic and, 169. See also Facebook;
Internet; social media; technology
global jihad, transformation of Afghan
jihad into, 95–96, 110–115, 209, 226n3
global war, Daesh and projection of,
202–203
glossary, 239–244
Goldberg, Jeffrey, 135–137
Goldziher, Ignaz, 223n11, 228n29
Google+, 179
GoPro cameras, 200
"green on blue" suicide attacks, 233n7
Guantanamo, 161, 200–201
Gul Sha'er (poet), 48–49, 224n1

Hadda, 83
hadith: End Time, evoked in Bin Laden's
"Declaration," 111, 123; Paradise for
martyrs, 233n5; Taliban and, 93
Hamas, 126, 136
Hamid, Mustafa, 105, 107, 109, 227nn11,16
Hanafi Islam, 108
Haqqania madrasa, 136
Haqqani, Badruddin, 179, 180–181,
234nn15–16
Haqqani, Maulavi Jalaluddin, 107, 179,
234n16
Haqqani Network, 131, 178–179, 180–181
Hasan, Syed Shoaib, 229n14
Hassan, Nasra, 125–127, 130, 136, 174
Hawaiians (ethnic group), 17–18
Hazaras (ethnic group), 76–77
Hegghammer, Thomas, 227n10
Hekmatyar, Gulbuddin, 77, 82, 108
Helmand, 75, 183
Hindu Kush, 2, 77, 111
Hindus, 75
Hizb-i Islami (Islamic political party), 65;
animosity with Jamiat-i Islami party,
77; contested religious authority of, 66;
friendships and, 193; and Jalalabad, siege
of, 108–109; leadership of, 77, 82; magazines commemorating martyrs, 7–8,
57–59, 61–64, 61, 63, 66; and methodology of text, 234n16; and precedence/
seniority of members, 60–63; tribal
poetry condemned by, 57. See also
magazines commemorating martyrdom
homeland (watan), 55, 143–144, 231n33
homo sacer, 87, 161–162
homosexuality, madrasas and, 137–138
honor: aid and, 231–232n40; American
occupation and affronts to, 145–147;
and Bin Laden's embrace of pre-Islamic
poetry and spirit, 113–115, 228n29;
Britain and eclipse of, 35; and face/
reputation, 185–186; and family visibil-
ity/invisibility, control of, 145, 146–147;
of female delegation suing for feud
peace, 29–30, 32, 34, 222nn4–5; importance of, vs. physical safety, 146; killing
as compensatory action for loss of, 144,
148, 151–152, 231n36; and land loss as

Islamic political parties in exile *(continued)*
soldiers by, 81; and refugee status, right
to determine, 66; relocation of, to
Kabul, 76, 77; seniority/precedence in
the movement, 60–63; shift to, from
tribal identities, 45, 47, 54, 67, 71, 86,
207–208; Soviets/communism as
symbol of infidelity to, 95; submission
to regime of, 193, 194; tribal poetry
condemned by, 57. *See also* coalition
government (1992–1995); madrasas;
magazines commemorating
martyrdom
Islamic State. *See* Daesh
Ismail, near sacrifice of, 29, 119–120
Israel: al-Balawi's motivations and, 155; in
Facebook posts by "Talifans," 177; as
suicide bombing target, 125, 126

Jaji base, 107, 111
Jalalabad: sales of Taliban music and videos
in, 163–164, 171; siege of, 108–109
Jalalabad School (*takfiris*), 109, 112
Jamal, Mullah Sayyid, 33, 34
Jamiat-i Islami (Islamic political party),
225n4; animosity with Hizb-i Islami
party, 77; friendships and, 193; magazines commemorating martyrs, 59,
60, 64; religious authority of, 66.
See also magazines commemorating
martyrdom
Jan of Nepomuk, 204, 205
jihad: compulsory, 67, 225n11; global,
transformation of Afghan jihad into,
95–96, 110–115, 209, 226n3; Internet as
battleground of, 129; madrasas teaching
themes of, 135; Pakhtu reading primer as
grounded in, 69–71; as requirement of
faith, 97–98; rulebook for (*Mufti
Sangar*), 66–68, 225nn10–11; Safi War
and desire for, 34
"Jihadi John." *See* Emwazi, Muhammad
jirga (tribal assembly): dispute adjudication
and, 27, 30, 31; drone strikes and break-
down of, 150
Jordan: Daesh and, 235–236n31; intelligence
officials' belief al-Balawi was undercover
agent, 154, 155–157, 158, 159, 161

Kabul, Afghanistan: destruction of, following Soviet withdrawal, 77, 90; moral
laxity associated with, under Soviet and
American occupations, 145; popular
media of, 168; relative modernity of,
3–4, 5, 11, 85–86; relocation of Islamic
parties back to, 76, 77; Taliban control
of, 73, 82, 85–86; traffic of, 11–12; and
U.S. invasion of Afghanistan, 11–13, 73,
145–146; walls of, and honor, 145–146;
Western perceptions of, xiii. *See also*
Taliban public punishments
Kabul Transit (film), 13, 221n5
Kabul University, 75
Kachagarhi refugee camp, 69
Kalashnikov AK-47, 43, 184, *184*, 200
kalimah allah, 68
Kandahar: Bin Laden and, 109–110; the
Taliban and, 81
Karmal, Babrak, 145
Karokhel, Danish, 130
Karzai, Hamid: and child suicide bombers,
133; and danger of association with
violators of Afghan honor codes, 145,
231–232n40; moral laxity associated
with state under, 145; security for, 13.
See also U.S.–backed government
Kennan, George F., "long telegram"
of, 216
Kevlar (bulletproof fabric), 146
KHAD (Afghan secret police/intelligence
service), 12, 82
Khales, Maulavi, 108
Khalid Sheikh Muhammad (aka KSM),
116, 129, 161
Khalil, Samir al-. *See* Makiya, Kanan
Khorasan, 111, 129, 159
Khorasani, Abu Dujaanah al- (pseudonym
of al-Balawi), 153, 155, 158–159. *See also*
Balawi, Humam Khalil Abu-Mulal al-
Khushal Khan Khattak, 36, 39, 50, 52, 224n1
Khyber Pakhtunkhwa, 36, 230n20
Khyber Pass, 8, 77
kinship ties: disconnected among mujahi-
din, 53–54; friendships between genders
and, 195; patrilineal, and honor, 142–
143; rivalries between paternal first
cousins, 142. *See also* tribal society

Kippenberg, Hans, 115
Kunar River Valley, 32–35

Lackhar, John, 141
landai (poetry form), 39–40, 102, 183, 188, 224n4
language, and pitfalls of psychological studies of terrorism, 142
Layla and Majnun, 172, 176, 233n10
Lebanon, suicide bombings and, 229n1
Lee-Enfield rifle, 42–43
Leno, Mavis, 72
Li, Daryl, 102, 226n7, 227–228n20
Lincoln, Abraham, assassination plotters of, 165
Lindholm, Charles, 52–53
Lindstrom, Eric J., 3
logic. *See* cultural logic
love. *See* romantic aspirations
luchak, 143

madrasas (Afghan): lack of alternatives to, 168; numbers of, 135, 230n20; orientation of, 229–230n19
madrasas (Pakistani): boarding schools, 135; education/training in, 135, 136–137, *136*; extremism and, 134–135, 229–230n19; functions of, 135; funding for, 135, 136; homosexuality and, 137–138; numbers of, 135, 230n20; orthodoxies of education in, 138–140; recruitment of foot soldiers from, 81; refugees and importance of, 135; student life in, 137–138; and Sufism, coexistence with, 134; suicide bombing and, 128–129, 133–141, 170, 229–230nn18–20; Taliban background and, 85; Taliban music singers from, 164; and women, portrayed as continual threat to male reason, 137–138
magazines commemorating martyrdom: authority of Islamic parties and, 62, 63–64, 66, 68, 207–208; and *caravan of martyrs,* as term, xiii–xiv; carried with mujahidin, 57, 224n6; cult of martyrdom as objective of, 174; eulogies and obituaries in, 59–63; foreign editions, 57; friendships portrayed by, 193; hierarchical ordering of the dead in, 60–63;

illustrations of, 59, *60–61, 63,* 64; and Jalalabad siege, 108; poetry in (martyr-centered), 57–59; as stage in cultural politics of Islamic resistance, 7–8
Makiya, Kanan (pseud. Samir al-Khalil), 119–120, 202, 236n35
Maktab al-Khadamat (Service Bureau), 97, 106
Malalai (Afghan heroine), 40
Maliki, Nouri al-, 179
Malinowski, Bronisław, 4, 5, 6
marriage: lack of opportunity for, 169, 172; photographs commemorating, 187. *See also* romantic aspirations
martyrdom: authority to confer status of, 24, 66, 68, 87; consumerism and instant gratification and, 128, 168–170, 198; Facebook material on, 174, 177, *178,* 188–192, *189,* 197–198, 235n23; feud dynamic disconnected from, 31; honor-centered poetry and disconnection from, 41–42, 49–50; Islamic political parties and tarnishing of, 86–87, 103, 208; Islamic political parties and tool of, 56, 63–66, 87–88, 96, 208; poetry centered in (vs. honor-centered), 47–56, *53–54,* 64, 95, 171, 193; Safi war (against the state) disconnected from, 34; the *sangar* (trench) and, 54–56; Sufi mysticism replaced by, 96, 99–100, 127–128, 209; uncertainty and, 23–24. *See also* magazines commemorating martyrdom; martyrdom, pursuit of; martyrs
martyrdom, pursuit of: as Afghan Arab pursuit, 95, 104–105; 'Azzam and development of, 25, 101–105, 129, 227n10; Bin Laden and development of, 25, 112–115, 129; commemoration and honoring by the living, 114–115; definition of, 25; denial of, by the state, 161; enchanted realm, Afghanistan as, 103–104; and fear vs. fearlessness, 104–105; focus on and frustrations of, and recruits, 105; and *jahiliyya* (martial glory of tribal culture), 113–115, 228n29; reclaiming martyrdom as path of redemption, 103; rewards of martyrdom evoking, 112–113; sexual desire and the figure of the houri

poetry: on Facebook, 176–177, 183, 188, 195, 235n24; and feud, logic of, 42, 45; and friendship/male comrades, 52–54, *53–54*; as galvanizing people to take up arms, 36, *37*, 39; honor-centered (Afghan tribal), 35–42, 45, 49–50, 51, 55, 57, 167, 183, 224n1; importance in Afghanistan, 35–36; importance in Middle Eastern Muslim societies, 223n11; *landai* form, 39–40, 102, 183, 188, 224n4; martyr-centered, 47–56, *53–54*, 64, 95, 171, 193; personal and confessional mode of, 235n24; pre-Islamic tribal, Bin Laden and, 113, 114–115, 228n29; by prisoners, 12; tapes of: provenance, distribution, and translation, 36, 167, 223n16, 224n1. *See also* Rafiq Jan

pornography, 169, 203

Post, Jerrold, 141

prisons and prisoners: Islamist parties and, 57–59, 62; in Kabul, 12, 58–59, 76; in Sufi narratives, 224–225n7; Taliban and, 74–75, 76

protective amulets, 68

Pul-i Charkhi prison, Kabul, 58–59, 76

purificatory rituals: September 11, 2001 as, 122–123; suicide bombing as, 138; Taliban public punishments as, 80–81, 85–88, 90

qisas, 91

Qur'an: delegation of women carrying copies of, 29; "martyred" (burned) copies of, 64; 9/11 manual and, 118

Qutb, Sayyid, 95, 97, 167; *Milestones*, 114

Rabbani, Burhanuddin, 225n4

Rabbani, Mullah Muhammad, 225n6

Rafiq Jan, and poetry of: biographical information, 36–38; eclipse of poetry of, by martyr-centered poetry, 51, 224n1; ethos of honor of, and disconnection from martyrdom, 41–42, 49–50; as inciting battle against Marxist regime, 38, 39, 49, 167; and Islam, 41–42, 49–50; Islamic political party condemnation of, 57; and morality, 85; as neutral moral arbiter, 40–41; and pre-

Islamic poetic traditions, 113; and shift of locus of honor from the tribe to political party, 45; tapes of, 167, 223n16

Rahman, Atiya Abd al-, 157

Rahman Baba (poet), 52, 224n1

Ramadan, 183

Raufi, Rahmatullah, 231n32

Raverty, H. G., 36

refugees (internally displaced peoples, IDPs), 77

refugees in Pakistan, 5; demographics of, 69; and madrasas, importance of, 135; party-run schools for, 69–71; status as refugee, power to confer, 66. *See also* Islamic political parties in exile (Peshawar, Pakistan); madrasas (Pakistani)

religion: and power of ritual sacrifice, 11, 20, 92–93; sacrifice not limited to, 92–93

reputation, and relation to feud, 27–28

Revolutionary Association of the Women of Afghanistan (RAWA), 72, 73–74, *73*, 225n1

ringtones of Taliban music, 164–165, 233nn6–7

ritual: definition of, 211; and emotion, 10; energy release and, 10; sacrifice as, 10–11; and the structure of the conjuncture, 17–18. *See also* sacrifice

"road tax," 80

Rohde, David, 149

romantic aspirations: as forbidden, except in imagination, 52–53, 172, 235n24; landai poetry form and, 39–40, 102, 183, 188, 224n4; and loss and incompleteness, acceptance of, 172–173, 233n10; marriage, lack of opportunity for, 169, 172; persistence of, despite cultural containment of, 172; promised for martyrs in Paradise, 169, 233n5; Taliban *tarana* songs and recruitment of martyrs via, 170–173, 233n10; and *Titanic* film, popularity of, 75, 225n2. *See also* honor

sacrifice: animal, xi, *xii*, 9–10, 29–30, 89, 122, 201, 222n5; as anthropological subject, 18–19, 222n10; changing registers from violence to negotiation, 30, 211; deep structure of, 211; delegation of women to present, 29–30, 32, 34, 222nn4–5; diversity of purposes of, 20, 23, 46, 92–93, 119, 211; energy released by, 10; honor killings as, 144, 231n36; Islam as basis of/as invoked by, 29, 30–31; as leverage over terror of death, 10; mediating contradiction between self-determination and social control, 30, 46; as metacommunication, 30; occasions for, generally, 29; as pathway between the sacred and profane worlds, 19, 23, 117–118; religion and power of, 11, 20, 92–93; as supreme act of political and personal self-assertion, 152–153; symbolism and, 30, 31; Taliban public punishments as, 86–87, 92–93; as term, linguistic indeterminacy of, 18–19; terms used for, 29, 222nn2–3; tripartite structure of both the rite and the division of responsibility, 19–20. *See also* feud dynamic of Pakhtun tribal society; purificatory rituals; sacrifice machine

sacrifice machine: act of giving something up as energy fueling, 21–22, 120–121; act of killing within container of ritual, 22; as analogue, 21, 213; as an appropriation, 21; and balance of Islam, tribe, and state, 46, 207; Czechs and, 205–207; definition of, 21; dehumanization of victims, 90, 120, 201; diversity/adaptation of purposes of, 22, 23–25, 119; energy conversion/direction/amplification by, 21–22, 23, 30, 88–89, 118–119, 213–214; and failure, possibility of, 23; and honor, exchange of, 211–213; as magnifying impact, 118–119; the profane converted to the sacred via, 23, 117–118; the "sacred" as surplus energy emerging from, 23; sexual energy and, 103; sustainability of, 93, 213, 215; vessel of ritual, weaknesses in, 22; voyeuristic entertainment and, 203; witnessing spectators of, 22–23. *See also* Daesh beheading/execution videos; martyrdom; September 11, 2001; suicide bombing; Taliban public punishments

sacrificer, 19

sacrificial crisis, 88–89, 90

sacrifier, 19, 66, 118–119

Safi tribe, 31, 39

Safi War, 32–35, 223nn9–10

Sahab, as- (al-Qaeda media organ), 155

Sahlins, Marshall, 17–18

Said, Edward, xiv

saints. *See* Sufi saints

Saint Teresa, 190, 192

Salafi Islam, 108, 135, 191, 229–230n19

sangar (trench or bunker), *48*; as center of fighting, 47; as Facebook users' "place of employment," 182; as liminal space, 54–56

Saudi Arabia: appeals to Taliban to preserve Buddhist statues, 84; 'Azzam and, 97; Bin Laden and, 109, 110, 111, 113–114; and madrasas, support for, 135; women's clothing style of, 181–182, *182*, 184, *184*, 187–188

Sayyaf, Abdul Rab Rasul, 108

scapegoating rituals of the Taliban. *See under* Taliban public punishments

self-determination (autonomy): vs. conformity to social norms, in tension and as balance, 28–29, 30, 224n4; honor and, 142, 144, 147; suicide bombers and loss of, 152. *See also* submission

September 11, 2001: cultural and religious context, focus on, 115; and "Declaration" of Bin Laden, 110–111; hijackers, 115, 116, *117*; hijackers' parents, 120, 121; and transformation of Afghan jihad into global jihad, 95–96; and undermining of al-Qaeda, 123–124; and undermining of traditional Muslim institutions, 123. *See also* September 11, 2001—as sacrificial ritual

September 11, 2001—as sacrificial ritual: amplification of energy and, 118–119; Bin Laden's enhanced prestige as sacrifier via, 118–119; dehumanization of victims, 120; diversity of function of, 119; emotional doubts and distractions, 117, 118, 120; as offering, 120–121; the profane converted to the sacred, 117–118; as purificatory ritual, 122–123; as

September 11, 2001 *(continued)*
ritual of remembrance for gifts from
God, 120; as "sacrificial transfer," 123;
spiritual manual for (document), 115–
118, 119–121, 122, 209; and templates for
ritual sacrifice, 119–120; and vengeance,
121–122
Seven-Party Alliance, 67, 225n10
sexual desire: and the martyr as willful
agent of his own demise, 102–103, 169.
See also romantic aspirations
sexual honor of women, 29, 143, 144,
222nn4–5
shahid, figure of, 103
Shahmund (informant), 27, 32, 35
Shah, Saira, 72
Shah Shuja, 145
shari'a law: nerkh (local precedents) as
acceptable to, 31; politicization of, by
Islamic political parties, 79; tribal law
superseded by, 79
Shia (Islamic denomination), 76, 199
Sima-yi Shahid (The Visage of the Martyr,
magazine), 57–59, 61–64, *61, 63*
SIM cards, 164–165
Šmíd, Martin, 236–237n2
Snowden, Edward, 175
snuff films, 203
social media: and *caravan of martyrs*, as
term, xiv, *xv*; and conformity, 196–198;
as decentralized form of communication, 174, 194; and incivility–conformity split of discourse, 196; and new
generation of martyrs, 198, 209–210;
and personal/confessional mode of
poetry, 235n24; platforms used, 179. *See
also* Facebook
Soviet occupation, of Czechoslovakia,
martyrs of, 204, 205, *206*, 236–237n2
Soviet occupation of Afghanistan: and
Afghan Arabs, 95, 97, 106–107; as
distanced compared to U.S. occupation,
144, 231n37; and honor of Afghans,
offense to, 143–144; invasion (1979), 47;
Islamic political party animosities and,
76–77; moral laxity of state associated
with, 145; mujahidin called "ghosts"
(*dukhi*), by Soviet soldiers, 231n37;

president Karmal brought to power by,
145; as symbol of infidelity to Islamic
political parties, 95; tribal role diminishing in wake of, in favor of Islamic
political parties, 45, 47, 54, 67, 71, 86,
207–208; weaponry of, *44*, 45, 50;
withdrawal of, 8, 76, 97, 108, 110, 143–
144. *See also* al-Qaeda; Marxist regime;
mujahidin
Soviet Union, and Cold War, 215–216
Sozanský, Jiří, 236–237n2
spectacle: Daesh beheading videos as,
201–202; September 11 as, and lessons
learned from, 124, 129; state prevention
of, 161; Taliban public punishments as,
73–74, 82, 84, 87
Sri Lanka, 16
Stern, Jessica, 141–142
submission: to Islamic party regime, 193,
194; madrasas and, 139; peer pressure as
source of conformity, 194, 196–198; Sufi
mysticism and, 59, 127. *See also* self-
determination (autonomy)
Sudan, 109, 110
Sufi leaders (*pirs*): erosion of authority of,
127; religious authority of, 56, 127,
224–225n7
Sufi saints: definition of, 191; destruction of
shrines of, 78; *lifting the veil*, 235n23;
martyrs as replacing, 99–100, 209;
practices of, 99–100; shrines of, 65, 83,
134, 191
Sufism: coexisting with madrasas, 134, 139;
decline of centers of, 134, 139; erosion of
mystical traditions of, 96, 127; "lifting
the veil," 235n23; miracle stories of, 59,
224–225n7, 235n23; mysticism of, martyrdom replacing, 96, 99–100, 127–128,
209; poetry of, image of "the Beloved"
in, 51–52, 172, 233n10; and resistance to
Marxist regime, 38; training and,
127–128
suicide, opprobrium Afghans attach to,
142, 231n32
suicide bombers: children as, 133, 134,
229n14; confessions of, 130–133; Daesh,
200; drugs and, 140; families of, 127,
169–170, 233nn5–6; and family, isola-

tion from, 140; increasing intolerance of, 215; number of volunteers increased as consequence of drone strikes, 152, 160; ordinariness of, 126; Pakistani madrasas and, 128–129, 133–141, 170, 229–230nn18–20; qualifications of "living martyrs" (in preparation), 126; training of, 126; videos made of, 126, 163–166, *166*, 169, 190–191, *191*, 200, 233nn6–7; women as, 188; YouTube material on, 189, 192, 235n20. *See also* Balawi, Humam Khalil Abu-Mulal al-; Facebook, "Talifans" and; suicide bombers—motivations of; suicide bombing

suicide bombers—motivations of: armed home searches, 147; cleansing of guilt for homosexual behavior, 138; commemoration/immortalization by the world, 126–127; drone strikes, 152, 155–156, 160–161, 214; Islamic ideology/religiosity and, 128–129, 133–134, 141, 148, 210–211; as Islamic religious duty/will of God, 148, 155–156, 158, 170–171; money, 134; political science/psychological studies analyses of, 141, 210, 230n28; purification, 138; as repayment for debt of honor, 148, 152; revenge, 148, 151–152, 229n13, 229n18; romantic desire of loss and incompleteness, 171–173, 233n10; shortest path to Paradise, 125; threats and inducements, 134, 140, 169–170, 229nn14,18, 233n5; unjust oppression, 148. *See also* martyrdom, pursuit of

suicide bombing: advent of, 16, 124, 125, 229n1; Afghan exiles in Pakistan and, 15; and agency, 16, 188; by army or police officers, 233n7; Bin Laden as first championing, 14–15; commonalities across cultures and, 124; initial expectation that Afghans would not participate in, 15; and martyr as willful agent of his own demise, 25, 161; Palestinian model of, 16, 124, 125–127, 158, 174, 209, 229n1, 231n33; "sacred explosions" as term for, 126; September 11, 2001 and, 124; social and political histories of, 210–211;

statistics on, 15; as tactic of war, 229n13; the Taliban and advent of, 14–15, 148; and Taliban, popularity of, 133–134; as term/terms for, 16–17, 221–222n9. *See also* suicide bombers; suicide bombing—as sacrificial ritual

suicide bombing—as sacrificial ritual, 124; prescribed words and actions, 126; purification, 138

symbolism, and sacrifice, 30, 31

Syria, 202, 209, 235n29

Tajik (ethnic group), 76–77

takfiris, 109, 112

Taliban: al-Balawi (suicide bomber) and, 154, 157; and Bin Laden, 111; education for girls confined to home by, 75; Facebook (official presence), 194; fall of, 73, 109, 164; founding of, and pacification of mujahidin, 80; journalism under, 75; and Kabul, 73, 82, 85–86; madrasas as background of, 85; music banning by, 13, 75, 166–167; Northern Alliance as enemy of, 93, 136; and opprobrium attached to suicide, 142; Pakistani government support for, 80, 81; photography and, 187; purification as avowed goal of, 80–81; remote-controlled truck bombs, 13–14; self-representation of, 80; September 11 and, 124; and suicide bombing, advent of, 14–15, 148; as target of U.S. invasion, 73, 93; technology and, 167. *See also* suicide bombing; Taliban public punishments; Taliban resurgence (post–U.S. invasion); U.S.-backed government

Taliban public punishments: authority demonstrated via, 87, 90–92, 208; and Buddha statues, destruction of, 83–84, 225n7; collective guilt and, 89–91, 93; commonality and difference of victims of, 89–90; degrading/dehumanizing the victim, 90; Islamic (shari'a) law and, 81–82, 83, 84, 91, 92; mimetic violence/retaliatory violence and, 88–89, 91–92; minority groups as victims, 90, 93; moral policing, 12–13, 75, 81–85, 93, 225n7; Najibullah execution, 82–83, 84,

doing Pakhtu; feud dynamic of Pakhtun tribal society; honor; kinship ties

Turkey, 235n29

Turkmani, Abu Muslim al, 236n35

Turkoman (ethnic group), 76–77

Twitter, 179, 186

U.N. Assistance Mission to Afghanistan (UNAMA) report, 134, 147, 229n14, 231n32

United Nations, 82

United States: Bin Laden's "Declaration" and expansion to global jihad, 111, 112; Cold War and containment policy, 215–216; embassy attacks, East Africa (1998), 98, 214; Internet surveillance, 175; losing face, meaning of, 186; and mujahidin as "freedom fighters," 6, 104; photographs as index of status in, 186; U.S. Marine barracks attacked in Beirut, 229n1; visibility, necessity of, 186. *See also* United States, invasion and occupation of Afghanistan (2001); war on terror

United States, invasion and occupation of Afghanistan (2001): aid, 129, 231–232n40; air attacks, 148; al-Qaeda as target of, 73; Bin Laden as target of, 73, 161; cost of, 129–130; drone strikes, 148–153, 156, 160, 214, 231–232nn41,43,45,56; in Facebook posts of "Talifans," 177, 180; home searches, 145–148, 149; and honor, affronts to, 145–147; intelligence gathering and, 144, 146, 149, 151, 160; and Kabul, 11–13, 73, 145–146; moral laxity of state associated with, 144–145; and music, lifting of restrictions on, 164; national-building task of, 73; suicide attacks on officers of, by army and police members, 233n7; Taliban as target of, 73, 93; Taliban songs and videos targeting, 170; video of Taliban execution of woman, effect of, 72–74, 73, 225n1; and walls, 145–146; women and, 13, 73, 145–147. *See also* U.S.-backed government

UNOCAL (oil development corporation), 72

U.S.-backed government: aid to, 129, 231–232n40; in Facebook posts of "Talifans," 177, 180; ineffectiveness of, 129–130; lack of alternatives to madrasas, 168; presidential election (2014), 177, 180; suicide attacks on, by army and police members, 233n7; and Taliban songs and videos, 165, 170. *See also* Karzai, Hamid; Taliban resurgence (post–U.S. invasion)

USS *Cole*, 96, 98, 106, 121

Uzbek (ethnic group), 76–77

Václav, Saint (King Wenceslas), 204, 205

Verdery, Katherine, 84, 87–88

victim (of sacrifice), 19–20

videos of executions: Taliban execution of woman, effect on U.S. invasion, 72–74, 73, 225n1. *See also* Daesh beheading/execution videos

videos of martyrs: suicide bomber al-Balawi, 153, 154–158, 159–160, 161–162; suicide bombings/martyrs, 126, 163–166, 166, 169, 190–191, 191, 200, 233nn6–7

violence: of Daesh, and sacredness of sacrifice, 201; reciprocal, 88–89, 91–92, 211–216; of state, and cult of personality, 202; symbolic dimension of (violation), 17

Wahhab, Abdul, 9

Wahhabi Islam: and Afghan objections to Afghan Arabs, 108; destruction of Sufi saint shrines by, 78; interdiction against veneration of martyrs, 108, 191, 227–228n20; madrasas and, 135, 229–230n19

Wakil (fieldwork companion), 1, 2

Warhol, Andy, 191–192, 235n22

war on terror: al-Balawi's martyrdom and, 160; *homo sacer* and, 160–161; as "state of exception," 161

wealth, feud dynamic and accumulation of, 28

weaponry: and changes to feud dynamic, 42–45, 43–44; lessons in madrasas, 136–137; Western donors for, 69; women and, 184, 184, 188

West: Cold War and containment policy of, 215–216; consumer culture of, 168–170; love songs of, 171, 173; music as omnipresent in, 172; weaponry supplied by, 69. *See also* United States

wireless communications network, 167. *See also* Internet; mobile phones

women: agency of, Facebook and, 188; burqa, 145, 146, 184, 187–188; as Daesh members, 199; delegation of, and feud, 29–30, 32, 34, 222nn4–5; excluded from madrasas, 137; Facebook *user profile* (Abida), 181–184, *182*, 187–188, 195–196, 234n17, 235n24; friendship between genders, 182, 185, 195–196, 235n24; honor killings of, 144, 231n36; houri, figure of, 102–103, 169; *landai* poetry and, 39–40, 102, 183, 188, 224n4; madrasa teachings about, 137–138; as *namus* (symbolically charged possessions), 142–143, 144; and photographs, 187–188; and *sangars* (trenches), 55; Saudi-style clothing of, 181–182, *182*, 184, *184*, 187–188; sexual honor of, 29, 143, 144, 222nn4–5; as

suicide bombers, 188; Taliban public punishments of, 72–74, *73*, 76, 225n1; Taliban rules for, 75–76; and U.S. invasion of Afghanistan, 13, 73, 145–147; and weaponry, 184, *184*, 188; Western clothing worn in Afghanistan, 5. *See also* romantic aspirations

World War I, 35, 205–206, *206*

World War II, 204, 205, 215–216, 237n3

Yahya Senyor (martyr), 100–101

Yousafzai, Malala

YouTube, "smiling martyr" videos, 189, 192, 235n20

Zahir Shah, King, 223n9

zakat (religious tax), 79–80

Zaman al-Wasl (Syrian opposition site), 235n29

Zarqawi, Abu Musab al-, 155–156, 159, 161, 198–199

Zawahiri, Ayman al-, 101, 154, 199, 203

Zeid, Ali Bin, 156, 157, 159

Zhawar (mujahidin base), 106–107